DATE DUE

AG 8 '97		
OCT 99		
AP 4 '02		

DEMCO 38-296

The Experts Welcome
Customer Bonding: Pathway to Lasting Customer Loyalty

"Forget everything you know about winning customer loyalty. *Customer Bonding* shows you how to go beyond marketing fads to beat your competitors at every turn. You can't afford to ignore this bold new pathway to marketing success."

Stan Rapp
Author with Tom Collins of bestsellers
MaxiMarketing and *Beyond MaxiMarketing*

"This book's cutting-edge treatment of customer development is must reading for all managers. It resonates far beyond the boundaries of the marketing department."

Alexander Hiam
Consultant, author of *Closing the Quality Gap*
Professor of Marketing, UMass, Amherst

"The most important force transforming business today is the growing power of customers. Cross and Smith show marketers how to make this force work in their favor. *Customer Bonding* is timely and useful."

Rosabeth Moss Kanter
Harvard Business School
Author of *When Giants Learn to Dance* and
The Challenge of Organizational Change

"Down-to-earth examples, step-by-step actions and great new ideas on how to profit from customer relationships. Right on target, *Customer Bonding* is a true masterpiece. Read it now!"

Philippe Bloch
CEO, PBRH
Co-author of French best-seller *Service compris*

"*Customer Bonding* is must reading in order to obtain the leading edge in the marketplace today and in the future."

Don W. Barrett, Jr.
President, INFOBASE

"Today's markets have changed dramatically. A company marketing a product or service faces an entirely new landscape, with advertising clutter, disintegration of media and anticommercialism. Richard Cross and Janet Smith explain the problems and how *Customer Bonding* can solve them. They write, 'You have to do more than just break through the din. You actually have to transcend it by managing in a true exchange of value with your customers.' If you're looking for a marketing advantage, your search is over."

Bill Olcott
Fund/Raising Management magazine

"Your customers can become your very best salespeople, and *Customer Bonding* shows you how. Step by step, Cross and Smith provide a prescription for success that returns trust, value, and loyalty to the forefront of customer relationships. *Customer Bonding* works!"

David E. Kennedy
Senior Vice President, Susquehanna Radio Corp.

"In today's media and marketing environment, the only permanent source of economic security is wholehearted commitment to the customer, no matter how complex and challenging that might be. The value of *Customer Bonding* is that it shows how to apply and demonstrate that commitment in a tangible and immensely satisfying way."

Peter M. Winter
Vice President—Market Development, Cox Newspaper, Inc.

CUSTOMER BONDING

Richard Cross and Janet Smith

Printed on recyclable paper

NTC Business Books
a division of NTC Publishing Group • Lincolnwood, Illinois USA

Cross, Richard
     Customer bonding : pathway to lasting customer
loyalty / Richard Cross, Janet Smith.
          p.   cm.
     Includes bibliographical references and index.
     ISBN 0-8442-3318-8
     1. Customer relations.   2. Customer service.   I. Smith, Janet
     II. Title.
HF5415.5.C8   1995
658.8′12—dc20   94-11504
                                                                CIP

Published by NTC Business Books, a division of NTC Publishing Group
4255 West Touhy Avenue
Lincolnwood (Chicago), Illinois 60646-1975, U.S.A.
© 1995 by Richard Cross and Janet Smith. All rights reserved.
No part of this book may be reproduced, stored in a retrieval system,
or transmitted in any form or by any means,
electronic, mechanical, photocopying, recording or otherwise,
without the prior written permission of NTC Publishing Group.
Manufactured in the United States of America.

4 5 6 7 8 9 BC 9 8 7 6 5 4 3 2 1

To our parents

Contents

Acknowledgments

Many organizations have shared their trial and error experiences for this book, including Air France, Airstream Trailers, American Airlines, Avis Rental Car, Ben & Jerry's, Benetton Group SpA, Birkenstock, The Body Shop, Burger King, Chesebrough-Ponds, Coca-Cola, DowElanco, Harley-Davidson, Holiday Inn, IBS, Intuit, Les Editions Play Bac, MCI, Microsoft Corporation, Nestlé Holland, Nestlé Sopad, Nestlé U.S.A., Ogilvy & Mather, Philip Morris, R.J. Reynolds, Salon Sebastian, Saucony, Sierra Club, Sonic Air, United We Stand America, *Utne Reader*, Volkswagen France, Waldenbooks, and Winnebago-Itasca. We thank all of their spokespeople and researchers and the many other organizations that supported this effort by providing data and ideas. Their reports from the marketing trenches illuminate and enrich the ideas put forth here.

We owe a special word of thanks to Mr. Thierry Hermant of Rapp & Collins/Piment in Paris, to his colleagues Veronique Maugé and Bérengère Malin, and to Rapp & Collins/Piment clients at Air France, DowElanco, and Volkswagen France for their generous time and assistance and for sharing their expertise with us.

Mr. Jean Luc Colonna D'Istria of Les Editions Play Bac, one of the first followers of the customer bonding system, willingly shared his evolving plans with us, even when it meant working until all hours to write up his careful notes on the program. We are particularly grateful to him for giving us a privileged look at his bold marketing outreach to parents across France.

We are also indebted to Stan Rapp and Tom Collins for pointing the way toward the power of customer bonding. Throughout our long association they have demonstrated that power time and again: first as agency principals showing their young whippersnapper client the secrets of customer loyalty; then as authors of *MaxiMarketing*[1], *The Great Marketing Turnaround*[2], and *Beyond MaxiMarketing*[3]; and, finally, as mentors and consulting colleagues in the brave new world of modern marketing. Although most of the concepts in this book are our own, many are built directly upon the foundation these two innovative marketers laid before us.

We also wish to thank Mollie Neal for publishing the initial article on customer bonding in *Direct Marketing* magazine and for her enthusiasm for and interest in our ideas.[4]

To illustrator Steven Meyers of Gorham, Maine, we owe the book's sprightly renditions of Charles the Customer and Albert the Advertiser. These two characters have taken on a life of their own since they first sprang from Steve's fax to ours.

Polly Goodwin's good-natured support was a boon at every stage of this project. She contributed not only her research, copy-editing, proofreading, and transcription skills, but also her unending patience and moral support.

Finally, we owe enormous thanks to Mary Jean Smith for her eagle-eye assistance during the final stages of this project.

Richard Cross and Janet Smith
Tarrytown, NY

What makes *you* different from the pack?
Good service? A great advertising gimmick?
A sophisticated customer database? The
best possible price?

None of these alone is enough. And, today,
much, much more is needed. The rules of
marketing have changed faster than even the
most forward-thinking companies ever expected.
Only organizations that systematically earn the
trust of their customers or constituents will
survive as prosperous players into the new
millennium.

What Is Customer Bonding and Why Should You Master It?

Bird's-Eye View

Whether it's selling business-to-business products or services or consumer goods, raising money for a charitable cause, or mustering support for a political candidate, marketing is getting tougher and tougher. A new approach is needed—one that uses all available marketing technologies in a systematic way to create and preserve customer loyalty.

This book presents just such an approach. *Customer Bonding* is a bold new system for initiating and sustaining lasting relationships with each customer or prospect. It offers a strategic framework for a new, more responsible, and customer-focused kind of marketing. No matter how well you're doing now, this book will challenge you to do better, to expand your vision of your organization, and to protect the trust your customers place in you.

This book is written for anyone who:

- has a new product or service and needs to find customers,
- has customers and wants to give them good value,
- wants to have more customers, and
- wishes current customers would stay forever.

It's also for:

- companies that sell a business product or service to other businesses,
- companies that sell packaged or durable goods to consumers,
- companies that sell consumer services,
- companies that consist of only a few people selling in a single, local market,
- multinational conglomerates with far-flung operations,
- nonprofit organizations and political candidates who want to build and maintain an active network of dedicated supporters, and
- the advertising and marketing agencies and consultants who support all those mentioned above.

Our goals are straightforward:

1. To help all of you become true experts in customer bonding.
2. To dispel the myth that brand-building image advertising and direct-response advertising (advertising with a reply mechanism such as a toll-free number or reply card built in) are mutually exclusive approaches to marketing. They are not. In fact, both play an important and mutually supportive role in creating and sustaining customer loyalty.
3. To show that customer bonding is much easier than you think. So easy, in fact, that there is no excuse for *not* doing it.

A Crying Need for Loyalty

Customer bonding is the process of building customer relationships that withstand the rigors of today's fragmented, overcommercialized marketplace.

As any marketer or fund-raiser knows, it's rough out there and getting rougher. We are not talking about temporary difficulties created by cycles of economic contraction or expansion. We are talking about the increasing difficulty of maintaining a lasting relationship with consumers of your products or services—whether they're individuals or businesses.

As we'll discuss in the next chapter, changing life-styles and an overwhelming explosion of commercialism have reduced the power of mass-marketing techniques. A convergence of cultural, technological, and demographic trends has made it imperative to create a new approach to marketing—one that values the creation and maintenance of relationships with individual buyers.

Many U.S. marketers have already begun favoring direct media that enable them to reach individual prospects and customers by name. Advertising that was once created for mass audiences and delivered through mass-media channels—primarily print (newspapers and magazines), radio, television, and outdoor—is now created for named individuals and delivered by mail and telephone. And many print and broadcast campaigns that once sought only to get share of mind for a brand image are now geared to get interested individuals to identify themselves by name, address, and telephone number. In fact, marketers in many industries are allocating more of their advertising budgets to direct-response activities—direct mail, direct-response print and broadcast campaigns, and frequency-marketing programs.[1]

An internal organizational struggle often ensues when marketers attempt to justify the use of targeted marketing. They come to us with questions like: "Is it possible to create or support recognition for our product or organization without some kind of mass appeal through image advertising, publicity, trade shows and events, and other familiar forms of marketing and promotion?" "Where should direct marketing and database marketing fit in our overall marketing plan?" "Is it possible to move from bombarding the market with mass-media advertising messages to more interactive relationships where we have informative dialogues with individual customers?"

The answer to this last question is an emphatic, "Yes." You *can* achieve the balance. But you need to create a comprehensive strategy, one that combines the best of traditional and leading-edge marketing and recognizes the unique conditions of your particular marketplace.

Done genuinely, and with care, this approach earns customer loyalty—for the long haul.

How This Book Will Help

This book offers you a bold new marketing system that does just that. It blends the best of the proven techniques with leading-edge marketing, creating a powerful strategic framework for building stronger bonds with your customers.

No matter how well you think you're doing now, we challenge you to do better:

- Does your current marketing strategy fulfill the needs of your customers and prospects, your political supporters, or your fund-raising donors in a way that wins their loyalty?

- Have you started building a database of your customers? If so, have you determined its role in your overall marketing, advertising, promotional, and sales strategies? Is the database the core of information that drives every strategic and tactical element of your plan?

- Are you doing the right things to create meaningful, sustainable relationships with your chosen customers?

To be masterful in the matter of earning and keeping strong customer bonds, you will have to become skilled in achieving—with each of your customers—the most important element of any good relationship: the trust and loyalty both parties feel toward each other.

This book will show you how to do it. It's not as hard as you may think. But you have to do *all* of the right things for your customers, and do them well. Sophisticated consumers, donors, and political supporters demand nothing less as the price for their loyalty.

In fact, self-serving half-way measures can do irreparable harm to your organization. Too many consumers have been irritated and offended by irresponsible and sloppy packaged-goods marketers who target their children with ads for products of questionable value or safety, by telemarketers who use intrusive technology to break into the privacy of the family dinner hour, by fund-raisers who shovel mail at them by the pound, or by a host of companies that promise product or service benefits that they fail to deliver. Business customers likewise have been offended and turned off by misguided communications, overzealous salespeople, and manipulative marketing tactics.

Customer bonding experts know that investments in advertising, publicity, and promotion can create powerful market impacts. But they also know not to abuse this power. They seek to create durable relationships based on mutual trust and respect, on a fair exchange of value, and on an ongoing dialogue that recognizes both parties' needs. We're talking about building the kind of bond that suppliers and customers had in simpler times: homemakers with the corner grocer; tradespeople with suppliers; young professionals with barbers or stylists; consultants with clients.

Fortunately, the information age, with its interactive telecommunications technology and sophisticated computer databases, has made building such personal bonds possible even when dealing with hundreds of thousands of prospects and customers with many different needs and profiles and across far-flung geographies.

Toward a Responsible, Customer-Focused Marketing Framework

In this book we hope to disabuse you of the myth that one marketing strategy is inherently better than another. (Note that from here on we will use the term "marketing" in the broadest sense, as a set of strategies and tactics that encompasses Kotler's "Four Ps" of product, price, promotion, and place.[2])

Rivalries among different marketing disciplines are legendary. Image-building advertisers, direct-response practitioners, sales-promotion specialists, public-relations gurus, direct salespeople, and event marketers—all are justifiably proud of their strategic contributions to the marketing mix and can make arguments as to why their component should be supreme. Friction between advertising agencies and direct-response practitioners has grown particularly pronounced as companies that used to rely solely on image advertising shifted more and more of their budgets into direct marketing. If you hire a direct-marketing or advertising agency for your firm, or work in one of these industries, you have no doubt noticed this competition for conceptual supremacy.

What often makes such rivalries bitter is the size of the advertising budgets at stake. But the debate is earnestly waged, with various practitioners believing the merits of their arguments and willingly falling into the "good guys/bad guys" morass.

We contend that all marketing disciplines have important roles to play in the new marketing drama:

- Image advertising, event sponsorships, promotion, and public relations are powerful tools for building awareness of your product or service and capturing a share of the customer's mind. But their payback is notoriously difficult to measure.

- Direct-response marketing practices such as direct mail, telemarketing, and direct-response print or broadcast advertising are versatile techniques that support sales promotions or let you build direct relationships with individual customers on a mass-market scale. But they may not always be the most cost-effective way to build awareness.

In terms of customer bonding, however, all of these marketing elements can potentially be combined as needed into a unified framework that supports your unique marketing goals and maximizes customer loyalty.

As we'll see, many marketers already intuitively combine many elements to good result. Not so the service providers who support them. In particular, the separate camps of mass-market advertising and database-driven marketing probably will not come comfortably together in any agency, as some promoters of "integrated marketing" would have you believe.[3] However, they *will* come together in your internal strategic marketing plan, where both can be positioned as synergistic tools for reaching and winning the hearts of customers, donors, and supporters.

Moving with the Times

Let us add two cautions before we begin.

As more and more companies develop customer databases and figure out how to use them, the customer bonding programs we'll be discussing in this book will *themselves* add to the din of commercialism. Consumers may eventually tune them out, just as they are already doing with mass advertising in the developed market economies of North America and Europe, and may eventually do in developing economies as advertising increasingly saturates people's lives.

This means that you probably face a finite window of opportunity and stand to gain much from mastering the customer bonding system right now. From American Airlines's launch of the world's first frequent-flier program in 1981 to General Motors's 1992 U.S. introduction of a cobranded credit card with a rebate tied to GM car purchases, we've seen that the first marketer in a category to capture the customer as a member of its "club" may gain a powerful and lasting competitive advantage.[4]

But the potential for saturation also suggests the need to stay on your toes. Don't get too attached to any single program or theory. Learn instead to listen to your customers. The very market information that will enable you to earn loyalty—information about what customers value and how to deliver it to them—is the same information that will enable you to see where your market is heading and to adapt yourself so you can greet it when it arrives.

How to Use This Book

This book is organized into three parts. The first three chapters make up Part I. They tell you (1) why old marketing approaches aren't good enough anymore, (2) what the customer bonding system is, and (3) what information-driven marketing means and why you can't succeed without it.

Part II consists of Chapters 4 through 8. They are the heart of the book. They review in detail each level in the customer bonding framework and discuss its characteristics, strengths, and weaknesses, and what you must do to make it succeed. Throughout, you'll find plenty of actual examples of organizations that are putting customer bonding into action (as well as a few that aren't). Chapters 1 through 9 also include a bonding checklist to help you apply the system to your unique situation.

In Part III we help you put the system into action. Chapter 9 reviews the entire customer bonding framework and offers a customer bonding checklist to help you work with colleagues and clients in developing your own system.

Chapter 10 shows what a full complement of customer bonding programs—covering all five degrees—could look like, and it does so for three different hypothetical companies—in publishing, resorts, and business services.

And because customer bonding is about enlarging your vision, the book closes with a look at what you could accomplish when you put customer bonding to work in *your* organization.

PART I

The Information Core

Chapter 1

Transcending the Din

Bird's-Eye View

Commercial clutter, rising anticommercialism, media disintegration. These are all factors that ultimately make consumer cultures resistant to traditional marketing, with its heavy reliance on mass advertising and promotion. From the computer screen to the noon sky above, there is little that advertisers won't consider as a medium. Even the "new marketing"—targeted, dialogue-oriented, and trust-building—runs the risk of further numbing populations already besieged with messages exhorting them to consume a host of goods and services. This chapter explores the reasons behind this tough marketing reality and measures the scope of the challenge.

> . . . Salesmanship, which at one point in history occupied a specific sector of the cultural arena, has come to occupy almost every facet of human experience.
>
> Stuart Ewen, Media Studies Professor, Hunter College[1]

As we approach the millennium, it's no secret that commercial messages fill what media professor Stuart Ewen calls "virtually every crack in people's lives."[2] It gets harder and harder to break through the din. Even if you offer a product or service of obvious value to a select group of people, finding and reaching those individuals is more difficult than ever before. And once you do reach them, you'd better have their interests genuinely at heart if you hope to gain—and keep—their trust and loyalty.

What Has Changed?

Several factors are converging to create a radically new marketing landscape that is redefining the marketing task for every organization. Let's take a brief tour to assess the change factors at work.

Overwhelming Clutter

In the United States, Canada, and Europe, advertising clutter is a growing and serious problem. For example, the average American is now subjected to more than 3,500 advertising messages a day, double the rate of just thirty years ago.[3] At the same time, ad spending in all media has risen over ten times, from $12 billion to $138 billion in 1993.[4] That means that U.S. manufacturers and service providers spend more than $555 per year on every man, woman, and child.[5] And the amount of sales-related mail alone has risen from one-hundred to more than six-hundred pieces per person per year in the United States, more than double the volume in Canada,[6] which has the next highest rate, and six times the rate in Switzerland.[7] This sheer volume creates a cluttered communications environment that burdens both consumers and marketers. And the problem will only increase, as marketers seek ever more targeted avenues for reaching micromarket niches.

Advertising clutter is less of a problem in other economies, but it is nevertheless a factor in places like the United Kingdom (U.K.), France, and Germany, where advertising growth has slowed to less than 5 percent in recent years. In growing countries like the "four tigers" of Asia (Hong Kong, Singapore, South Korea, and Taiwan) and Latin American growth economies like Venezuela and Argentina, markets are less saturated with advertising, and marketers may have a profitable and relatively uncluttered playing field for some time to come.

Explosion of Products

All of this communications activity is driven by an explosion of goods and services that promises to fulfill every real and imagined need. When a baby pops out of the womb, marketers are waiting with a dozen ways to keep her bottom suitably dry and comfy. By the time she's old enough to notice advertising herself, a host of tantalizing goodies—toys, food, and entertainment programming—are offered to entice her. In fact, the older she gets, the more objects, images, and services are waiting to suit her every fancy. On grocery shelves alone, the 6,000 product choices of the 1980s[8] have proliferated to 30,000 today.[9] There are even products and services for the afterlife. (How about videotaping a last message for your loved ones or purchasing perpetual gravesite maintenance, for example?)

Media Disintegration

As you already know if you do any advertising at all, the need to promote an exploding array of products has created an equally explosive media landscape. Advertisers in mature and developing market economies are increasingly challenged to spread that expenditure across ever more fragmented media to reach their chosen targets. That's partly because the advertising industry, seeking productive ways to deliver finely tuned segments of buyers to clients, keeps inventing new communications channels. Virtually any medium may carry advertising messages—from ubiquitous public transportation to milk cartons or even screen-saver software that sends Eveready Energizer bunnies or Nike shoes cavorting across your computer screen. You can even get your product associated with global space research, thanks to a fledgling space-marketing industry.[10]

Here are a few other examples of what we mean by media proliferation:

- In 1994 Americans can choose their reading material from more than 11,000 different magazines, 10,000 newsletters, and 1,600 newspapers.[11] Business readers are offered more than 4,700 trade publications in the United States, a number that keeps increasing steadily.[12] According to recent data, advertisers in India can choose from as many as 20,000 consumer magazines and 3,000 trades. Japan surpasses the U.S. for newspaper publishing, with over 3,500 different newspapers published in the late 1980s.[13]

- New customization capabilities could soon make all of those numbers look pretty meager. From McGraw-Hill's *Business Week* to the National Farmer's Union's *British Farmer*, leading-edge publishers around the world are starting to put customer databases and selective-binding techniques to work, creating multiple versions of each issue to suit the interests of multiple micromarkets. The fledgling technology is currently used by only 20 percent of the U.S. publishing industry, and *British Farmer* is the first selective-binding publisher in Europe, but we expect this trend to grow rapidly in Western economies as more companies build and use customized databases.[14]

- Competition is fiercer than ever in the U.S. radio broadcast industry due to the proliferation of radio formats and the fragmentation of the listening audience. Stations struggle to gain fractional share-point advantage over competitors. However, radio is growing in popularity in many developing economies. Print media in other markets vary widely. Print advertising jumped noticeably in Australia, Hong Kong, India, Israel, Malaysia, the Netherlands, Norway, Sweden, Taiwan, the U.K., and the former West German Republic through the late 1980s.[15]

- Network television in the United States continues to lose ground to the burgeoning cable industry, which has seen advertising expenditures rise from $45 million in 1980 to almost $2 billion today.[16] There are currently about seven-thousand cable systems in the United States, representing approximately 50 million subscribers, that carry advertising and receive advertising revenues.[17] Argentina has more than 950 cable channels, and Japan has close to 300. In several European countries, cable has penetrated close to 90 percent of all households.[18] By the year 2000, viewers may have hundreds of programming stations to choose from on cable television. Cable is also growing—although at a lesser rate—in Europe, which has 165 stations today and is expected to grow by 65 percent by the year 2000.

- Traditional consumer couponing reached new highs in the United States in the early part of the decade, although redemption rates are running below industry expectations. Manufacturers distributed 310 billion coupons in 1992, of which 7.7 billion were redeemed.[19] That number remained relatively constant in 1993, and some experts expect traditional couponing to decline with the anticipated growth of electronic coupons that consumers can obtain as they shop.[20]

- The United States is by far the most advanced country in the use of direct mail. Expenditures tripled during the 1980s[21] as the medium extended far beyond its former limited use by catalogers and mail-order firms to become a major tool for both consumer and business-to-business marketers. Direct mail's popularity as an advertising medium is also growing rapidly in most European countries, as well as in Japan, Singapore, Australia, and New Zealand, as marketers discover the benefits of targeting their marketing programs to individual prospects and customers.

- New media, such as in-store couponing and interactive shopping aides, interactive television, broadcast facsimile (enhanced fax), and even on-line computer shopping, are also proving their commercial viability:

  —France Telecom provides on-line directory information, research services, and home shopping to six million French citizens through its Minitel terminals. On-line shopping promises to be a growth market in the United States in the coming years. And, following the passage of the North American Free Trade Agreement (NAFTA) in the fall of 1993, CompuServe announced plans to court subscribers in Mexico as part of an international expansion.

  —Dedicated television broadcast channels such as Whittle Communication's in-school Channel One and the birth of dedicated, upscale home-shopping cable channels in the United States, France, and Japan demonstrate the tireless march of niche marketing. Some experts predict the value of home shopping sales in the United States alone could be $25 billion by the year 2000.

  —New services—such as USAir's FlightLink or a new syndicated program from TV Answer and Transactional Media—are experimenting with combining entertainment programming and interactive shopping.[22]

—Other retailing innovations abound. Safeway Foods in San Francisco, for example, has rolled out an interactive food-shopping service that lets customers place orders from their PC or Macintosh computers at home or in the office.[23]

What we're actually witnessing is media *disintegration* resulting from the splintering of target markets and the concurrent redistribution of advertising budgets. Advertising as it existed for most of the twentieth century is rapidly fading into history. Marketers are being challenged to mix old and new media in ways no one has ever tried before, in the search for ever narrower and more elusive targets. The "cocooning" American consumer has turned into what trends forecaster Faith Popcorn calls "burrowing" anticonsumers of the 1990s,[24] making marketing success more and more dependent upon your ability to microtarget your communications to every individual in your marketplace.

Commercial Culture and Anticommercialism

Even if you *do* break through the din of competing messages and media, you still have to win the loyalty of consumers who, by and large, have grown weary and suspicious of advertisers' boisterous claims. The 1993 Yankelovich MONITOR®, an exhaustive survey of American consumers, confirmed that Americans have lost faith in all institutions. And few stand lower than the advertising industry. The only things that consumers gave lower confidence marks to were the claims of car salespeople and the statements corporations issued when stating their point of view on an issue! Worse yet, perceptions of product quality are declining.[25]

This portends a significant cultural shift that has radical implications for marketing directives. Dr. Ewen, Dr. George Gerbner of the University of Pennsylvania, and others who study consumer trends argue that commercialism has all but played itself out in the United States. Futurist Faith Popcorn predicts a shakeout, a consumer revolt so profound that she terms it a "socioquake":

> "We'll be buying, yes, but buying carefully with a new awareness that buying is a political act having ramifications all the way up the chain of life. This socioquake will be consumer-driven, which is why business people will want to get in on the act. Companies will have to realize that you don't sell only what you make. You sell who you are."[26]

According to Popcorn, what makes consumers choose one product over another is increasingly going to be a "a feeling of partnership with the seller."[27]

What does it take to become a partner with your customers? *You have to do more than just break through the din. You actually have to transcend it by engaging in a true exchange of value with your customers.*

Some marketers do this by becoming proactive supporters of social causes that they and their customers care about. The Body Shop is a well-known example. A specialty retailer of cosmetics and toiletries, The Body Shop grew from a single shop in Brighton, England, to a global franchise operation with 1,000 stores in 44 countries and sales of $574 million in 1993. Such growth was accomplished without spending a single penny on traditional advertising. Instead, the firm invests in publicity initiatives on behalf of various causes, such as cosmetics and toiletries created without animal testing, environmentally friendly packaging, voter registration, and social justice for third-world peoples. Founder Anita Roddick has, in effect, translated her personal activism into a set of principles that imbue the product set and retail operations of the global enterprise she built. She calls this approach "profit with principles."

Italian apparel manufacturer Benetton Group SpA (United Colors of Benetton in the United States) follows a different path to break through the din. A $1.63 billion marketer of colorful apparel with more than 7,000 stores in 100 countries, Benetton uses mass-media advertising to stir up controversy on socially oriented themes such as multiculturalism, racial harmony, and world peace. The strategy is notable for two reasons: (1) Benetton's advertising content generally stakes out highly visible—some might even say risky—positions on touchy social issues, and (2) the content of Benetton's social advertising lacks any connection to the product the company offers.

The fall/winter 1991 campaign, for example, consisted of such company-commissioned photographs as a nun and a priest kissing on the lips, a display of unrolled pastel-colored condoms, a human baby still attached to the umbilical cord, a white infant nursing at a black woman's breast, and black and white toddlers embracing. (See Exhibit 1.1.) This last image drew fire in the United States because the black child's dreadlocks looked like devilish horns while the white child's blonde, curly locks made her look almost angelic. So many people

Exhibit 1.1 Benetton Campaigns Spark Controversy.

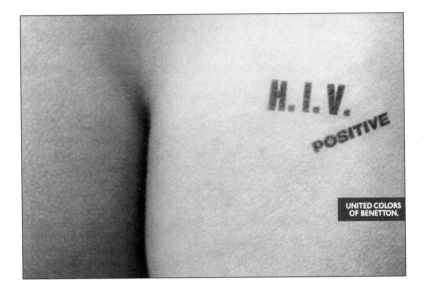

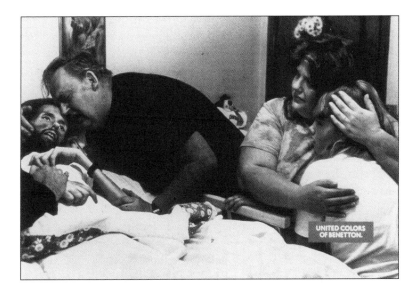

International clothing retailer Benetton Group SpA breaks through the din with its controversial advertising campaigns. For several years, the firm has run awareness campaigns on social issues such as multiculturalism, discrimination, and world peace. The ads were notable both for their riskiness and their lack of relationship with Benetton's products.

called to complain that the company provided its customer-service operators with a special address for ad comments. Even some Benetton store owners were upset, and sales were uneven.

The spring/summer 1992 campaign switched from commissioned photography to existing works by well-known photojournalists, but it, too, became a lightning rod for anticommericial sentiment. The photographs depicted real human suffering, such as a grieving family at the deathbed of an AIDS patient; a car exploding from a terrorist bomb; and strong images of immigration, AIDS, terrorism, and violence. The campaign drew wild praise for its breakthrough creative approach and heavy criticism from anticommercialists, who deemed the campaign "a prime example of the most craven kind of consumer democracy."[28]

Benetton remained unapologetic and continued on its social-awareness path until the spring of 1994, when Benetton executives finally apologized after a campaign intended as a "plea for peace" provoked a furor around the world. The campaign showed the blood-soaked uniform of a fallen Croat warrior, with a letter supposedly written by the slain soldier's father. When the father challenged Benetton, saying the photograph was not of his son, the Vatican called the ad tantamount to terrorism and authorities in some countries banned the ad from use. But whether this uproar will impact sales any more than prior upsets remains to be seen. Meanwhile, Benetton Group SpA reported that worldwide sales increased 13 percent in 1993, despite enduring recessions in its major markets.

While social values are increasingly important marketing factors, so, too, is an organization's service orientation. Customers are no longer content with multiple-choice options bearing little relationship to their unique requirements. They expect and demand more from suppliers than ever before and are increasingly angry when they don't get it. In the business-to-business arena, this translates into customers who expect suppliers to be partners in a strategic "value chain," where each player in the chain puts the interests of the whole chain before its own. In the consumer arena, it means customers who demand new products, services, and marketing approaches that accommodate increasingly diverse needs. In the United States, for example:

- The nation's 25 million Hispanic Americans, with buying power of $200 billion and a projected growth rate through the year 2000 of 41 percent, make up 10 percent of the U.S. population and are its fastest growing ethnic segment. The group's purchasing power has grown 70 percent since 1982, compared to 33 percent for mainstream white Americans. But the market is fragmented by country-of-origin variants in cultural values and language and is heavily concentrated in five states.[29]

- Ethnic marketing to other immigrant populations remains fragmented and difficult. According to the U.S. Census Bureau, 14 percent of U.S. residents over the age of five speak a language other than English in their homes. Most marketing is still done locally via print, radio, and even broadband media for communities of Koreans, Japanese, Indians, Mexicans, Russians, Poles, and the many other "melting pot" communities. Nevertheless, 70 percent of packaged-goods manufacturers and service providers surveyed by Donnelley Marketing were engaged in ethnic marketing in 1991, the most recent year in which the Donnelley survey tracked this practice.[30]

- Among more established American populations, African-Americans make up the nation's largest minority group. This group is growing at twice the rate of the white population and has been largely ignored except by a few consumer marketers.[31]

- American seniors, the so-called "third lifers," with twice the median net worth and a faster growth rate than any other age group, have very specific product and service requirements across virtually every category.[32]

- The "new" American woman, starved for time and energy, is not the attentive shopper of the past, and is less interested in the task of product comparisons. She buys tried-and-true brands from well-known companies to minimize the risk of a bad choice. Three out of four women report that once they make a successful purchase, they tend to be loyal re-purchasers. They also are less responsive to Madison Avenue's definitions of femininity and want to be addressed directly, as individuals.[33]

- The upcoming generation of 46 million eighteen- to twenty-nine-year olds—variously dubbed "busters," "twentysomethings," "slackers," "Generation X" (from the Douglas Coupland novel of this name), "Xers," "post-boomers," or the "shadow generation"—represent a $125 billion market and will fuel future growth for many product categories. But these individuals are also hard to reach. Traditional print and television media are still largely geared to aging "baby boomers." And don't expect materialistic values to play well here. As one advertising executive says, "As soon as they think you're trying to sell them something, they turn off and walk away."[34]

A Global Challenge

The stinging global recession of the early 1990s left its mark on many companies, teaching the tough survival lesson that smart marketing pays. But smart marketing is not always easy to practice globally. Disparate marketing infrastructures in different geographies can impede the best laid plans. In Europe, for example, overall advertising expenditures are rising faster than in the United States (see Exhibit 1.2). But targeted marketing techniques are difficult to practice in markets like Germany, where steep postage costs and tough privacy laws impede the use of database marketing and direct-mail techniques. And it may be impossible in the new economies of Eastern Europe or the emerging economies of Asia and South America, where customer lists are unreliable and hard to find.

Another barrier can be cultural. While new market economies in Central and Eastern Europe, the Pacific Rim, South America, and Africa are hungry for products, sophisticated West European consumers are—like their American counterparts—increasingly resistant to advertising messages. Says Fabienne Petit, marketing manager for Sopad Nestlé in France, "Studies show that the consuming society is finished. People are looking differently to products. You have to seek techniques whereby you can bring real service to consumers, so that they get the feeling you are really helping them as a brand and are not only trying to make them buy your product."

Thierry Hermant is training manager for Rapp & Collins/Piment, the European direct-marketing arm of the third largest advertising agency in the world. He believes European marketers must overcome ignorance of database-driven marketing to meet these marketing challenges in the 1990s. "The new challenge is to be profitable in a depressed economy where the rules of the golden past thirty years are no longer operating," Hermant explains. "Database-driven marketing is among the new solutions, but few operating models exist. How do you keep track of purchases and cost-efficiencies, especially for fast-moving consumer goods products? And with short-term profit goals and frequent turnover among product managers, the long-term investment required to build a marketing database can be a problem."

The problems of advertising clutter and anticommercialism are less evident in Eastern block countries and in fast-growing Asian markets like Taiwan, Singapore, Malaysia, and the Philippines.[35] China is also a virgin market with vast potentials for growth. Asian consumers have not been exposed to the glut of advertising seen in Western markets.

Exhibit 1.2 Growth of Major Media Expenditures in Europe, the
United States, and Japan: 1982–1992. (Unit: Index = 100 in 1982).

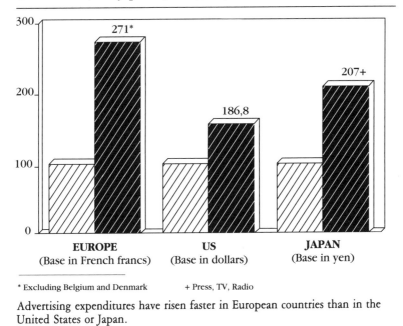

| | EUROPE
(Base in French francs) | US
(Base in dollars) | JAPAN
(Base in yen) |

* Excluding Belgium and Denmark   + Press, TV, Radio

Advertising expenditures have risen faster in European countries than in the
United States or Japan.

Source: 10 Années d'Investissement Publicitaires 1982–1992, Association des Agences
Conseils en Communication (AACC), Paris, France, February 1994.

Direct marketing is also becoming accepted practice and, while mailing
lists are difficult to come by throughout the region, other supporting
infrastructures are falling into place. The region's first frequent-flier
program, "Passages," was launched in 1993 by four of its most important
airlines.[36]

Japanese consumers, despite recent economic and political upheaval,
remain an important market for high-quality, name-brand goods, and
they are drawn to prestige products. They tend to become fiercely loyal
to chosen brands. They are highly responsive to mail-order programs,
perhaps because of the premium placed on leisure time and the difficulty
of shopping in crowded urban centers. Direct-mail saturation has not
yet occurred and, indeed, direct-mail expenditures are growing at 15
percent per year, compared to less than 5 percent for all advertising in
Japan in 1994.[37] Alternate media are appearing, too. In early 1994, the
Home Shopping Network, Inc. of Florida announced plans to bring
home shopping to Japanese consumers in cooperation with TeleCommunications Inc. and Japan-based Sumitomo Corporation.[38]

India's huge middle class, estimated at 300 million, presents an interesting market opportunity that is attracting companies like Coca-Cola, Kellogg, GM, Fujitsu, BMW, and DuPont. Bausch & Lomb has been selling pricey sunglasses and contact lenses there for two years. And Bank of America is betting that Indian consumers are ready for Western-style credit cards. While only about 750,000 cardholders existed in 1992, the bank believes that number could rise to 30 million by the end of the decade.[39]

In the Middle East, Israel and highly developed Arab oil-producing nations offer important markets that are still growing and are highly responsive to advertising, and especially to direct mail. The Near East economies of Pakistan, Bangladesh, and Sri Lanka are expected to grow as they move more toward market-oriented economies.[40]

And in Latin America, free markets are taking hold all over. Mexico offers an important growth opportunity, with a developing middle-class consumer segment of 30 to 40 million people hungry for goods and services. One-third of the country's 85 million-person population owned credit cards by the early 1990s, and the infrastructure for advertising and direct marketing is quickly maturing. Mexico has 320 newspapers, 200 major magazines, and 900 radio stations, plus a sophisticated telemarketing industry.[41] CompuServe, a major U.S. on-line information service, expanded its direct service to Mexico in early 1994, with Spanish language capability provided through partners Infoaccess and Infotec. Jim Ryan, director of international development, expects new trade opportunities to open up for both Mexican subscribers and U.S. marketers who use CompuServe in the wake of the North American Free Trade Agreement.[42] Indeed, as the prospects for regional trading blocks continue to develop in Latin America, expect further economic development and the emergence of other well-defined consumer markets with supporting marketing infrastructures.

At a dizzying pace, global economies and political shifts are creating new opportunities for marketers. Many of these emerging markets seem to offer growth potential for years to come. The key for savvy marketers is to tap this potential with comprehensive strategies that have as their common goal the maximizing of customer loyalty. Companies operating in more than one global market will undoubtedly have to offer different customer bonding programs in each market. But the customer bonding framework can help both local and multinational companies to achieve synergy in all their marketing efforts.

Global Opportunity or Global Clutter?

As advertising usage rises around the globe, clutter and anticommercialism will eventually become greater obstacles in marketing efforts everywhere, and marketers will have to seek new ways to bond with customers.

Moreover, marketers who have a systematic approach—one that is easily adapted to each market—will be able to stay on the leading edge, despite rapid changes at local levels. The customer bonding system we will be discussing in this book offers that flexibility. It can be used on either a local or global level. Indeed, the firm that is first to demonstrate real concern about customer relationships in *any* market may win a lasting competitive advantage.

Recap and Where-To

It's not too hard to find the obstacles to customer bonding. Advertising clutter, the disintegration of media, and anticommercialism are growing problems in the United States and in Europe. Government restrictions, supporting marketing infrastructures, and consumer attitudes towards marketing have to be evaluated in other global markets.

What all this means is that the golden days of marketing and advertising are over in well-developed Western economies and have a finite window elsewhere. Paradoxically, the very technologies that have opened new marketing opportunities have also made it harder for marketers to create lasting relationships with customers. So it is more crucial than ever before that marketers become experts in earning and keeping customer loyalty. In the next chapter, we'll show you what the customer bonding system is and discuss how it can help you maximize loyalty in all your markets.

Checklist

Answering the following questions will help you get a clearer picture of your current marketing situation. If you operate in more than one geographic market, be sure to answer the questions for each region or country. Local advertising, marketing, and direct-marketing organizations can help you locate detailed information about your marketplace. Future chapters will help you develop strategies to cope with your unique marketing challenges.

1. How would you characterize your major markets in terms of their current exposure to advertising?

   • Are you trying to reach prospects and customers who are already overwhelmed with advertising messages? How are you trying to overcome this competition for attention today? Is it working?

   • Is there a segment of your market that is highly resistant or even hostile to mass advertising? How does this impact your marketing challenge? What are you presently doing to acknowledge the sentiments of this segment? Is it working?

2. How well-developed is the marketing infrastructure in each of your target markets? Which media are you currently using and how well does each reach your target customers? Which ones are your competitors using and how well do their campaigns seem to be working? What other media are available to you?

   • Television advertising. Must you rely on network broadcasts or are targeted cable channels a viable option? Is interactive shopping an option, and would it work for your customers?

   • Direct mail. (This includes direct-mail solicitations sent to the home or office.) Are prospects and customers in this market accustomed to receiving direct mail? In what form (direct-mail letters, newsletters, catalogs)? Do they read it? How responsive are they? How are they used to responding—by mail, telephone, or some other means?

   • Telemarketing. Is your target audience responsive to outbound telemarketing? Can you incorporate advanced interactive technologies such as integrated voice, fax broadcast, or fax-on-demand?

   • Radio. What is the penetration of radio in this market? How well would broadcast radio work to reach your target customer base?

   • Outdoor. What options are available to you for outdoor advertising? Can your product be explained easily enough in outdoor advertising's condensed format?

   • Alternate media. Are there other media, such as in-store, on-line, and event sponsorship, that you could exploit to reach your targets? What media offer breakthrough potential because of their newness to the market?

3. How do you prioritize these marketing elements today in each of your markets? In general, how widely are each of these media used in each market?

- Image advertising
- Co-op advertising
- Direct-response advertising (including direct mail, telemarketing, print ads, and broadcast direct response)
- Outdoor advertising (billboard advertising)
- Sales promotions
- Alternative media (on-line, supermarket carts, matchbook covers, and so forth)
- Publicity (may be linked with social-cause sponsorship)
- Direct sales
- Event sponsorship
- Relationship marketing programs (such as frequent-buyer programs)

4. Have you examined your marketing strategy to see where you could be achieving greater global synergy? Are you maximizing customer loyalty in all your markets?

Chapter 2

The Information Core

Bird's-Eye View

Many organizations fail at customer bonding because they define marketing according to outdated models. To create winning loyalty strategies, you must build them around a dynamic database of information about prospective and actual customers, donors, or supporters. The dynamic record of these interactions becomes the Information Core. It informs all of your marketing activities and provides synergy and cohesion between all elements in your marketing mix.

We call this the new Information-Driven Marketing Model. It is the only marketing approach that can support higher levels of customer bonding. Information-driven marketing replaces the "image-based" model of earlier, simpler times. It is also more effective than the much-discussed Integrated Marketing Communications Model advocated by advertising agencies and some academics.

In this chapter, we will examine how the Information-Driven Marketing Model works—how it supercharges your marketing with "Datamotion." We'll also discuss the roles played by a marketing database, by customer dialogue, and by direct media—three essential ingredients for higher-level customer bonding programs. Last, but not least, we'll look at how you can stretch your marketing dollars further with "Dollar Doublers."

The battle for customers in the future will be won by marketers who understand how and why their customers *individually* buy their products—and who learn how to win them over, one customer at a time.
                    Rob Jackson and Paul Wang, *Strategic Database Marketing*[1]

As we prepare to look at how the customer bonding system can solve the problems of advertising clutter and consumer resistance—or insufficient marketing support structures in some markets—you need to know a few essentials that will enable customer bonding to work for you. This chapter offers a structural model for organizing your marketing activities. Hang a copy of Information-Driven Marketing: The Complete Model (Exhibit 2.4) on your office wall and refer to it daily. Share it with your colleagues, your consultants, and your marketing-services suppliers. Use it to help everyone in your organization understand that you are engaged in a new kind of marketing. It may take some time and effort to get everyone on board, but we promise you it *will* be worth it.

Information Is at the Core

How should an organization approach customer bonding? Where does it fit into your current activities? What levels of bonding can you shoot for and how? Should you try to achieve more than one level at the same time? Is customer bonding part of a larger program or is it the whole program?

To help you formulate answers for your unique situation, we're going to give you a new organizational model for your marketing activities. At its core will be a database of information about each prospective or actual customer, donor, or supporter. This information will form the underlying foundation upon which all of your new marketing choices will be made. It will form an "Information Core" that will inform and empower every element in your marketing mix, helping you to achieve real synergy and make the most of every opportunity to earn or reinforce the loyalty of your constituents.

As we'll see in Chapter 3, customer bonding is not just a marketing program. It is not just another *piece* of the marketing puzzle. It is a systematic marketing approach that can help you solve the *entire* puzzle. Successful bonding involves everything you do. It is an overarching strategy that eventually manifests in every tactical program, every communication, every contact you have with your prospects and customers, and in the very products and services you offer or the causes or candidates for whom you seek support.

The Battle for Conceptual Supremacy

To really understand the power of information-driven marketing, it helps to contrast it with the two other marketing models in vogue today. You may well be following one of these approaches already or may have felt pressure to do so from your own management or from external suppliers.

The two models we are referring to are (1) the Image-Based Marketing Model and (2) the Integrated Marketing Communications Model. Both share several characteristics that limit their usefulness as models for building or enhancing customer loyalty:

- Both are driven by product-based considerations, by virtue of their definitions and their origins in the advertising communications industry.

- Neither is driven by a self-replenishing supply of information about individual customers.

- Both are dominated by advertisers and their agencies rather than by information obtained from real prospects, customers, donors, or political supporters.

The Image-Based Marketing Model

The image-based marketing approach, depicted in Exhibit 2.1, has been the predominant model in most consumer product categories throughout the century, and it is also used by business-to-business marketers to support corporate identity. And, ever since political candidates discovered the power of television as an image creator in the 1960s, image advertising has dominated political elections almost to the exclusion of old-fashioned, grass-roots organizing.

As its name implies, image advertising's goal is the creation and support of a particular image for your product or service, your candidate, or your cause. As such, this model is heavily weighted toward image-oriented advertising, usually through mass media. To the extent that other goals and activities are desired, their success is frequently measured by how much they enhance the desired image.

Image is largely an intangible, making the measurement of one's success—or failure—in promoting it highly subjective. Lacking rigor-

Exhibit 2.1 The Image-Based Marketing Model.

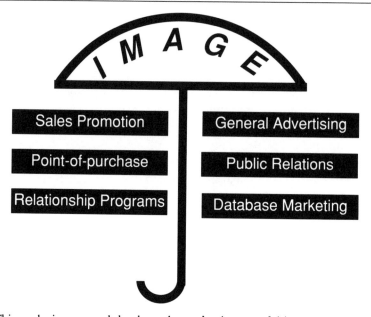

This marketing approach has been the predominant model in most consumer product categories throughout the century. Its goal is the creation and support of a particular image for your product, service, candidate, or organization.

ous measurements, this model relies largely on broad, bottom-line sales goals as yardsticks of performance. Individual line-item expenditures are more or less taken on faith as efficient and useful, and accountability is, of necessity, minimized.

This is a fairly comfortable arrangement for the executive or agency responsible for building and maintaining the image. But it is scarcely adequate for organizations trying to determine the effectiveness of current expenditures or to justify new expenditures on customer bonding programs. For these reasons, organizations operating under the image model often find it difficult to introduce programs that focus on measurable and tangible results.

If this scenario sounds familiar to you, starting a customer bonding program will require a significant change in approach. That change is sure to meet with resistance, both from your own staff or colleagues and from agencies and service suppliers who have a stake in maintaining the status quo.

Can you overcome the resistance? Emphatically, yes. But, to do so, you will need a clear strategic plan for improved customer bonding—a plan that others in your organization can comprehend and support. Your plan must include the development of a database; the use of direct media to reach your customers; a means for carrying on dialogue with your customers; plans for collecting, storing, and analyzing information collected from your customers; and a variety of other functions related to knowing and addressing your customers on a one-to-one basis.

Generally, you will find that the image-based marketing approach is not useful as a model for customer bonding programs because of its singular dedication to image building and its resistance to those marketing communications that call for direct customer contact. To achieve lasting customer loyalty, you will need the comprehensive marketing model offered in this book.

The Integrated Marketing Communications Model

Another model has been challenging the image-based model of late. It is also a message-driven approach, and it is commonly known as integrated marketing communications. This approach, depicted in Exhibit 2.2, emphasizes the importance of delivering consistent messages through all of the elements in your marketing mix. In theory, each element—direct marketing, sales promotion, publicity, and other approaches to customer communications—is recognized as a legitimate contributor to an overall strategy of market penetration or defense. In practice, however, we find that general advertising is often given more weight than other activities.

The integrated marketing communications trend began during the 1970s, when general advertising agencies started buying up direct-response and promotion agencies. More recently, it has found proponents in the academic community and among advertising agencies struggling to adapt to their clients' changing needs.[2]

Integrated marketing communications is a big step forward from image-based marketing because it recognizes the importance of other goals besides image creation and support. It also recognizes that these goals can be achieved through means other than general advertising. It even appears—at least on its surface—to provide a rational framework for allocating resources.

Exhibit 2.2 The Integrated Marketing Communications Model.

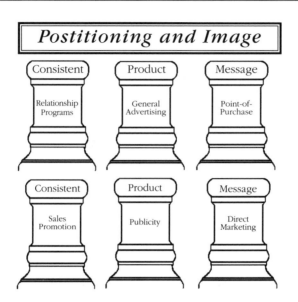

This model recognizes the interdependence of all your marketing programs and emphasizes the importance of consistency among the media carrying your message, but still aims to support product positioning.

However, upon closer examination, this model also has a number of serious problems:

1. What does it mean to be message-driven rather than market-driven? It means that your marketing programs are carefully orchestrated to serve a common theme and goal. But they may lack any ability to dynamically respond to the marketplace because the model does not require you to empower every element with information coming *back* from the marketplace. So if you're missing the market, it will take time to find that out, and even more time (and expense) to adapt all the pieces of the integrated program to new goals.

2. The apparent democracy of this approach is often benevolent tyranny in disguise, and it frequently fails to put each marketing discipline to its best use. Integrated marketing communications campaigns attempt to make advertising, publicity, sales promotion, distribution, and direct marketing live harmoniously side

by side. This is a laudable goal. But can a message that works well in one medium, such as mass-media advertising, really perform optimally in another, such as direct mail? And can you really create harmony among a diverse team of professionals whose disciplines sometimes compete with and confound each other? Cats don't bark and dogs don't meow. And, unfortunately, most "integrated" campaigns we've seen are still integrated around one master—and that master is most often product-oriented image advertising.

3. A third weakness of this model is structural. Creating a control center for your integrated campaign can be a daunting task. Many large advertising agencies that promote the integrated approach have expanded their services in order to provide one-stop shopping, and it may seem sensible to turn the reins over to such an agency. But doing so may mean abandoning suppliers who already know your business and do good work for you. Perhaps a better approach is to develop a strong in-house team to manage and coordinate a team. How you handle the structural controls of your marketing will determine the extent to which your program is truly integrated and how democratic it really is.

In sum, we find the integrated marketing communications model to be problematic. However, we applaud the idea behind it and see it as a tremendous conceptual breakthrough for advertisers. The jury is still out on its future. Certainly, it is not yet practiced by the majority of companies. And the advertising industry is just beginning to figure out how to integrate the various advertising and promotion disciplines while maintaining income.

Information-Driven Marketing and Datamotion

Information-driven marketing both supports image building and transcends it. It is far more flexible than either of the other approaches because it is fueled by actual information about the customer and the marketplace—dynamic information that is derived from interactions with the individuals that make up the market for your product. It also encourages the maximizing of all of your marketing programs because of the rich rewards that flow from the use of each element of customer information as your central resource. It starts with the assumption that each contact with a prospect or customer (or with prospective or existing donors or supporters) provides an opportunity to learn something more about that individual, and that what you learn can be stored in a database and used to drive virtually every aspect of your marketing and promotion plans.

Exhibit 2.3 presents the Information-Driven Marketing Model at its simplest. The key difference between this model and the image and integrated marketing communications models is the Information Core. This is your database of information about the individuals in your marketplace—created and constantly replenished from a variety of sources, including incoming calls to your sales- or customer-service departments, product-registration cards, replies to surveys or promotional offers, and the like. All of this information becomes a strategic asset that enables you to choose the most appropriate market activities

Exhibit 2.3 The Information-Driven Marketing Model.

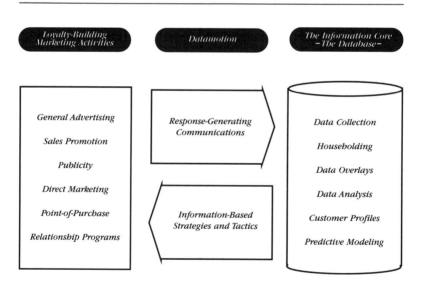

This model relies upon the information core. It is your database of information about the individuals in your marketplace—created and constantly replenished through calls to your sales- or customer-service departments, through product-registration cards, from replies to surveys or promotional offers, and the like. "Datamotion" describes the flow of data as you use information to determine marketing plans and as you bring fresh data in from new customer interactions.

that will build sales and create strong bonds with your customers. Based upon what you know about your markets and the objectives you decide to focus upon at any given time, the information you collect will help you decide how to allocate marketing budgets to get the maximum impact out of all your communications.

Crucial to this model is the idea that the information you're working with is constantly in motion between the marketer and the marketplace. This is what we call "Datamotion." When you use your existing data to determine marketing plans, your data are moving from the information core to impact the marketplace. But just as critical is the movement of new data back into the information core, which can occur every time you make contact with an individual in your universe and record their reaction.

Because information-driven marketing relies on information the market is giving you, it allows each marketing element to perform optimally. Rather than seeking to make advertising, publicity, relationship programs, and point-of-purchase all conform to the same look and message, each discipline can be used for the functions it performs best. The only constraint that is placed upon the people creating each element in the mix is that they must seek, wherever possible, to add a dialogue component to their communications, so that the maximum amount of usable information is derived back from every point of contact with a real, live prospect or customer.

Having an information core enables you to define and implement marketing strategies and supporting tactics based upon the most complete, up-to-date market information available.

Let's say that your core strategy is to increase the loyalty of existing customers while acquiring new ones, and you want to simultaneously position your organization to defend against competitive encroachments. With the data in your information core, you have many new options for meeting that strategy. Exhibit 2.4 shows you some of these options.

Information-Driven Marketing: The Complete Model

We know that the information core is the key strategic asset that enables you to define your strategies. And we've discussed how it powers a host of new tools and tactics for achieving those strategies.

Now let's put it all together in one diagram. This is the one we want you to put on your wall, carry in your briefcase, and pass out

Exhibit 2.4 Information-Driven Marketing—The Complete Model.

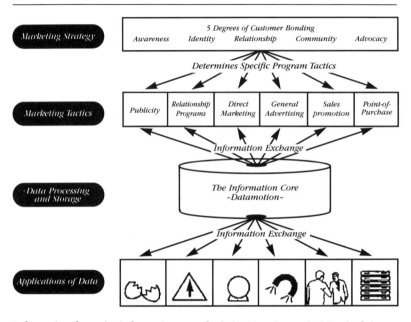

Information from the information core feeds back to the tactical level of the system, providing guidance for future activities on new business opportunities, partnering opportunities, routes for enhancing lifetime value, information acquisition, and market predicting.

to all your colleagues. Because once you really grasp the power of it, you will wonder how you ever got along doing business the old way! Here we see that the information core is at the center, the information crossroads, of your entire marketing strategy.

Let's say that strategy, shown at the top of the chart, is to build customer loyalty using customer bonding. How will you do that? Start by evaluating your marketing program options according to the contributions each can make to further customer bonding. Design each to feed information into the information core, the database. This information feeds back to the tactical level of the system, providing guidance for each succeeding round of activity. Meanwhile, the information core is an invaluable source of reliable, information-driven guidance on new business opportunities, partnering opportunities, routes for enhancing customer lifetime value, and a host of profitable new business activities.

New Product Incubator

This is a hatchery for all kinds of new developments. Based upon your information base, you might decide to launch a new customer club to retain the loyalty of current customers and/or to add a new product-line extension to attract new ones.

Lifetime-Value Enhancer

You can use your database to increase the cumulative value of every customer or supporter in your base. Using the information you have, along with media that let your prospects and customers communicate directly with you, you can shift light users from the base of the customer pyramid up towards the top by encouraging larger or more frequent purchases. (Fund-raisers can shift small donors up the donor pyramid by encouraging them to give more and/or to give more frequently.)

Crystal Ball Predictor

This describes the use of the information core to analyze what you are doing today and to direct your future based on that analysis. Using the information core to do predictive modeling helps you assess likely responses to any given marketing activity before you begin, thereby minimizing risk and maximizing the potential for positive results.

 New Customer Attractor

To know with whom you should talk next, you have to know with whom you are successfully talking already. That's the power of the database when it comes to expanding your customer base. By evaluating your current customer base to understand who your best customers are, you can target your new customer-acquisition efforts to people with similar profiles.

 Partnership Stimulator

The database can help you find the right marketing partners by giving you an accurate picture of what third-party tie-ins your customers would find attractive and by making an alliance valuable to prospective partners. As we'll see later in this chapter, partner-marketing can really multiply your competitive options, giving you access to new prospects, new products, and new ways to enrich the benefits you offer to your best customers.

Information Accumulator

Once you have collected information in your electronic file cabinet, the information core enables you to segment your marketplace based on whatever variables you choose. No longer do you have to make decisions about a mass market based only upon assumptions derived from statistical sampling. Now you can segment your actual markets to determine which activities to direct where.

Reaching Higher Bonding Levels: The Three D's

Unlike image-based marketing or integrated marketing communications, information-driven marketing places actual customer information at the center of your strategic planning. It lets you base all of your marketing plans upon live information about what the individuals in your marketplace think, how they respond to your actions, and what they want from you next. This information can guide your selection of messages and media and it supports targeted testing and promotions. And it is particularly valuable as you try to establish stronger customer bonds, as we'll see in future chapters.

The strongest customer bonds require what we call The Three D's—Database, Dialogue, and Direct Media. These three elements are the heart and soul of deep and lasting customer bonds.

If you live in the United States or Canada, you have already experienced The Three D's in action in your business life or as a consumer yourself. No doubt you belong to a frequent-flier or frequent-shopper club, for example, and get plenty of direct mail, magazines, or newsletters from suppliers. Your name, no doubt, is in countless marketing databases, and you are the recipient of appeals from suppliers who believe you may want what they have to offer. The most advanced among them only send you offers geared to your known interests, and they measure your response to every offer they send through various interactive techniques. Such marketers know about The Three D's.

Can you think of any cases of organizations that engage in such activities with you where you've come to expect their offerings as a *routine and desirable* part of your every day life? If so, that organization has locked in your business. Start noticing who has won your loyalty in this way, because you will certainly want to learn from what they do.

It's quite possible to create awareness for your product or service or cause without The Three D's. In fact, as we'll learn in Chapter 4, awareness bonding relies almost exclusively on one-way communications aimed at the market through mass media. The same is true of identity bonding, as we'll see in Chapter 5. But both are fairly fragile and vulnerable to competitive attack. To create stronger loyalty with customers, you have to move to the higher-level bonds—relationship, community, and advocacy. It's harder to break away from a relationship than to just change your mind about something—to adjust your image or impression. To create the relationship means you have to: (1) know what the individuals in your marketplace like (database), and (2) keep learning more about them (dialogue), which requires that you (3) have some way of communicating directly with them (direct media).

Database

Marketers still sometimes make the mistake of thinking that advertising alone builds relationships. But it's impossible to have a relationship with someone you can't name or that you see only as a set of demographic or psychographic characteristics.[3] A relationship requires a certain amount of sharing and interaction. And that requires a database. You have to know who your customers are by name and address to interact with them directly and effectively.

Database marketing has received lots of ink in the marketing trade press and continues to be a hot topic on conference rostrums in many industries. In fact, a whole industry of consultants, publications, trade events, and seminars has sprung up to fill the growing demand for database-marketing assistance. From radio broadcasting to publishing to banking to pharmaceuticals to politics and more, marketing professionals are trying to get their hands around the technology and application of the database.

But, for all the talk, most companies seem to be stuck working at the most rudimentary stages of database building and database-driven promotions. These efforts are often designed to achieve only short-term sales goals and to operate at the lowest levels of the customer bonding system. Some companies aren't even aware of the potential to form higher-level customer bonds. Or they consider the investment in creating stronger bonds too expensive. It is remarkable, for example, how few think to ask customers for referrals. (Word-of-mouth advertising is known to be the most powerful form of advertising, and buyer-get-a-buyer programs are an old and familiar way for direct marketers to create new business.) Fewer still have incentive programs such as MCI's Friends and Family Calling Circle, which empower and give customers the incentive to pass along good deals (see Chapter 8).

We are *starting* to see more organizations working at building long-term relationships with customers. These firms are beginning to make the necessary commitments of time, personnel, and technology to capture meaningful customer data and launch outbound relationship-building programs. Their stories are inspirational. You'll read about some of them in upcoming chapters of this book.

Much of the public discussion about marketing databases focuses on technological micro-issues at the expense of strategic questions. The technical issues can indeed make—or break—a database-driven marketing program and are worthy of your study and attention, but not until you have decided on a strategic direction that maximizes your chances for success. Technological decisions should be driven by your marketing goals, which must include closer ties to your customers.

A marketing database is a repository for the information you need in order to have a mutually rewarding relationship with your customers. For purposes of building such a relationship, it should include these three categories of information:

1. Customer name and address.

2. Relevant information about that individual and other household members, such as age and income level, family status, and buying intentions, that you collect yourself and obtain from other sources.

3. Data captured whenever you and the customer have a transaction. This includes behavioral data, such as what, how, when, and why (in response to what stimulus) the customer interacts with you—whether it is to call your toll-free number for information, to respond to a survey, to send in an order, or to contact your customer-service line with a complaint or question.

What information you capture within these categories will depend upon your strategic goals. Exhibit 2.5 presents a sampling of what kinds of information database marketers in various industries have been collecting.[4] You'll notice that those with a direct-response orientation (the cataloger and publishing segments) were much more likely to monitor customer lifetime value and other nonpromotional information than were manufacturers, wholesalers, and financial-service providers. We attribute that to the relative inexperience of the latter segments in making information-driven choices.

When it comes to customer bonding, you should update your database with information every time you make contact with someone in your database. Every mailing you send out is an opportunity to gain valuable information as well as an order. Every customer purchase presents you with an invaluable opportunity to enhance your understanding of how your customers like to do business. If such critical data sources are overlooked, your flow of information about customers and prospects will stop, hobbling any information-based marketing programs you try.

Dialogue

Dialogue is the process of interacting directly with your prospects and customers (or, if you're a nonprofit or political organization, with your donors and supporters). To foster dialogue, you have to provide ways for these individuals to react directly to whatever communication you send them, be it an advertisement or FSI (free-standing insert) in the mass media; a catalog, newsletter, letter, or bill insert sent to their home or place of business; or a telephone call asking for them by name. Dialogue continually refreshes the database of marketing information you are building, enabling you to stay alert to what prospects and customers want from you.

If you are not convinced that direct communications and dialogue are important these days, just consider the case of Michael Dell, who used it to build the fourth largest personal computer company in the world. Dell founded Dell Computer from a dormitory room in 1984, bringing custom configurations, direct mail-order selling, and unprecedented service guarantees to a field previously dominated by IBM's monolithic sales approach. Both corporate buyers and small businesses alike flocked to Dell's new channel and brand, sparking a revolution in the way PCs are sold worldwide. Dell set the standard that IBM

Exhibit 2.5 What's in Your Database?

	Total	Manufacturing	Cataloger	Wholesale Trade	Financial Services	Publishing
DOLLAR VALUE OF PURCHASE	67.5	78.5	84.2	79.8	55.6	64.3
HOW LONG INDIVIDUAL HAS BEEN A CUSTOMER	64.3	65.0	78.9	62.8	66.7	73.8
NUMBER OF PURCHASES ANNUALLY	61.5	68.4	84.2	63.8	53.7	61.1
DOLLAR VALUE OF PURCHASES ANNUALLY	55.7	68.4	73.7	69.1	35.2	48.4
SOURCE OF ORIGINAL LEAD/CONTACT	55.3	55.4	52.6	47.9	74.1	66.7
TRACK PROMOTIONAL EFFORTS	34.0	31.6	42.1	26.6	50.0	38.1
ADD COMPANY INFORMATION	20.2	20.3	0.0	17.0	33.3	22.2
BY SURVEY	55.6	47.2	0.0	50.0	44.4	67.9
BY OVERLAY	40.7	44.4	0.0	50.0	50.0	35.7
TRACK NON-RESPONDERS	18.9	18.6	15.8	11.7	38.9	19.8
ADD SOCIO-DEMOGRAPHIC INFORMATION	18.5	13.0	5.3	12.8	40.7	19.0
BY SURVEY	57.6	69.6	0.0	50.0	45.5	62.5
BY OVERLAY	48.5	43.5	0.0	33.3	68.2	50.0
INFORMATION ON ON OTHER PURCHASE INFLUENCERS AT THE SAME ADDRESS	16.6	18.1	15.8	12.8	25.9	14.3
TRACK RENTALS OF YOUR CUSTOMER'S NAME	6.7	5.1	10.5	3.2	5.6	11.1

METHODOLOGY: This survey was commissioned by Direct magazine and conducted by Jacobson Consulting Applications of New York, N.Y. The names were selected on an nth-name basis, primarily from Direct's circulation list. The survey closed on September fifth and 535 completed questionnaires were returned, for a response rate of 27.9%. The survey was confidential.

What's in Your Database? Who knows what? The types of data gathered and kept in a database vary from the obvious (dollar value of purchase) to what might *seem* obvious (name rentals) but isn't.

and others had to follow. And the standard was based on dialogue. Writes *Target Marketing* editor Denison Hatch, "Dell has learned to talk to its customers, while IBM is talking to itself."[5]

Many marketers suffer too much anxiety about dialogue because they erroneously believe that it is difficult to establish. This anxiety is especially acute in organizations that have heretofore avoided direct contact with their constituents. They may lack the facilities and knowledge required to maintain a dialogue and may have no idea how to make direct customer contact work for them.

But anxiety is no reason not to act, especially with competition for customer loyalty increasing in every industry, as well as in the public and nonprofit sectors. And listening and learning from actual constituents is only daunting if you usually rely on focus groups, third-party research, statistical surveys, or "gut feel" to inform your marketing decisions. You will soon discover the benefits of putting an ear to the market and listening carefully:

- Your future interactions will be driven by accurate information about each prospect or customer as an individual rather than as a demographic statistic.

- You will have ongoing and reliable input from the people you need to know best—your customers or supporters—about what you are and are not doing right. Every customer transaction provides a research and testing opportunity for your products and services, your pricing, your messages, and your business operations.

- You will have a reliable base for trying out new product ideas, for approaching new strategic business partners, for identifying new prospects based on your known customer profile, for launching customer-get-a-customer programs, and for all your customer bonding activities.

Some organizations hold back from creating dialogue because they fear that the mere act of listening will obligate them to act on all the wishes and whims of their audience. It does not. Nor does it mean that you personally have to do all the listening. Think about it for a minute. In the United States, when President Clinton talks about putting in a toll-free number at the White House for citizens to call and register their views, few callers actually expect to reach the President personally. Those who want to interact are usually content to make do with automated-answering systems that let them navigate to the issue of their choice and leave a voice-mail message. Others are content to send letters or postcards. They are often less concerned about *how* they are heard than they are simply that they *are* heard. (Indeed, as Ross Perot and Bill Clinton graphically demonstrated both during the 1992 presidential election and since, people will use almost any forum you make available—including dial-in talk shows—if they have a desire to interact with you or your organization.)

As more marketers embrace the idea of dialogue, they are refining old techniques for customer interaction and adding innovations:

- Preprinted surveys and questionnaires that use ink-jet and laser printing to fill in basic information such as customer name and address, freeing the customer to focus on substantive responses.

- Opinion polls conducted via organization-sponsored newsletters or magazines, through direct-response print ads, or via telemarketing or direct mail.

- Product registration forms that ask for detailed demographic and psychographic data needed to develop customer profiles.

- On-line customer-service systems that let your service representatives collect valuable marketing information while they record and categorize customer complaints or problems.

- Event admission forms that ask for basic attendee information.

- Surveys inserted into magazines and newsletters.

- Even just a few key questions added to an invoice or order form.

Of course, maintaining dialogue is not always easy or cheap. You have to have a dialogue plan before even building your database. And for mass marketers, the cost of maintaining individualized customer relationships can easily run as high as $10 to $20 per customer per year. (See Chapter 6.)

Creating effective two-way communication also requires an in-house champion who can convince every person and every department in the organization to do business in this new way. What do you do if you are that person? Sell the concept as a new *attitude* toward your customers. Ask everyone to participate and contribute to it. You will probably find untapped enthusiasm for customer dialogue among your colleagues. Once people in your organization get a taste of direct feedback from customers, they will want more. They will find out how great it is to stop guessing what the market wants. Eventually, everyone will understand that this is a much smarter, much easier, and much more rewarding way to run a business.

Direct Media

New communications technologies are making it easier than ever to create dialogue with customers. Direct-mail, interactive voice response (IVR) systems, interactive facsimile, on-line conferencing, electronic mail—even interactive TV—are increasingly affordable and workable tools for interacting directly with your constituents. With some ingenuity, you can even link telecommunications-based media directly with your computerized database to automatically record each exchange of information you have with your constituents!

Mail is still the most popular direct-response medium. In the United States direct-mail usage has more than doubled since 1980 and, in virtually every business survey we could find, marketers acknowledge the medium's growing importance as a communication channel. But even traditional advertising media—print, TV, radio, and outdoor—are increasingly used for direct response. In fact, these media are starting to profit from the trend.

NBC television, for example, announced a new service for advertisers in July 1993—a toll-free number advertisers can promote for additional product information. In a way it's like a magazine's bingo card in which the medium carrying the message takes on responsibility for handling resulting inquiries. Of course, the telephone is a much more powerful response device than the bingo card. In addition to just getting a name and address from responding viewers, it permits companies to take orders and establish live dialogue with prospects and customers, with donors, or with supporters. The advertiser pays for the calls, of course. There's enough of a margin built-in so that NBC profits from the service as well.[6] What an opportunity for NBC to learn more about its viewers and to speak to them directly! Armed with direct information about what type of advertising works best in combination with its programming, NBC's sales force has an entirely new way to sell air time and a new telemarketing profit center to boot.

The best direct media, however, are often "private media," meaning that the sponsoring organization owns them. A company that sends a monthly newsletter to customers with their bill, or that produces a customized quarterly magazine, has created a private channel of communication. The use of private channels permits the sponsoring organization to create highly customized communications, with all kinds of interactive devices. They can combine nonselling formats with selective selling, creating very effective "adazines" and "adletters." Companies that publish mail-order catalogs are increasingly giving selling space over for interesting editorial material because they have found it can increase readership, retention, and response. (The resulting hybrids are sometimes called "magalogs.") Moreover, the sponsor can choose whether to make the channel available to other marketers. Many do include ride-along offers or other advertising from carefully selected marketing partners. The partner can provide extra value to readers and also offset costs.

Although no one has an accurate count, company-sponsored newsletters and magazines appear to be one of the fastest-growing vehicles for targeting prospects and customers. (According to *Business Marketing*, customer-targeted magazines are growing at an explosive rate.[7]) This is a good indicator that corporations are taking relationship-building seriously, because these publications are frequently quite expensive to produce and require a real commitment. Customers expect to see them regularly, and they generally require either a dedicated staff or ongoing partnership with a contract publisher. Some, like *Nintendo Power*, are tied into frequency-marketing programs that promote product or service sales and customer feedback. Many offer useful tips and advice related to the company's products and services. Others are oriented to image-building, with the best of these relying on reader research and letters to the editor or on surveys to determine their editorial content.

Magnifying Your Impact with Dollar Doublers!

The power of The Three D's—Database, Direct Media, Dialogue— can be magnified using another essential element that we call "Dollar Doublers." These are techniques that permit you to get more of a wallop out of every marketing dollar you invest. Adding value without adding cost is a good trick, and dollar doublers help you do exactly that!

There are three reliable ways to double the impact of your marketing dollars:

1. Add "double-duty advertising"—something that every marketer should be doing by now—to your marketing objectives.

2. Issue "private money" to your customers—"currency" that is good only for "purchasing" products or services from you or others.

3. Team up with marketing partners (usually suppliers of non-competing goods and services) to offer your customers valuable rewards for their loyalty.

Double-Duty Advertising[8]

Make every communication accomplish more than one loyalty-building activity. That is the idea behind double-duty advertising.

An example that is particularly ingenious is a print campaign that supported the launch of Microsoft Excel version 3.0. While neither the company nor its agency, Ogilvy and Mather, retains files on the campaign today, it appears to have accomplished several objectives simultaneously. The first two-page advertisement ran in major computer magazines in late 1991 and featured the large, bold headline:

> "9 out of 10 Mac spreadsheet users use Microsoft Excel. What are we doing wrong?"

The only other elements on the page (besides mail-in instructions) were a large rectangular space for writing comments and the appeal:

> "Tell us what's on your mind and it could end up on your screen."

Think about the headline for a moment. If "9 out of 10 Mac spreadsheet users use Microsoft Excel," then Excel has 90 percent of the market. That's quite a record and speaks well for the product without seeming to boast. "Tell us what's on your mind and it could end up on your screen" is the invitation to dialogue with the company about product improvements users would like to see. The clear message is that Microsoft is a company that cares about what users have to say; that's an important message to users and nonusers alike. When you think about it, most mass-media advertising is intended to recruit new customers. But in this case, Microsoft addressed its appeal to *both* prospects and existing users of Excel. That's double duty.

But there's more. The clear message is that Microsoft is preparing to launch an upgrade of one of its most popular products. And although the upgrade is months away from being available, this ad puts users on notice. To those who depend on computer spreadsheets, an upgrade that removes program glitches and adds timesaving features can be a godsend. What a terrific way to build suspense for a product introduction.

Microsoft received some 800 responses from Excel users. Each was answered with a personal letter. The next ad in the series (see Exhibit 2.6), which appeared several months later, actually showed some of those customer responses, complete with users' hand-written comments and drawings and the bold headline:

Exhibit 2.6 Microsoft Excel Advertisement Does Quadruple Duty.

The second flight in a two-stage campaign by Microsoft helped the software company launch its Excel spreadsheet upgrade while also collecting invaluable user feedback on the product *and* demonstrating the company's commitment to listening to customers. Moreover, Microsoft addressed its appeal to both prospects and existing users of Excel. That's quadruple duty!

"New Microsoft Excel version 3.0. The result of an exhaustive correspondence course."

The two-stage campaign actually demonstrated quadruple-duty advertising. With one campaign, the company (1) built awareness for the product, (2) asked for dialogue with users, (3) created a direct-response vehicle for both new users and upgrade sales, and (4) recognized the contribution that users made to the upgraded product.[9]

Private Money

Ever since consumers discovered the rewards of collecting frequent-flier miles, company-issued scrip has been moving into mainstream marketing. Airlines, hotels, grocery stores, credit-card issuers, and even running-shoe manufacturers are rewarding frequent shoppers with credits toward future purchases. According to Michael Schrage, writing for *The Washington Post*, such private money is becoming "the S&H Green Stamps of the 90s." He postulates that as information technology makes it easier for companies to establish and manage private currencies such as frequent-flier miles and purchase points, blocks of corporate credits will emerge. "Consumers will decide if they want to purchase goods and services with cash, credit card, charge card, or credits [*sic*] cards—just as today's frequent fliers now purchase air travel, rental cars, and hotel accommodations with their pseudo-currency mileage coupons," he writes. He also quotes Arthur J. Rolnick, research director at the Federal Reserve Bank of Minnesota and an expert on the history of American scrip, who says, "[Private money] is not a bad gimmick to use to promote brand loyalty."[10]

In Chapter 6, we'll look more closely at how such programs work to create customer loyalty. For now, let's just consider how private money can become a dollar doubler.

When you issue private money as a way to reward customers for their loyalty, you must be careful not to cut into your existing profit margin. If, for every $100 of purchases I make at a book store, I automatically get $5 in scrip (private money) to spend at the store, the book store has merely given me $5 from their profits. The worst thing that can happen, from the store manager's point of view, is to have 100 percent redemption! No book store could withstand that sort of attack on its margin, nor could most any other business.

This does seem like a paradox. All the books on the new marketing shout, "Reward your best customers!" (This book is no exception to that rule.) *But you had also better find a way to reward loyalty without cutting into profits if you want to keep your organization from financial ruin!*

The solution? Build your program around two complementary concepts: reward customers for reaching specific purchasing or activity goals, and expect that some rewards will not be redeemed. (This is what is commonly known as "breakage.") These two variables, rewards and breakage, are what will turn private money into a Dollar-Doubler for you.

Here's how it works. Private money becomes a Dollar-Doubler when customers are asked to accumulate credits or points toward a reward goal. An easy one to relate to is accumulating airline flight segments (rather than miles) toward free flights. When airlines run these promotions, they typically offer fliers a free ticket for flying a certain number of flight segments in a limited period of time. This goal encourages existing customers to buy more (it can include offers to update to gold-card status or other special privileges) and can also attract new customers from competing airlines. The net impact of the reward program is to increase overall business from both new and loyal customers.

At the end of the promotion some fliers accumulate fewer than the required number of segments and get no reward. Others accumulate more than are required for one free ticket but fewer than they need to get a second free ticket. In either case, they have generated incremental revenues. The airline takes into account that many participants will overshoot or fall short of the reward mark. And, of course, many rewards will never be redeemed. That creates the benefit to the sponsor known as "breakage." How much additional revenue such programs can generate depends upon how many customers would ordinarily reach the target without an incentive and how reachable the promotion target is (which also determines the level of participation). It's a numbers game—whether counted in your nation's currency or your firm's private money.

Partners

Also known as "strategic alliances," marketing partnerships are a mainstay of modern marketing precisely because they are one of the most effective ways to double the impact of your marketing dollars.

As more companies put loyalty-marketing programs in place, they quickly find that they need new ways to expand the value these programs provide to loyal customers. Programs that include the goods and services of another firm as rewards for demonstrating desired behavior are a tried-and-true method. According to one recent survey of U.S. marketing executives, three-quarters have already tried tie-in promotions and 90 percent plan to do so in the future.[11] And, overseas, leading-edge marketers are using the same techniques.

So when you fill up at participating New England Mobil stations these days and get a voucher towards a free ski weekend at one of the area's larger resorts, you're participating in a global trend to dollar-doubling. It's really just a question of economics. Mobil does not want to give away free gas as a reward for loyalty. So they team up with ski areas who want to reach Mobil's audience with their offer for discounted lift tickets. All the consumer has to do is fill up three times with Mobil gas and turn in the receipts for a discount coupon. For Mobil, the program builds continuity and loyalty. For the ski area, the signage at Mobil stations is nearly free advertising. Talk about win-win marketing!

That such partnerships work has been amply demonstrated by the plethora of cooperative-marketing programs in the marketplace. According to Ira Mayer, publisher of *The Licensing Letter*, tie-ins are growing rapidly in the licensing and entertainment marketing industries. And judging by reports in the marketing and advertising press, it appears that they are growing in virtually every other category as well.

Tie-in offers give both parties several advantages:

- As the sponsor of a reward program, you can (1) add value to existing customer relationships at little or no incremental cost, (2) reward your best customers by offering deals on someone else's product, and (3) protect your profit margins by giving away someone else's product.

- As the partner who provides the reward you get (1) exposure to a market you might not otherwise reach economically, and (2) promotion at places or times not otherwise accessible, such as at point-of-purchase or in private communications between the customer and the program sponsor.

The advantages of marketing partnerships make them increasingly attractive in this age of clutter. But the risks should be carefully evaluated, too. Many companies were left in an awkward mess when Air Miles, an eighteen-month-old program that gave subscribing consumers airline mileage for shopping with sponsoring companies, folded its U.S. operation in 1993. Air Miles's parent, Air Miles International Group, pulled out of the United States altogether in order to concentrate on its more successful operations in Canada and the United Kingdom. This left U.S. corporate sponsors, such as AT&T, Citicorp, Prodigy Services, Gillette Company, and Procter & Gamble, trying to figure out how to compensate customers who had bought goods from them with the lure of free airline mileage. (For additional background on the Air Miles decision, see page 139.)

While it may not be possible to prevent such problems altogether, the Air Miles example certainly underscores the importance of choosing your marketing partners carefully and cautiously. Always make sure you have a contingency plan in the wings.

Recap and Where-To

The heart and soul of maximizing customer bonds is information about real customers, real prospects, or real supporters. By adopting an information-driven approach, you empower your marketing with dynamic, up-to-the-minute information. This enables you to earn the respect and loyalty of your customers by structuring future communications and promotions to suit their individual interests and preferences.

Structuring your marketing so it can be driven by information may not be easy at first. You're bound to meet resistance from people in your organization and advertising agency who will probably regard the new approach as a threat. But with courageous leadership you can soon prove to all that listening to customers is actually the easiest and most effective way to do business.

Armed with your database capability and a commitment to a customer bonding strategy, you can supercharge all of your marketing activities. You'll soon master the use of direct media and dialogue and wonder how you ever did business any other way.

Some other essential tools will come in handy along the way. These are Dollar-Doublers, which include marketing partnerships and your own special loyalty rewards, known as "private money."

Checklist

1. How would you describe your overall approach to marketing your product or service?
   - Image-driven?
   - Marketing communications-driven?
   - Information-driven?

   How well is your current approach working for you? What improvements would you like to see?

2. Is the goal of building strong customer relationships at the center of your marketing strategy? Do you see or experience a conflict between strategies intended to enhance image and those that build one-to-one customer relationships?

3. What devices can you use to get information back from customers each time you interact with them? How can you increase the number of interactions so that you can collect more information while building your relationship with them?

4. What rewards for loyalty do your customers really want? Are you using rewards provided by business "partners" to recognize your loyal customers?

5. How can you use the concept of "private money" to make your loyalty-reward system more valuable and interesting to your customers?

6. Do you use awareness advertising to let prospects know about your reward program?

7. What information would you like to have about your customers that would help you design a relationship program?
   • Launch new products?
   • Increase sales of existing products?
   • Approach potential marketing partners?
   • Increase customer lifetime value?
   • Segment your customers into groups for targeted communications efforts?
   • Predict the future of your business?

Chapter 3

The Customer Bonding System

Bird's-Eye View

In this chapter, we will introduce you to the customer bonding system. Customer bonding may be an entirely new marketing approach for your organization, or you may already be doing some aspects of it. We'll give you an overview of the system, including the characteristics, strengths and weaknesses, and critical success factors for each level of bonding.

We define the customer bonding process broadly. It begins with the creation of awareness for your product or service, grows to become an ongoing bond based on the customer's relationship with your organization, and can even extend to other customers. Supporting it is the marketing triumvirate of (1) a strategy that emphasizes customer loyalty, (2) an honest appeal, delivered through targeted media, and (3) a product/service experience that meets or surpasses every expectation. We conclude this chapter with a note for any manufacturer who is trying to solve the vexing problem of trade bondage.

. . . Your objective—once you have customers—should be to woo them and excite them so that they continue to buy over and over again. In other words, bond them to you. Successful direct marketers achieve this by making their customers feel they are talking directly to them in a highly personal way. Poor marketers simply send out more and more offers.

Denison Hatch, Catalog Business[1]

As we saw in Chapter 1, reaching customers and gaining their trust is getting harder, especially in highly developed Western economies that have heavy use of advertising, splintering media, and growing consumer resistance. Even in less developed countries, global competition is fueling the growth of marketing industries that are quickly importing sophisticated marketing ideas. That is why it is becoming much more crucial, no matter where you market, to create lasting bonds with customers. To do that, you must be willing to take a fresh look at your approach to marketing.

There are a few other requirements:

- You will need a new strategic framework in which to position all of your interactions with your prospective and existing customers, donors, or supporters. You will have that by the time you finish reading this book.

- You will need a willingness to try new things; to experiment with a different marketing mix; to change your organization; to change the way you apportion responsibilities between your own people and the vendors who provide you with marketing services such as advertising or information management. (If you're one of these marketing-service suppliers yourself, you may have to adjust the kinds of services you offer and develop or hire in new skills.)

- You will need someone in your organization to provide leadership, acting as change agent, salesperson, advocate, and inspiration. Ideally, this leadership will come from the top, because cross-organizational cooperation is required to really create and sustain the highest level of customer bonding.

- You will need to pretest each new marketing effort very carefully, constantly monitor results as each is rolled out, and be prepared to make continual adjustments as you learn how the marketplace reacts to it. The new marketing environment demands accountability, and the new marketing technology affords the means to get it. Hard information must drive both strategic and tactical decisions. Focus groups and other forms of market research can define issues and give you a feeling for what customers are thinking, but they seldom provide true measures of the market. And why settle for less, when today's marketing technology enables you to determine the real interests of customers every day? (Chapter 2 discusses this all-important point in depth, and explains the new information-driven model that supports customer bonding.)

This may sound like a lot of change, but it's doable, as innovative companies around the world are proving. This book will start you on the new path. We're going to give you the framework you need— The Customer Bonding System. You'll be surprised at how much it will help you and the rest of your organization develop a workable— and profitable—approach to marketing that will carry you through the 1990s and beyond.

In the chapters to come, we'll show you in some detail how each level of customer bonding works. You'll discover that much of your current marketing activity fits somewhere in the customer bonding model. You'll also see where you could augment or modify your activities to be more effective.

The Customer Bonding Players

Without further ado, we would like to introduce a couple of characters who will help us illustrate the customer bonding system throughout the rest of the book. Allow us to present Albert, the Advertiser, and Charles, the Customer.[2] (See Exhibit 3.1.)

Albert the Advertiser

Albert is a marketer. Think of him as the collective organization you direct or work for.

This may be a stretch, particularly if you work in the public or nonprofit sector. But the fact is, whether you are a consultant selling your services through word of mouth, the head of a multinational conglomerate plying your wares through sophisticated channels, a bureaucrat in a government agency delivering services to communities you serve, or a fund-raiser in a nonprofit lobbying group, you must find, win, and keep your "customers" to prosper. That means you must engage in marketing.

Exhibit 3.1 Albert the Advertiser and Charles the Customer.

Albert the Advertiser is the company, government agency, nonprofit
organization, or political campaign that wants to win, and keep, the allegiance
of customers, donors, or supporters. Charles the Customer's overriding concern
is to get what he wants or needs for a reasonable price and to be treated fairly
in the process. He gets attached to products, services, or organizations that
meet this concern, and he tends to do business with them repeatedly.

Of course, marketing is much more than just advertising. We
should mention that, despite his name, Albert the Advertiser will be
engaging in many activities in this book in order to communicate with
his prospects and customers.

Albert the Advertiser probably does not have all of the skills he is
going to need to respond to the needs of savvy consumers like Charles.
It used to be that he could rely on one or two pretty straightforward
methods for getting Charles' attention—a good ad campaign or maybe
just word-of-mouth referrals. But, as we saw in Chapter 1, the competition for Charles' attention is fiercer than ever before. Moreover,
information technology has moved the competitive frontier to the
formation and use of databases filled with information about individual prospects and customers.

Therefore, Albert the Advertiser faces a new challenge. He has to
learn a new approach to marketing, one that involves new disciplines
and a new mind-set. That mind-set is "customer bonding."

Charles the Customer

Charles is the prospect you would like to transform into your customer. He is also the customer with whom you would like to do more business. If you're part of a nonprofit organization, think of Charles as the person you would like to have in your base of supporters. If you're a political candidate seeking office, think of him or her as the individual who's going to make or break your next election. (Charles may also be instrumental in supporting your success once you're in office and will certainly be crucial in future reelection bids.)

Who is Charles? Well, his exact profile will vary. But there are some things that you can pretty much take for granted. First, you can be sure that he's a savvy consumer. He knows a good deal when he sees one and, in most cases, he's willing to shop around for it. (However, Charles, like most of us, also has an indulgent streak and sometimes makes decisions on pure whim.) Charles generally knows what he likes in the way of quality and service from suppliers, and he reacts negatively when he doesn't get the attention he feels he's entitled to. Oftentimes, that means taking his business elsewhere.

Secondly, Charles generally seeks information from one or more sources about the products and services he purchases or the causes he supports or participates in. He may prefer one source over another for a given informational need, but his options will certainly include the following:

- Referrals from friends and associates.
- Independent news sources such as trade or consumer journals, newspapers, radio or TV talk-shows, and the like.
- Advertising and promotion: image- or direct-response ads (through all mass media, including TV, radio, print, point-of-purchase, and outdoor).
- Direct-response literature that arrives in his mailbox, including catalogs, videos, newsletters, bill inserts, and free-standing inserts (FSIs) in local newspapers.
- Salespeople—individuals who approach him by phone, make a personal presentation at his home or office, or are available to help him when he goes to a retail outlet or calls a mail-order operation.

As a buyer, Charles' overriding concern is to get what he wants or needs for a reasonable price and to be treated fairly in the process.

He gets attached to products and services or to organizations that meet this concern, and does business with them repeatedly. Sometimes Charles feels a bond with the product or service because he knows he can rely on it to make him feel a certain way. (He feels hip on the town in his Nike shoes or secure in an American automobile with anti-lock brakes and air bags.) In some cases, Charles bonds as much with the provider of the product or service as with the product or service itself. (He feels conscientious when he contributes to an environmental or social-service organization that advocates values he agrees with or to a political candidate or group whose work or positions he admires.)

What Is Customer Bonding?

At this point, a definition of customer bonding is in order:

- From a global standpoint, customer bonding is the process through which Charles the Customer and Albert the Advertiser develop and sustain a trusting, mutually rewarding relationship.
- From Charles the Customer's viewpoint, customer bonding is the decision process that goes into selecting the organizations he will buy his goods and services from or donate his hard-earned money and time to.
- For Albert the Advertiser, customer bonding is a long-term strategic vision that will empower and inspire every element in the marketing mix.

The Five Degrees of Customer Bonding

The customer bonding system encompasses five different levels—or "degrees" of customer bonding.[3] Each has different characteristics, different strengths, and different weaknesses. And each places different requirements on the marketer.

As we'll see in later chapters, the customer bonding levels are hierarchical in the sense that each involves a greater bond between you and your customer than the one that precedes it. But the goal is not necessarily to move your customer from one level to another. Customer bonding is *not* about racing to the top of some loyalty ladder!

Rather, your unique market situation and your own business goals will tell you which levels are desirable for your purposes. And the resources available may well determine some of your strategic choices.

When you approach marketing with customer bonding as your goal, you are simply interested in choosing a marketing mix that optimally serves that goal. As we'll see, other goals—such as building short-term sales volume or tactical competitive responses—can also be handled within this framework. But when you choose customer bonding as your strategic marketing model, long-term customer loyalty becomes your primary goal, informing every choice you make about your marketing mix.

In Exhibit 3.2, Charles and Albert depict the five degrees of customer bonding. Exhibit 3.3 summarizes the characteristics, strengths, weaknesses, and critical success factors for each level of customer bonding. Let's look briefly now at these levels. We will explore each in detail in Chapters 4 through 8.

Exhibit 3.2 The Five Degrees of Customer Bonding.

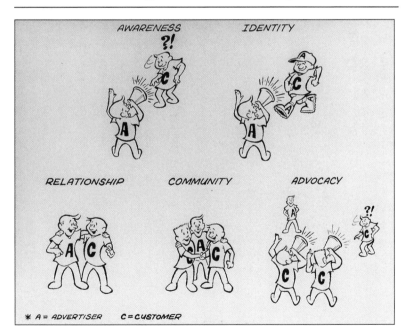

The customer bonding levels are hierarchical in the sense that each involves a greater bond between you and your customer than the one that precedes it, but the ones that are key to you will vary depending upon your unique circumstances.

Exhibit 3.3 The Customer Bonding System.

Bonding Degree	Characteristics	Strengths	Weaknesses	Critical Success Factors
Awareness	Gains share-of mind. Often a one-way monologue to unknown prospects or customers. Mass-media advertising, public relations.	Establishes brand recognition. Supports higher-level bonding.	Fragile, easily disrupted by competitors and consumer influencers. Expensive. Measurability and accountability difficult. Nothing learned about individual customer.	Repetition. Reach. Creative execution.
Identity	Prospect identifies with values and emotions embodied by your product, service, or organization. No direct interaction required. Consumer may desire/display items bearing your logo.	Stronger than awareness. Encompasses interest, desire, and action. Associates life-style preferences and attitudes with product/service or brand.	Fragile, easily disrupted by competitors and consumer influencers. Expensive. Measurability and accountability difficult. Nothing learned about individual customer.	Communications must appeal to values, emotions. Excellent product/service experience.
Relationship	Known customer. Two-way dialogue. Database driven. Uses direct media. Rewards prospect or customer for desired behavior.	Stronger bond: difficult for customer to give up benefits. Customer is individual. Highly targeted. Helps differentiate commodity product.	Competitors may copy. Can be expensive. Requires long-term commitment.	Recognition. Reward. Continuity.
Community	Marketer fosters interaction and relationships between customers.	Deep, durable bond. Hard for competitors to copy.	May be difficult to control. Heavy company involvement.	Event or group driven. Life-style related.
Advocacy	Customer becomes salesperson. Referrals not always known. Word-of-mouth flourishes. The ultimate customer-marketer relationship.	Highest level of loyalty. Based on dedication to product or service. Most powerful form of advertising.	Customer's credibility on line. Customer may resist efforts to organize program.	Excellent follow-through. Incentives. Empowerment.

Customer bonding occurs every time a prospect or customer interacts with your product, your service, your organization, or some component of your marketing programs. Every contact represents an opportunity for finding out more about the customer or prospect and for strengthening the customer bond. And every marketing activity must be carried out with an eye to doing just that.

1. Awareness Bonding

Awareness is the first level of customer bonding. It begins with no relationship at all and ends up with the customer or prospect being aware of what you are offering, forming some impressions of it, and perhaps making a first purchase or a donation. This is where you gain the share of mind required to move your product or service or candidate ahead of your competitors' in your prospects' minds.

Awareness bonding does not require any actual interaction with the prospect or customer or supporter. In fact, it almost always is accomplished using some sort of one-way monologue from the marketer, generally through mass-media advertising.

Awareness bonding gains share of mind. It establishes brand recognition and perception. These are important assets in a cluttered consumer landscape, and very important supports for higher-level bonding activities. But it is also the most fragile of bonds. It is easily broken by competitors who outspend you or who broadcast a message that the consumer finds more compelling. This bond can also be damaged or broken if consumers become more educated about the category and discover information unfavorable to you. Moreover, establishing awareness bonding can be very expensive, and reliance on mass media can be limiting, both in terms of the desirability of available communication channels and the difficulties of measuring the impact your advertising is having on your business.

Critical success factors at this level will be familiar to advertisers everywhere; they are the repetition and reach of your communications to your chosen markets and the inherent creativity of your advertising image.

2. Identity Bonding

At the next level of bonding, prospects or customers identify with your organization, your candidate, or your product or service. They attach to it values that are important to them, such as belonging, status, or self-fulfillment. Remember when owning a VW "Bug" was a social statement?

The action at this level of bonding is all done by the prospect or customer and does not require any interaction with your organization. The consumer may pass from interest through desire and on to action. He or she may even wear or display your logo, as we see Charles the Customer doing in Exhibit 5.1.

No direct interaction is required to achieve an identity bond. In fact, it can and does commonly occur as a response to the marketer's one-way awareness advertising. That is also its greatest weakness. Usually, the advertiser still has no dialogue with the supporter, prospect, or customer and is vulnerable to the same disruptions as in awareness bonding.

There are only two things the advertiser can really control at this level, and they are critical success factors. The first is the nature of your communications, which should appeal to Charles's values and emotions. The second is the quality of Charles's experience with you. Beginning with your advertising and continuing through his sales and service contact and his experience with your product, Charles must have an *excellent* experience. The same is true whether you're running for mayor of his city or seeking his support for equal rights. To maintain the emotional bond we call "identity," you must continually demonstrate your credibility and earn your customers' trust. (This is actually key to all levels of bonding, as we'll see shortly.)

3. *Relationship Bonding*

When you move into relationship bonding, you enter the higher levels of the customer bonding system. Now you are moving past one-way monologue into an interactive dialogue with your constituents. You and your prospect or customer or supporter are no longer at arm's length. Your customer is now actively involved and you are interacting directly with him. This requires a marketing database.

Some of the best-known models of relationship bonding are the frequency-marketing programs of airlines and hotel companies. These programs clearly demonstrate another characteristic of this level: a direct exchange of benefits between both parties. For Charles the Customer, the benefits may include recognition and rewards such as added-value offers for doing business with you. (As we'll see in Chapter 6, how you structure the benefits you offer is very important.) Albert benefits from every interaction with Charles by gathering more information that can be used to guide future marketing choices.

A relationship bond is considerably stronger than either awareness or identity bonds, particularly if you structure a reward system that will encourage Charles to return to you again and again. He will then have a vested interest in maintaining communications with you. He may even come to regard competitive communications with disdain.

Achieving such loyalty is not without its cost, however. It takes both an up-front and an ongoing commitment, and may be fairly expensive. Success at this level demands the support of a database, the use of direct media (such as customized direct mail, newsletters, monthly statements, and so forth), and a solid reward system that builds continuity, which we define as making each purchase a customer makes increase the value to that customer of the next purchase.

4. Community Bonding

Few companies have actually ventured past the relationship bonding level. But those who do find it exciting and rewarding. The community bond extends the marketer-customer relationship to a third party. Your customers are now bonding not only with you, but with each other. They desire interaction with others who share their interest in your organization, your cause, or your product or service. Your job is to foster such interaction.

Classic examples of community bonding are found in recreational vehicle industries (campers, motorhomes, and motorcycles), where rallies and conventions are commonplace. But as we'll see in Chapter 7, new examples are springing up in some surprising places—in travel, publishing, auto retailing, and even politics.

The community bond is very durable. But the marketer doesn't always have control over the process. (In fact, we'll look at one example where the marketer largely steps back and lets the community run the show.) If you're thinking about encouraging such high-level bonding, you should create lots of opportunity for interaction. Mass media will probably play no role at all in maintaining this bond. In fact, it may detract from the exclusive nature of the relationship you wish to maintain with these customers. Typically, community bonding requires events or activities centered around the life-style interests of your customers or supporters.

5. Advocacy Bonding

The highest form of bonding, of course, is when your customers take up Albert the Advertiser's megaphone on your behalf. If your customers or supporters think highly enough of you to refer you to others, you have achieved the very highest level of trust.

Of course, your current base of customers or supporters may refer others to you quite independent of any marketing action on your part. Or, like MCI with its innovative Friends and Family Calling Circle, you may find a way to tap the power of referral selling.

The advocacy bond is strong and durable. But an element of risk is also present. At this high level of bonding, the individual supporter's relationship is now visible to others. So you'd better be prepared to follow through promptly and professionally on any referral, and to make the new recruits feel as valued and important as the advocates who recommended them. Disappointed customer referrals can become a fierce and insurmountable liability.

Aside from MCI and a handful of others, very few companies have developed the power of advocacy bonding in any meaningful way. Perhaps that's because marketing activities at this level must be handled with so much care and delicacy. MCI's model was to provide a financial incentive for people to sell the MCI service to others, and it continues to be highly successful. Indeed, empowering your advocates with something they can offer as an incentive to recruits may be helpful when you're trying to create this kind of bonding. But if your customers are highly loyal already, they may also resent your efforts to stimulate referrals in this way.

What If You're Already Bonding with Your Customers?

The concept of a customer bond has been knocked about by marketers before. So you may be asking yourself, "What's so new about customer bonding? We've already tried all the usual techniques to bond customers to our products. What more can we do?" Or, your organization may focus more on building customer relationships than on bonding the consumer to your brand. If you consider yourself successful at that task you may be asking, "We're already meeting our goals. What more should we be doing?"

The answer, in either case, may be, "Nothing." You are undoubtedly already doing *some* of the elements of the customer bonding system we are about to describe. That may be sufficient for your current business goals and competitive environment. You may even find that you are already involved at *all levels* of the customer bonding model, with results to your satisfaction. In either of these cases, just consider these concepts a framework within which to assess your progress as your marketing environment changes. *In our experience, no matter how well an organization is doing, there is always room for improvement. And continually assessing your strategic vision enables you to stay ahead of changes in your corner of the world and in your competitive landscape.*

For many of you, however, reading this book may make it stunningly clear that you aren't even scratching the surface of your customer bonding potential:

- You may be failing to gain the attention of individuals who could easily have an affinity with your product, your service, your cause, or your candidate.

- You may be losing people to competitors because you fail to develop relationships with new customers once they sample what you're offering.

- You may be spending a lot of money developing awareness of and identity with your product, only to lose out when a competitor outspends or outsmarts you in the advertising arena.

If you think you are missing the loyalty-marketing boat, the framework we are offering will help you get on board quickly. It will enable you to get a clear picture of how to proceed and how to prioritize your efforts. You'll be surprised to learn how easy it really is. In fact, it's so easy that there is no excuse for not doing it.

Breaking Free of Trade Bondage

The customer bonding system will come as especially welcome news to packaged-goods manufacturers, or anyone who relies on retail channels to get goods to market. Why? Because the loyalty created by this marketing system offers a way out from the profit squeeze that retailers have put them in.

According to Brian Sharoff, president of the Private Label Manufacturers Association, "Retailers have consolidated and grown large enough that they can exercise real power in the consumer market. The buzz in the packaged-goods industry is the drive to squeeze unnecessary costs out of the system. The cost the retailer would like to drive out of the system the most is someone else's cost."[4] In other words, the manufacturer's profits are getting smaller and smaller.

This "unbearable squeeze," as David Martin calls it in his book *Romancing the Brand*, has made price—rather than value—the name

An Absolute Prerequisite: Excellent Products and Services

You can use innovative advertising and promotion initiatives to build lasting bonds with each customer, each donor, or each supporter. But you must also provide a consistently high-quality experience of your product, your service, and your organization.

How many willing new donors have turned bitterly away from nonprofit or political organizations that heaped requests for more money on them after their initial donation, with never even the courtesy of an update on the group's activities?

How many consumer or business prospects have been moved to respond to an advertisement or promotion only to be angered by the treatment they received from disinterested or poorly trained clerks, telemarketers, or salespeople?

How many customers have *you* lost after one purchase because they couldn't get through to your customer-service department with a problem or because they had a disappointing experience with your salespeople or with the product itself?

Open up your thinking when envisioning the kinds of customer bonds you want to create, and base your marketing programs on:

1. A strategic vision that emphasizes the creation of loyalty with each prospect, customer, donor, or supporter;

2. An honest, persuasive appeal, delivered through media that reach the individuals you want to target; and

3. A real product or service value that meets or surpasses every expectation in your claim.

Your effectiveness in creating and sustaining bonds with your customers will generally have a direct, measurable correlation to your share of market.

of the retailing game. With retailers charging admission fees to put your product on the shelf or take it off, you are at the mercy of the trade until you can command enough demand to create consumer pull-through. Says Martin, "Soon only the fittest, with solid category share, will survive."[5]

That is because the trade has learned how to dominate manufacturers' expenditures on customer loyalty by demanding a fee for the customer's in-store attention. In 1975, according to Martin, 20 percent of sales in the United States were made because of coupons, sales programs, or other promotions. Sixty percent of advertising and promotion budgets were spent on developing the brand's equity. By 1989, the retail squeeze had shifted this proportion so that only 30 percent of a manufacturer's budget was available for brand building.

(This phenomenon is even more pronounced in Europe, where retail distribution is generally quite concentrated in a handful of chains. According to an analysis by *Business Week*, the trend to off-brand buying has spread from big northern countries to Spain and Italy. And consumer companies that were once invincible are facing slow growth or declines.)[6]

"The little cats pay up or drop out unless consumer loyalty kicks in as an override," writes Martin. He adds that if you hold less than 20 percent of your market in any category, you are likely to find that the retailer controls your price. Unless you can find a unique product benefit that fuels consumer demand, or in some other way increase your market share, you may be forced to "ransom" your brand by cutting back on distribution and building a smaller share in niche markets.

"Consumer loyalty is the key, and brand uniqueness (or the perception of added value) is the essential ingredient," notes Martin.[7] And the customer bonding model can empower marketers to create such loyalty. You can go far beyond perception to become a truly unique force in your category.

Recap and Where-To

There is a way out of the morass of consumer clutter, disintegrating media, and antimarketing hostility we see rising in developed consumer economies. It's also the way to earn early and lasting loyalty in emerging market economies. Customer bonding is a system through which marketers can rethink all of the choices they make about their marketing mix. It focuses on earning and keeping customer trust. And it goes far beyond traditional marketing or customer-service solutions.

Are you ready to do some customer bonding? Then let's turn now to the first level of our system and look at the awareness bond.

Checklist

1. Which of the five degrees of bonding does your organization's marketing strategy actively participate in currently and how?
   - Awareness
   - Identity
   - Relationship
   - Community
   - Advocacy

2. Which of the five degrees of bonding do you actively participate in as a consumer? How?

3. Which of the five degrees of customer bonding do you find most appealing as a consumer? Which intrigues you the most? Can you identify why?

4. How do you yourself usually discover a new product? Mass media? Direct mail? Advice from friends and family?

5. Would you say that you are open to or skeptical of advertising messages as a consumer?
   - Do you like to receive mail from organizations you support? Of what kind?
   - Are you someone who joins frequent-buyer award programs? Do you look forward to receiving your monthly statement from these programs? Why or why not?
   - What kind of community activities draw you? What kind would draw your mother? Your kids?

6. What companies or organizations do you identify with the most? What products are you wearing or using right now that make some statement about who you are? What is the basis of that identification? Do you ever buy products that don't make you feel good about yourself?

7. How did you decide which political candidate to vote for in the last election? Do you have a political party affiliation? If so, how does that party keep you as a member? If not, what do you think it would take for a political candidate or organization to get through to you?

8. Do you feel close to any cause? How do you express your support? How does the organization you support show you that they appreciate your support?

9. Do you have any relationships with companies or organizations that you would find difficult to end? Would there be some "cost" involved? What would you be giving up?

10. Do you attend events sponsored by or related to companies you do business with? Trade associations you belong to? Companies whose products you consume?

11. When was the last time you recommended a product, service, or company to a friend or associate? What was it that motivated you to make that recommendation? Were you satisfied with the way the recommendation turned out? What happened that made you satisfied?

PART II

The Five Degrees of Customer Bonding

Chapter 4

Awareness Bonding

Bird's-Eye View

Awareness bonding is the first and most fundamental level of customer bonding. It is where you capture "share of mind." Prospects become aware of your brand, your product or service, your candidate, or your cause, and form impressions about it. Existing impressions may be reinforced or changed. The bond may also go beyond impression to bring about a desire to sample the product or service. It may even be strong enough to move the individual to action.

Awareness bonding does not require knowing who the individual consumer is by name. It need not involve a dialogue (direct interaction) with the prospect or customer, either. It is generally achieved most cost effectively through mass-media advertising or other forms of one-way monologue, such as public relations and event sponsorship. Critical success factors for marketers trying to achieve consumer awareness are the repetition, reach, and creative content of the communication.

Awareness bonding sells products and elects presidents. And it can provide a critical platform upon which to build higher levels of loyalty. But, by itself, it has several major weaknesses: it is fragile; it can be quite expensive to create, maintain, or repair; finding the right media mix is often a challenge; and accountability and measurability are very difficult to achieve.

> . . . Advertising is the wind on the surface, sweeping all before it when
> it blows with the tide but powerless to prevent a shifting of greater
> forces.
>
> Martin Mayer, *Madison Avenue USA*[1]

One day after April Fools' day 1993, a day thereafter referred to as
"Marlboro Friday," U.S. cigarette-maker Philip Morris announced
major price reductions for Marlboro cigarettes. The move acknowl-
edged the marketing muscle of store brands, which had gobbled up
almost a third of the $47 billion cigarette market in the United States.
It sent Philip Morris stock plummeting 23 percent and sparked wildfire
sell-offs in the stocks of other consumer-product companies, many of
which face similar private-label competition in their categories.

Whatever happened to consumer loyalty for the Marlboro Man?
How could the cigarette with one of the most widely recognized brands
in the world be forced into a price war with store brands?

The answer lies in the nature of awareness bonding. You probably
can't live without it, but you can't survive on it alone.

What is Awareness Bonding?

Awareness bonding establishes a perception in the consumer's mind
about your product or service, your brand, your cause, or your candidate. It is what advertisers typically call "share of mind." It is a crucial
foundation to any higher-level customer bonding you want to achieve.
But it is getting harder and harder to establish, and it is fairly unstable,
as we'll see shortly.

As Albert and Charles demonstrate in Exhibit 4.1, awareness bonding is created through a monologue—a message that moves in one
direction from advertiser to consumer. The advertiser's goal—at its
most basic—is to gain the consumer's attention. This job is commonly
performed by image advertising in the mass media or by other mass-
communication techniques such as mass-media promotions, public
relations, or event sponsorship. Awareness bonding can create some
loyalty, but it is usually very limited in focus; the emphasis is on
making sure the consumer *recognizes* and *remembers* the brand or
the product, so that it will be in the consideration set when he or she
is ready to make a purchase. If a strong enough perception of product
difference is created, the image advertising may actually move the
consumer through interest and desire to action, motivating the first-
time consumer to trial and existing customers to repeat purchases.[2]

Exhibit 4.1 Charles and Albert: The Awareness Bond.

Awareness bonding is created through a monologue—a message that moves in one direction from advertiser to consumer. The advertiser's goal—at its most basic—is to gain the consumer's attention. This job is commonly performed by image advertising in the mass-media, promotions, public relations, or event sponsorships.

Image advertising increases brand awareness. Various studies, including one by the Strategic Planning Institute (SPI) and Cahners Publishing Company, demonstrate a definite link between a firm's investment in image advertising and an increase in brand awareness levels, with a corresponding rise in market share. (See Exhibit 4.2.) According to the SPI study, image advertising also exerts a strong influence on consumer perceptions of product quality and, therefore, on the price the market will bear for a product.[3] Success stories in image advertising fascinate everybody.

- Perhaps you're old enough to remember when Avis Rental Car first mustered support as the underdog with its slogan, "We're Only No. 2, We Try Harder." That campaign boosted Avis's profitability and stand in the U.S. leisure and business travel markets, and it helped the company to become number one overseas. (See Exhibit 4.3.) Although the company has gone through many changes since then, including an employee buyout, the "We Try Harder" slogan is still the center of the company's image and promotional advertising.[4]

Exhibit 4.2 Advertising's Impact on Awareness and Market Share.

Level of Advertising	Price Index & Relative Product Quality		
	Low	Medium	High
None	101	103	106
Medium	101	104	108
High	102	106	109
Percent Change	+1.0%	+2.9%	+2.8%

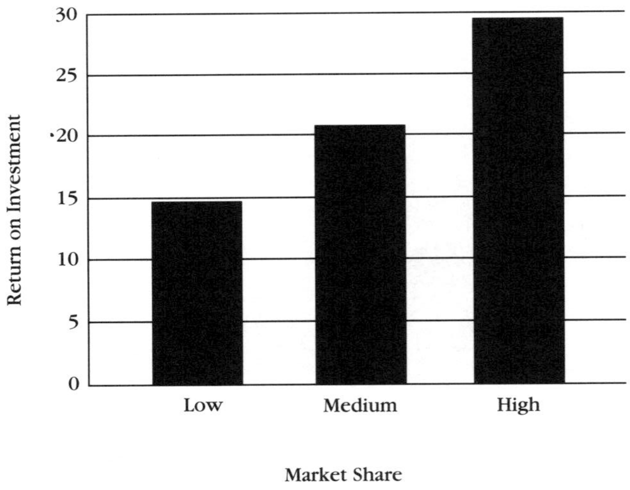

Return on Investment

Market Share

Here is direct evidence of what can happen to the price of products as you increase the amount of advertising. The table shows that as the advertising increases there is an increase in the price of products at all quality levels. The biggest increase is for products in the medium and high quality brackets.

Next we want to look at how advertising can help increase market share. But first, take a look at why market share is so important, and why everyone in business strives to increase market share. This table tells the story. It shows that businesses with high market share have about twice the ROI (Return on Investment) as business with low market share.

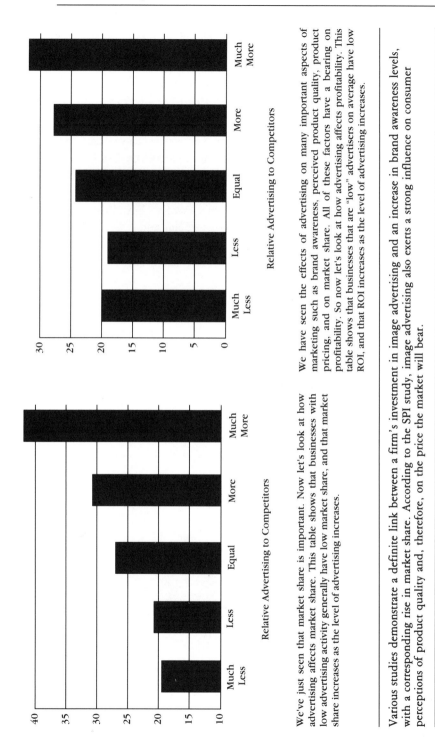

Relative Advertising to Competitors

We've just seen that market share is important. Now let's look at how advertising affects market share. This table shows that businesses with low advertising activity generally have low market share, and that market share increases as the level of advertising increases.

We have seen the effects of advertising on many important aspects of marketing such as brand awareness, perceived product quality, product pricing, and on market share. All of these factors have a bearing on profitability. So now let's look at how advertising affects profitability. This table shows that businesses that are "low" advertisers on average have low ROI, and that ROI increases as the level of advertising increases.

Various studies demonstrate a definite link between a firm's investment in image advertising and an increase in brand awareness levels, with a corresponding rise in market share. According to the SPI study, image advertising also exerts a strong influence on consumer perceptions of product quality and, therefore, on the price the market will bear.

Source: Strategic Planning Institute and Cahners Publishing Company, Cambridge, MA.

- The Coca-Cola Company brought back its "red disk" Coca-Cola logo for its 1993 campaign, "Always Coca-Cola" and quickly surpassed Pepsi-Cola's advertising for memorability. Sales of Coca-Cola in the United States, where it leads the soft-drink market, grew faster than total industry sales for the period.

  The Coca-Cola trademark, estimated to be worth almost $25 billion, is the world's most recognized commercial symbol.[5] (See Exhibit 4.4.) To maximize market presence, Coca-Cola uses a combination of image advertising, event sponsorship, and what it calls "interactive marketing"—a strategy of getting closer to customers epitomized by a new retail store in New York City. All three prongs were in action for the 1993 and 1994 Olympic games. Advertising, merchandising, and promotional campaigns all featured the trademark Coca-Cola bottle being guzzled by computer-generated bears.[6]

- "Retro-awareness" seems to be catching on as a strategy. J.B. Williams Company announced plans in 1993 to revive Brylcreem's "A little dab'll do ya" slogan and "There's something about an Aqua Velva man."[7] (The next thing you know, we'll see a middle-aged Gunilla Knutson stroking her Nordic locks across a 1990s boomer as she shaves with Noxema, saying "Take it off. Take it all off.")

Exhibit 4.3 Avis Tries Harder.

When it was launched in the 1960s, Avis's "We Try Harder." campaign boosted the rental-car company's profitability and standing in the U.S. leisure and business travel markets, and it helped the company to become number one overseas.

Exhibit 4.4 Coca-Cola Everywhere.

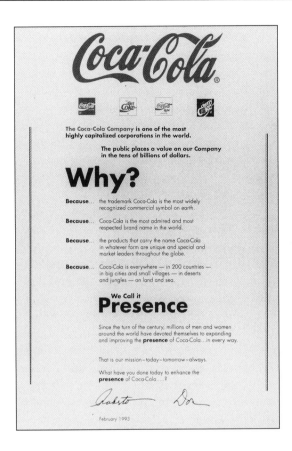

The Coca-Cola trademark, estimated to be worth almost $25 billion, is the world's most recognized commercial symbol. To maximize market presence, Coca-Cola uses a combination of image advertising, event sponsorship, and what it calls "interactive marketing"—a strategy of getting closer to customers, epitomized by a new retail store in New York City.

In the United States, political candidates are also "products" to be pitched. Since the 1950s, political campaigning has increasingly depended upon television. The average U.S. senatorial or gubernatorial campaign produces and airs about twenty to thirty advertisements.[8] The 1992 presidential campaign saw double that quantity by the Bush/Quayle team.[9]

A Strong Base to Build On

A strong awareness bond provides a foundation for all of your other marketing efforts. Targeted direct-mail campaigns, for example, often get sizably better response when the market has been primed with awareness advertising for the brand.[10] The trick is to think of awareness bonding in a larger context of loyalty-building activities.

As you read this book, we encourage you to think about engaging in multiple levels of bonding. Even as you undertake more targeted activities that bring customers to you and keep them with you over time, don't discount the importance of keeping a base of awareness support. Even sophisticated marketing programs that create high levels of bonding benefit from such support.

Holiday Inn Worldwide's Priority Club frequent-traveler program is a good example of how this works. It is one of many case studies we conducted in preparing this book, and it is of great interest because it involves virtually every level of the customer bonding system. A heavy base of awareness bonding supports the entire program.

The Priority Club was the first program of its kind in the hotel industry. When it was first launched in 1983, the club gained four market-share points for Holiday Inn hotels in the United States. By 1986, when frequent-traveler clubs had become a competitive necessity, Priority Club was completely revamped and relaunched. Today it encompasses every level of customer bonding in some way. Its U.S. members, primarily frequent business travelers, spend 60 percent of all their hotel-lodging nights at Holiday Inn properties.

Forty percent of the company's marketing budget goes to image advertising for the Holiday Inn brand. Another 40 percent is spent on promoting and running the club. Price promotions account for only 10 to 20 percent of the firm's total marketing budget.

"We have found that with our image advertising reaching the market segment that our relationship programs are placed with, the impact and awareness is increased," says Ken Pierce, vice president, frequency marketing. "We're not decreasing what we spend on image advertising because we have a loyalty program. What we are doing is increasing the impact of the expenditure with certain segments."

The Priority Club benefits greatly, Pierce explained. "Our Priority Club members are typically very highly aware of our advertising and the image we are trying to portray," he said. "Of all our market segments, they typically have the most positive image of our brand."

Indeed, Holiday Inn's awareness studies show that over 99 percent of American lodgers, and 97 to 98 percent of European lodgers, recognize the Holiday Inn brand. And independent studies of frequent-traveler programs show that the Priority Club has the highest awareness of any of the hotel-frequency programs (58 percent versus 46 percent for the next closest competitor).

Because of its huge worldwide franchise (1,800 hotels worldwide), Holiday Inn stands to gain significantly from its recent expansion of the Priority Club. Kathy Hollenhorst, director of global frequency marketing, explained that while U.S. and Canadian residents had always been able to earn rewards for stays at any Holiday Inn property

Exhibit 4.5 Holiday Inn Priority Club.

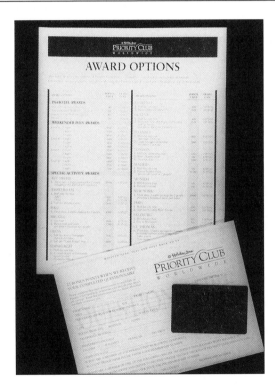

In late 1993 and early 1994, Holiday Inn began recruiting in Europe and Asia for its Priority Club. With a global network of 1,800 properties and strong awareness, the program was able to build upon Holiday Inn's established prestige image in these markets.

worldwide, residents of other nations could not. But in the fall of 1993, the company prepared for a pan-European launch of the Priority Club, recruiting from its European corporate accounts 70,000 members. In March 1994, the company launched a public recruitment drive though a combination of broadcast, print advertising, and direct communications. The rewards, which include amenities and points good toward Holiday Inn stays, are customized to local country needs. (See Exhibit 4.5.) So in Germany, for example, where frequency-marketing is hampered by privacy laws, Holiday Inn teamed up with Lufthansa to offer air mileage rewards.

Says Hollenhorst, "Our goal is to have one global program, but we are currently very unique in that we customize it to the taste of each locale. Our European advertising and fulfillment is now prepared in five languages. Ultimately, we hope to market Priority Club on a global basis."

In November, the Priority Club began recruiting in Asia and the Pacific Rim countries in partnership with Thai Airways International and Asiana Airlines. As of April 1994, however, the Priority Club began its own direct recruitment in key Asia-Pacific markets, primarily through print advertising and point-of-sale.

The Creative Challenge

Image advertising sells products, promotes causes, and elects presidents. But in cluttered media environments, creating impressions about a brand or a product or service is harder than ever before. Millions of hours and millions of dollars are spent every year trying to create campaigns that will break through the clutter and capture the consumer's attention.

Indeed, the images offered often have little to do with the advertiser's product or its performance. As we saw in Chapter 1, recent campaigns from Italian apparel manufacturer Benetton Group SpA promote social consciousness through memorable visual images. They arouse strong emotions, but do not make any obvious visual connection to the company's products.

Likewise, the TV and print campaign for the launch of the Infiniti automotive line showed lots of landscapes but not a single car. Advertising did not always have to reach so far. The classic Hathaway shirt campaign that ran throughout the 1950s in *The New Yorker* and other upscale publications made a household word out of a small Maine clothing firm. The early ads were copy-heavy, full of detailed information about shirts and shirt care. (See Exhibit 4.6.) But by 1956, the stylishly upper-crust character, Baron Wrangell, was so beloved by viewers that the ads could run without copy or even the name of the product. "Customers were buying an image, not a sales pitch," wrote Stephen Cox in *The Mirror Makers.* "The success of the Hathaway man, as [Hathaway's] annual sales tripled, rebutted the usual assertion that image advertising could not move merchandise."[11]

Another wrinkle in the creative challenge is how to translate successful national advertising and marketing campaigns into global marketing usage. The Japanese like lots of information in their ads, while the French prefer style and entertainment. Some popular U.S. tag

Exhibit 4.6 Hathaway Shirts and Baron Wrangell.

Hathaway reveals the truth about men who wear drip-dry shirts

The classic Hathaway shirt campaign that ran throughout the 1950s in *The New Yorker* and other upscale publications made a household word out of a small Maine clothing firm. The early ads were copy-heavy, full of detailed information about shirts and shirt care. But by 1956, the stylishly upper-crust male character, Baron Wrangell, was so beloved by viewers that the ads could run without copy or even the name of the brand.

Source: Reprinted with permission of Warneco.

lines, like Kellogg's Rice Crispies's "snap, crackle, pop," are unpronounceable in other languages, such as Japanese.

Some problems are prevented with careful homework and local guidance. On the other side of the globe, IBM found that its Charlie Chaplin campaign was not transportable to Chinese-speaking Asia, where the character was viewed negatively. And Pepsi-Cola killed its plans to launch the "Come alive with Pepsi" campaign in Japan when it learned the phrase means "bring your ancestors back from the dead" in Japanese.[12]

Other problems are tougher to foresee. When Procter & Gamble used direct mail sampling to introduce its popular Wash & Go shampoo in Poland, it got an expensive surprise when thieves stole the samples and irate consumers demanded reparations. Nor did IBM mean to stir up nationalist anger when it tried to please both Czechs and Slovaks with local-language billboard advertising.[13]

Other Routes to Awareness

As we mentioned earlier, image advertising is not the only technique that is used to establish awareness bonds. Publicity campaigns, promotional advertising, and event sponsorship are all ways to get your brand, your product, your cause, or your candidate into your consumer's consciousness. Even targeted communications such as direct mail can be used to create awareness bonding. And sometimes direct selling or personal contact is the best or only route to awareness, particularly in business-to-business situations.

Let's take a brief look at some examples.

Public Relations

While traditional image advertising growth has flattened out, the use of publicity is growing. An annual review by the Public Relations Society of America of corporate advertising expenditures in the United States found that real dollar investments declined between 1988 and 1992.[14] A Conference Board report found that corporate advertising budgets were the most commonly cut item in communications between 1989 and 1992. In the same period, publicity budgets for media and press relations grew considerably.[15] This continued a trend of the mid-1980s, when more marketing managers began viewing public relations as an integral part of the marketing mix. A 1985 survey determined that three out of four marketing managers used public relations for marketing purposes, particularly for building brand awareness for new or established products.[16]

In the early 1990s, use of infomercials and advertorials grew rapidly as a publicity technique, blurring the lines between corporate image advertising and editorial and programming content. These are informational formats that resemble the content of the medium they are carried in more than they do traditional advertising.

Infomercials (sixty-second to one-hour television spots). By one account, there were more than fifty infomercials on direct-response television stations in 1992, and viewers of this advertising purchased more than $1 billion worth of products.[17] And, aided by the legitimizing effect of Ross Perot's infomercial-based presidential campaign, 1993 and 1994 were boom years for the format.

Advertorials (print advertisements designed to resemble editorial material). So pervasive is the use of advertorial matter in the United States that the American Society of Magazine Editors (ASME) recently established strict guidelines to differentiate them from true editorials. Stephen B. Shepard, ASME president and editor-in-chief of *Business Week*, told *The New York Times* that editors were being increasingly pressured to blur the distinction between advertising and editorial. "The integrity of magazines demands that there be a distinction or both the editorial and the advertising lose credibility," the paper quoted him as saying.[18]

Publicity can be much less expensive than media advertising, but just as effective in generating awareness. "The problem is to generate events or issues associated with the brand that are newsworthy," writes David Aakers in his text on brand awareness.[19] Sponsoring events, underwriting causes, giving away product—these and other methods are commonly employed.

A master at using publicity to build awareness is The Body Shop. As we saw in Chapter 1, this global retail chain was built without any advertising. Rather, the company discovered early on that "profits with principles" could be newsworthy, and that being newsworthy was as valuable to market awareness as full-scale image advertising. Its first paid public-relations consultant got permission for the company to hand out free samples of Peppermint Foot Lotion to runners in the London Marathon. Writes founder Anita

Roddick, "It was a cute little story that made many of the newspapers the next day, and Peppermint Foot Lotion became one of our best-selling products."[20]

Roddick quickly became a devotée of publicity. "We could not see any point in paying to advertise if we could get free publicity through editorial coverage in newspapers and magazines," she wrote. According to a company spokesperson, each year the firm runs several publicity campaigns around the causes it has selected to sponsor, with full support through the stores.

Mass-Media Promotion

Promotional advertising has a shorter-term focus and typically involves a direct-response device—a toll-free number, a coupon, a reply card—and an incentive for the consumer to use it. Promotional expenditures are growing in the United States, particularly for consumer promotions. Instead of putting more dollars into retailers' pockets through trade margins, packaged-goods marketers are going straight to consumers.[21]

Chesebrough-Pond's "Pond's Institute" is an interesting example. The institute concept was inspired by the firm's research centers in Connecticut and New Jersey. The campaign was designed (1) to expand awareness for Pond's facial cleansers and moisturizers, and (2) to position Pond's as a company that has been caring about women for ninety years. Evidently it did more than that. The campaign kicked off in March 1993 with TV spots and print ads inviting consumers to call the Pond's Institute toll-free number for a free "Skin Discovery Guide." It generated 100,000 calls by mid-summer and moved Pond's cleansers from fifth position to second in the skin-care category.

(A company spokesperson indicated that the program also was the company's first attempt to build a customer database. But our experience with the program so far leaves us wondering how. After receiving the fulfillment kit, respondents are supposed to receive a newsletter with information on women's concerns, skin care, and beauty. The fulfillment kit we requested was slow in coming, and as we went to press months later, the newsletter still had not arrived.)

Let's look overseas at another example. Packaged-goods manufacturers face even greater retailer concentration in Europe. Increasingly, manufacturers are responding with consumer promotions and database-building initiatives of their own.

Nestlé, the world's largest food company, offers many good examples. The firm has revamped its worldwide marketing strategy to
support awareness and loyalty for its brands. An early example of
this strategy in action came from its operation in Holland. Using a
combination of retail and consumer promotion quite unique for Dutch
marketing, the company achieved a 40 percent market trial with the
launch of Gourmet premium cat food in 1991. Hank Kwakman, marketing manager for consumer products, said that the effort netted
Nestlé an 8 percent share of the huge and growing market for premium
cat-food products and distribution in 80 percent of the nation's highly
concentrated retail trade.

Exhibit 4.7 Nestlé Holland Gourmet Cat Food Campaign.

To obtain distribution of its new premium cat food, Gourmet, and maximum
efficiency from each marketing guilder, Nestlé Holland devised the trick of
offering free samples to consumers through paid ads in retailers' in-store
magazines. Upon sending in the glued-on coupons, consumers received a
handsome kit containing a sample can of Gourmet, an information leaflet,
and a coupon. The sample was a stimulus to move the product, and the
coupon guaranteed a minimum turnover for each store that participated.

"Our biggest competitor had five times the budget we had," said Kwakman. "And with distribution concentrated at levels of 40 to 50 percent and competitive penetration at 20 percent, the classical advertising waste would have been tremendous."

To obtain distribution and maximum efficiency from each marketing guilder, Kwakman devised the trick of offering free samples to consumers through paid ads in the retailers' in-store magazines. Upon sending in the glued-on coupons, consumers received a handsome kit containing a sample can of Gourmet, an information leaflet, and a coupon. The sample was a stimulus to move the product, and the coupon guaranteed a minimum turnover for each store that participated. (See Exhibit 4.7.)

According to Kwakman, the short-term promotion fully achieved the firm's goals for distribution and awareness. Nestlé is now planning the next phase: an informational campaign to build direct relationships with these customers, whom it now can identify by name. He has also used this technique successfully to gain consumer trial for other consumer products in Holland.

Direct Marketing

There are many occasions when mass media are not the most effective way to reach a given audience. When appropriate, a direct-mail campaign to a list of names can be a much more potent method for establishing awareness.

Volkswagen A.G. France (V.A.G.) offers an instructive example. Working with direct-response agency Rapp & Collins/Piment of Paris, the company broke new ground with an innovative program that accomplished both awareness and promotional goals for the launch of the new Volkswagen Golf in France.

The carefully orchestrated campaign broke in November 1991. A total of 170,000 owners of the earlier Golf model were mailed an invitation to attend an exclusive evening of entertainment and cocktails at the Zenith exhibition center in Paris on January 6, 1992. (Because the company had no customer database, all names were procured from the federal automotive registry.) Four percent responded, including 820 who took the trouble to say they would not be able to attend. The remaining 5,800 were mailed VIP tickets for themselves and a companion. A total of 11,000 Golf customers and their friends or families actually attended the evening's festivities on

January 6. They were treated to food and drink, entertainment, and the unveiling of twenty new Golf models.

According to a Volkswagen A.G. France direct-marketing executive close to the project, this was the first time in France that customers were invited to an event specifically designed to introduce a product. "Our competitors never dared to make such a wager," we were told. "But the bet paid off for the launch of the new Golf."

The day after the event, V.A.G. dropped another mailing to the same 170,000 Golf owners, and to 90,000 Polo and Jetta owners, along with an invitation to visit local showrooms on January 17 to test drive the new model.

The third mailing, which went out the next day, was targeted to V.A.G.'s dealers. It contained a local promotion kit with which dealers could create their own local mailings and advertisements for the January 17 launch. Over 1.1 million mailings were requested, an unprecedented response, according to Volkswagen.

The Golf promotion not only met its immediate objectives, but also enabled the company to begin creating relationships with the owners of its products. "Over 2 million messages were delivered nationally and locally to clients and prospects for the Golf launch," a spokesperson told us. "Such a volume is unprecedented at Volkswagen France."

Respondents to the mailings now receive the quarterly newsletter, *VW News*, and they and their families may eventually be offered membership in a customer club. "This is the first time that we have used all of the means of direct marketing together to complete the launch of a product," explained V.A.G.'s spokesperson.

Interactive Marketing

Emerging technologies geared to getting customers to respond directly can also generate awareness. Consider broadcasting information by fax, promoting your product on the so-called "information superhighway" of on-line computing networks, or joining the ranks of marketers selling their products through home-shopping networks.

Separating fact from visionary fiction may at times be challenging, but there is no doubt that new developments in interactive marketing offer tremendous potential for customer bonding at many levels. By definition, these media have built-in response capabilities, so prospects and customers can tell you—instantly in many cases—whether they're interested in getting more information.

Pontiac tested two one-hour programs on the Home Shopping Network (HSN) in late 1993, in part to determine the feasibility of an all-automotive channel that Hachette Filipacchi Magazines is considering. A company spokesperson called the test "very successful." While state laws prevent direct selling of automobiles except through dealerships, the programs did offer viewers reasons to call a toll-free number: Pontiac merchandise, an automotive maintenance package, and information on particular models, as well as a free premium. The company also is reportedly evaluating interactive computer disks,[22] as are several consumer and business-to-business catalogers in the United States.

Event Sponsorship

Event sponsorship is an increasingly popular means for achieving awareness. Worldwide expenditures on this form of marketing amounted to $9.6 billion in 1993, up from $8.5 billion the year before. U.S. firms spent more than $3.7 billion on event sponsorship in 1993 and are expected to spend $4.25 billion in 1994.[23] From golf tourneys to concerts, sponsorship offers opportunities to build awareness bonds. It is particularly effective when combined with other customer bonding initiatives that build identity, relationship, and advocacy.

In an interesting twist on the traditional sponsorship model, Ben & Jerry's, the popular Vermont ice-cream maker, launched its "Traveling Road Show" in 1992. Since then, the company's brightly painted ice cream buses have criss-crossed the country, bringing family entertainment (acrobatics, juggling, music, and magic) and free ice cream to residents in more than 150 communities across the United States. The company also sponsors its own music festival in support of its chosen cause, the Children's Defense Fund. In 1993, the company launched a newsletter with information on these and other activities. (See Exhibit 4.8.)

Direct Selling

Not every marketer has the means to employ some of the methods we've discussed in this chapter. Nor is every market suitable for these techniques. There are many situations in which direct, face-to-face selling is still the best, or only, means of creating awareness.

The classic example is in business-to-business situations. In many industries and geographies, awareness building is done through trade

Exhibit 4.8 Ben and Jerry's Traveling Show Promotion.

In an interesting twist on the traditional sponsorship model, Ben & Jerry's, the popular Vermont ice-cream maker, launched its "Traveling Show" in 1992. Since then, the company's brightly painted ice cream buses have crisscrossed the country, bringing family entertainment (acrobatics, juggling, music, and magic) and free ice cream to residents in more than 150 communities across the United States.

shows and by establishing relationships with a small group of the industry's inside players. Publicity and print advertising may play a role, too. For smaller firms without lots of capital or contacts, the support of middlemen is essential. Distributors, brokers, sales representatives, and other knowledgeable players with the necessary contacts can create the one-on-one relationships such firms need.

These challenges are compounded when you're trying to do business in regions that are unaccustomed to awareness-building strategies. IBS, a New Jersey software consulting and reseller concern, faces this situation in the South American markets in which it operates. Founder Mel Herskovits, a former IBM executive who has spent many years building Latin American ties, believes he is years ahead of any other firm offering packaged business software solutions to this region. "The

Latin American environment is not like the U.S.," he explains. "There aren't a lot of computer publications and people aren't as attuned to getting their information from them. It's much more important to have personal contacts and prestigious affiliations."

Herskovits establishes credible awareness in several ways. He picks reliable business software packages, often from big-name companies like Xerox and IBM, and introduces them to Brazil, Argentina, and Mexico through local distributors. He demonstrates the products at workshops sponsored by the big-name computer companies. IBS also is affiliated with the largest consulting firm in Mexico, SOFTTEK, which gives the firm credible technical support, contacts and clout.

Of course, if you are a big name company in one world market, you may be able to leverage awareness in that market abroad. That appears to be what U.S. Big-8 consulting firms Arthur Andersen, Ernst & Young, and Coopers & Lybrand have been able to do in Central Europe. According to a report in *Forbes*, these three firms have been soaking up business as auditors and advisors to local companies and governments as well as Western firms looking for acquisitions. And all without any real advertising effort.[24]

In countries like Germany, where restrictive laws and steep postal costs make direct marketing difficult and targeted mass-media are insufficient for some categories, direct selling may be useful for consumer marketers, too. Japanese electronics manufacturer Sharp, for example, used a third-party direct-selling service to test its Viewcam video camera in 250,000 German households in late 1993. The service company, Felicitas, put 1,100 uniformed hostesses to work visiting 4,000 households a day to demonstrate the Viewcam. At the end of each visit, the hostess left behind a postcard with a code number to take to a local dealer. According to published reports, the effort raised query levels 70 percent in a few months and cost a fraction of what direct-mail targeting would have cost. The service has also been successfully used by Procter & Gamble and Quelle.[25]

The Weaknesses of Awareness Bonding

The bond created by image advertising and awareness-building programs has several major weaknesses that any marketer must take into account when evaluating its marketing mix. Using the customer bonding system, it is possible to design an overall approach that uses awareness bonding as the foundation, but strengthens consumer loyalty with higher-level bonding initiatives. Holiday Inn, Ben & Jerry's, The Body Shop, Chesebrough-Ponds—indeed, all of the companies cited in this chapter established awareness that they can leverage into higher levels of bonding.

Vulnerability to Competitive Moves

Awareness bonding is a relatively fragile bond. It can be easily disrupted by external forces such as a competitor who outspends you, outcreates you, or undercuts your price in the marketplace.

Just look at Marlboro's experience. Leo Burnett's "Marlboro Man" and supporting western themes have been the focus of Marlboro's image for twenty-nine years and contributed to making it the "biggest-selling cigarette in the world."[26] In 1992 alone, Philip Morris invested $125 million in the Marlboro Man's western image. But R.J. Reynolds created "Joe Camel," an illustrated character who has helped the company maintain market share at a time when all other leading brands, including market leader Marlboro, have been losing share. And Joe Camel's fame now reaches beyond the target adult smoking audience and is almost as widely recognized among children as an average cartoon character.[27] (The company claims that children have an overwhelmingly negative perception of the character.)

Strong price competition can also upset well-established premium brands, as we see happening with Marlboro. Consumers have proven to be quite willing to throw over long-established favorites for lower-priced alternatives—often private label, no-frills brands created by retailers.[28] When your distributors become your competitors, or your product becomes a commodity, brand awareness alone is an insufficient basis upon which to compete.

The advertising industry's response to the brand crisis has so far missed this crucial point. "A brand is a covenant between a marketer and the customer," writes advertising researcher Larry Light, head of the Coalition for Brand Equity.[29] "The value of that brand is directly proportional to the value of the trust people have in that mark."[30] True enough, but how do you create and sustain that trust? Light's model, which he calls "Brand Relationship Marketing," seems to be little more than a way to allocate marketing budgets between advertising and promotion.

The fragile awareness bond can also be broken by buyer education. When a buying decision is important, buyers will not rely on impressions gained from image advertising only. To guide their purchase they will seek further information: from labels, from expert reviewers in the press, from prior customers, from research services, and from friends, family, and associates. Even if the emotional appeal for a product is strong, the buyer's purchase decision can still be swayed by negative information.

Awareness Bonding Is Expensive

Establishing an awareness bond takes time and money. In today's economic climate, under pressure to produce short-term results, few marketing or advertising managers have the luxury of either one.

Writes UCLA professor David Aakers, "For many businesses the brand name and what it represents are its most important asset—the basis of competitive advantage and of future earnings streams. Yet, the brand name is seldom managed in a coordinated, coherent manner, with a view that it must be maintained and strengthened. Instead of focusing upon an asset such as a brand, too often American fast-track managers get caught up in day-to-day performance measures which are easily available."[31]

Although a bond can be established with a single ad, repetition is needed for maximum effectiveness. Indeed, most studies of advertising frequency confirm that individuals must be exposed to multiple advertisements within a purchase cycle.[32] And with prime-time network exposure selling for as much as $325,000 per thirty-second spot,[33] it's getting harder and harder to spread advertising budgets far enough.

It Is Difficult to Measure or Assign Accountability

Of course, anyone who has done traditional image advertising knows that it is very difficult to measure its effectiveness. Measures of brand recognition and recall are helpful. Promotional advertising is easier to measure because it has a direct impact on sales during the promotional period. But any advertising expenditure that goes into a mass-media communication vehicle is ultimately not going to be precisely measurable. And that raises the question of accountability. How do you determine whether your program is successful, and how do you pinpoint the source of a failure?

Nothing Is Learned about the Customer

Last, but certainly not least, awareness bonding seldom produces any new insight about your individual customers. At least in the case of one-way communications, such as image advertising and publicity, you won't know who's responding to you by name when the campaign is over, and you will know nothing more about his or her individual preferences for doing business with you than you did at the outset. (This is not true when your awareness program builds in an interactive component that lets you begin to develop a relationship with each individual respondent.)

Critical Success Factors

Despite its weaknesses, awareness bonding nevertheless has an important role to play in the creation and maintenance of customer loyalty. It elects presidents and helps create the demand that pulls products through their chosen channels. It also sets the stage for other activities that can build upon it to create higher-level bonds.

There are only three requirements at this level. They have all been touched on already, so we will just repeat them here:

1. Repetition. Memorability is established only with repeated exposure, so you have to have a sufficient budget to make sure your target audience will hear your message repeatedly.

2. Reach. Selecting media that reach all of your target audiences is critical and often challenging.

3. Creative execution. An ongoing challenge is crafting a message that your target audience will find interesting enough to notice—and remember— amid the daily barrage of commercial messages.

Information-Age Awareness Bonding

Mass-marketing techniques arise when societies shift from an agricultural to an industrial base. In the United States, the process of using national advertising to create awareness for and loyalty to branded consumer goods began in the later nineteenth century.[34]

As we approach the end of the twentieth century, we are deep into the transition from an industrial-based to an information-based global society. The imperatives of marketing are reorganizing around the new powers of information-driven communications. But we disagree with proponents of "integrated marketing communications," like author Dr. Don Schultz, when they claim that technology has "killed" the mass market.[35] Technology has simply opened up new possibilities, such as the key capability of holding a dialogue with millions of consumers over an extended period of time.

Indeed, many of the techniques devised in earlier, simpler days can be updated and adapted to the Information Age. Consumers now demand more than just quality products: They want quality *information* about products, as well.

Marketers who understand the importance of providing that information will treat consumers with growing respect and not just seek to find new ways to offer selling messages. New generations of consumers are sophisticated and skeptical and know the difference between hype and substance. Navigating the fine lines between under- and over-informing, entertaining, and exciting people about products and services will be a continuing challenge.

New information-based tools seem to complicate the picture, but in reality they are simply providing new choices for reaching prospects to make them aware of your product and for supporting your relationships with existing customers through continual reinforcement of your brand image.

Recap and Where-To

The concept of branded products, born in the Industrial Age, remains just as viable in the Information Age and can be applied to services, cause-related organizations, and even political candidates. But marketers need to be smarter about how they create and support awareness. The key is not to rely too heavily on awareness bonding alone. It is the weakest of the bonds and easily overcome by competitive maneuvers or adverse consumer education.

Creating an awareness bond merely means that you've captured your prospect's attention and created awareness and interest in your product or service. Even if the consumer is motivated to desire and then samples your wares, the awareness must be considered just a supporting element in a larger strategy that encompasses the higher levels of bonding.

Mass media is often the most efficient way to create awareness and sometimes to maintain it. However, every situation is different, and marketers may also make good use of tools such as direct marketing, public relations, and even selective use of short-term promotions.

In the next chapter, we'll look at what happens when your customer moves beyond awareness and actually identifies with your product or company brand. Identity bonding is somewhat stronger than awareness bonding, and it can be actively encouraged.

Checklist

1. To what extent have you succeeded in establishing awareness in your target market? How have you accomplished this? If you don't know, how might you find out?

2. Can you measure the strength of your awareness bonds with your prospects and customers? How does it compare with that of your competitors?

3. What media have you used to create awareness? Which might be viable routes to explore?
   • Mass-media advertising (television, radio broadcast, print, outdoors)
   • Direct marketing
   • On-line shopping networks
   • Home shopping networks
   • Facsimile
   • Telephone (telemarketing)
   • Direct selling
   • Other

4. What techniques have you used to create awareness? What might be viable routes to explore?
   • Image advertising
   • Infomercials
   • Publicity
   • Interactive marketing
   • Event sponsorship
   • Other

5. What were the results of your campaigns?
   • Which campaigns worked best?
   • How many different elements did you test in each campaign? Do you really know what worked and what didn't and why? How could you improve your knowledge the next time?
   • How well do you think you executed each campaign? What would you do better the next time?

- Did you try to run a single campaign in more than one global market? With what result? What did you learn? How could you improve on your global marketing in the future?

6. Do any of your communications do double-duty for you, accomplishing more than one marketing goal for the same budget? How could you make them do so?

7. How can you make sure your message is reaching the right audience?

8. What can you add to the creative execution of the message that will guarantee it breaks through the clutter?

9. Are you relying too heavily on awareness bonding? What would you do if a competitor came along and attacked your public image? If a product disaster occurred? If you got a bad review in a public forum? What are your other vulnerabilities and what might you do to strengthen the bonds your audience has with you?

Chapter 5

Identity Bonding

Bird's-Eye View

Identity bonds are formed when customers admire and identify with values, attitudes, or life-style preferences that they associate with your brand or product. Customers form an emotional attachment based on their perception of those shared values. They may even want to wear or display your logo as an outward sign of their affinity.

Identity bonding, like awareness bonding, is created primarily through one-way monologue from advertiser to consumer. It relies heavily on the awareness bond—advertising and publicity usually stimulate its formation. No direct interaction between advertiser and customer is required, although the consumer is usually actively involved in sampling or using the product.

To encourage identity bonding, you must appeal to values and emotions in your communications. You must also ensure that the consumer's experience of your product, service, organization, or candidate is excellent.

The identity bond is less vulnerable to competitive challenges than awareness bonding. But it is not easily established for all products. And it shares many of the weaknesses of awareness bonding: it's difficult to measure and relies heavily on mass-marketing techniques.

> In a consumer society, people express themselves and their values by
> the products they consume.
>
> Faith Popcorn[1]

One of us traveled to Thailand a few years ago and bravely ventured
off the beaten tourist track to a couple of remote villages along the
Mekong River near Laos and Burma. This was not the smartest place
for a Westerner to travel solo, and if it weren't for the kindly company
of a British mystic who happened upon him, our hapless traveler
might not have fared as well as he did. But that's another story.

As it was, he managed to return with some interesting tales to tell
and one fewer item of clothing. No, it's not what you think. He merely
found that well-known branded goods such as Calvin Klein jeans were
as valuable as cash. Such items were status symbols, external markers
of sophistication and wealth for Thai individuals prosperous enough
to own them. After receiving numerous offers from admiring Thais
wanting to buy the pants, he finally gave in. "Keeping my pants
seemed a bit selfish," he said wryly, "and the price was finally too
good to pass up!"

In our consumer-driven world, people choose products and services
that reflect the way they perceive themselves or the way they want
to be perceived by others. This is true whether the items in question
are staples or luxuries. It is true for young and old, for corporate
purchasing managers, and for individual consumers.

Get close to some leather-clad Harley-Davidson riders, and you'll
find quite an assortment: corporate presidents, U.S. congressmen,
Japanese businessmen, yuppies, and old-fashioned rednecks. What
they all share is their attraction to the image of independence and
strength of character that the Harley product intentionally
symbolizes.

Examples of identity bonding abound. Peek into any business office
and you'll discover clusters of computer users, each with deep allegiances to their chosen computer brand. Watch Nike-, L.A. Gear-, or
Reebok-clad kids on the playground for a lesson in "footwear-speak."
Stand on a city street and pick out the individuals who display their
environmental concerns by carrying National Wildlife Federation or
Sierra Club tote bags. Or consider the millions of passionate sports
fans, the world over, who display their support for their chosen teams
by adorning their clothing and cars with team logos.

In each case, consumers have formed bonds based on their perception that they share the values, attitudes, and/or life-style preferences

a product or service symbolizes to them. They become emotionally attached to the brand and its perceived ability to fulfill a need, be it prestige, security, comfort, recreation, or whatever. This process of identification with the brand or the product or service lies at the heart of identity bonding.

Putting the Advertiser on a Pedestal

Identity bonding is similar to awareness bonding in many respects. It requires little or no direct interaction between Charles the Customer and Albert the Advertiser (and therefore no customer database). As depicted by Albert's megaphone in Exhibit 5.1, image advertising, publicity, or some other one-way communication is usually the source for Charles's impressions of the product. This also means that Charles is still a passive recipient of Albert's advertising messages, although he may move through several stages of the buyer-behavior model— from interest, to desire, and on to action, where he uses your product or service, donates to your organization, or votes for your candidate.

Exhibit 5.1 Charles and Albert: The Identity Bond.

Identity bonding is similar to awareness bonding in many respects. It still involves little or no direct interaction between Charles the Customer and Albert the Advertiser (and therefore no customer database). As depicted by Albert's megaphone, image advertising, publicity, or some other one-way communication is usually the source for Charles's impressions of the product. Charles forms an emotional attachment based upon his perception that he shares the values embodied in the product. He may even wear or display the product's logo as an outward sign of his affinity.

Exhibit 5.2.

When Charles the Customer moves past awareness into identity, he bonds with the reflection of his own values in Albert the Advertiser's product, service, or company, and forms a strong emotional attachment to it.

What *is* different is primarily what Charles brings to the picture. When he moves past awareness into identity, he bonds with the reflection of his own values in Albert the Advertiser's brand or company, and forms a strong emotional attachment to it. He may be inclined to display his feelings about the brand, product, or service by wearing or displaying merchandise that bears Albert's logo.

In fact, the customer puts the advertiser on a sort of pedestal and, by using the product, joins him up there (Exhibits 5.2 and 5.3). His beliefs about the product or service, or the company behind it, are all favorable, whether they are based on personal experience, on the persuasive power of advertising, or on references from the press or elsewhere.

Allegiance on Display

The cigarette industry has recognized the power of this emotional attachment in recent promotional giveaway programs. Eben Shapiro, writing for *The Wall Street Journal,* noted that tobacco executives consider those programs "an effective way to reward adult smokers for buying brand-name cigarettes." A closet full of Marlboro clothing, he writes, "creates a powerful emotional connection between a smoker and a brand."

Exhibit 5.3.

In fact, Charles puts Albert the Advertiser on a pedestal, and, by using Albert's product, joins him up there.

In 1993 alone, according to Shapiro, the industry was expected to lay out $600 million for merchandise giveaways. Since 1990, Philip Morris alone gave away twenty million T-shirts adorned with its various brands.[2] And its 1993 Marlboro Adventure Team program, in which smokers sent in on-pack coupons for Marlboro-branded merchandise such as jackets and rucksacks, generated 600,000 merchandise orders and 300,000 contest entries in the first three months.[3] We will examine the database-building facet of the tobacco industry's recent merchandising promotions in Chapter 6.

A consumer's desire to wear or display products bearing a manufacturer's logo can be a powerful indicator of his or her attachment to a brand. *The Licensing Letter* reports that about a third of all licensed products sold through retail channels in the United States and Canada (i.e., about $22 billion in 1993) are products bearing privately owned trademarks and brands (Exhibit 5.4). According to publisher Ira Mayer, many of these products are used exclusively as promotional premiums. Others, like those offered by Disney and Coca-Cola, are also sold through company retail stores and catalog operations.

The Sierra Club recently tapped the licensed merchandise tactic for the express purpose of building images and identity. Working with LucasArt, the nonprofit environmental organization has launched a line of premium Sierra Club products: T-shirts, shoes, crosswords, and even a screen-saver with an on-screen membership application. The program has a two-fold purpose: to expand awareness of the

Exhibit 5.4 1993 Licensed Product Retail Sales by Product Category
and Property Type, United States and Canada.

1993 Shares of All Licensed Products Retail Sales, by Product Category
(Dollar Figures in Billions; U.S. and Canada only)

Product Category	1993 Retail Sales	1992 Retail Sales	% Change 92/93	% of All Sales
Accessories	$6.20	$5.90	5.1%	9.3%
Apparel	11.60	10.70	8.4	17.4
Domestics	4.20	4.00	5.0	6.3
Electronics	1.06	$1.00	6.0	1.6
Food/Beverages	5.24	5.00	4.8	7.9
Footwear	2.03	1.90	6.8	3.0
Furniture/Home				
Furnishings	0.75	0.70	7.1	1.1
Gifts/Novelties	6.00	5.50	9.1	9.0
Health/Beauty	3.70	3.50	5.7	5.6
Housewares	2.18	2.00	9.0	3.3
Infant Products	2.16	2.00	8.0	3.2
Music/Video	1.18	1.10	7.3	1.8
Publishing	4.23	4.10	3.2	6.4
Sporting Goods	2.25	2.10	7.1	3.4
Stationery/Paper	3.10	2.90	6.9	4.7
Toys/Games	7.26	6.60	10.0	10.9
Videogames/				
Software	3.26	3.00	8.7	4.9
Other	0.20	0.20	0.0	0.3
TOTAL	$66.60	$62.20	7.1%	100.0%

Figures may not add up exactly due to rounding.
Source: *THE LICENSING LETTER,* © Copyright 1993 EPM Communications, Inc. Reprinted with
permission of the publisher.

1993 Shares of All Lincensed Product Retail Sales, by Property Type
(Dollar Figures in Billions; U.S. and Canada only)

Property Type	1993 Retail Sales	1992 Retail Sales	% Change 92/93	% of All Sales
Art	$4.74	$4.40	7.7%	7.1%
Celebrities/				
Estates	2.55	2.40	6.3	3.8
Entertainment/				
Character	15.80	14.10	12.1	23.7
Fashion	11.80	12.00	−1.7	17.7
Music	0.97	0.90	7.8	1.5
Non-Profit	0.65	0.60	8.3	1.0
Publishing	1.50	1.40	7.1	2.3
Sports	13.14	12.10	8.6	19.7
Trademarks/	12.64	11.60	9.0	19.0
Brands				
Toys/Games	2.55	2.50	2.0	3.8
Other	0.26	0.20	30.0	0.4
TOTAL	$66.00	$62.20	7.1%	100.0%

**Figures may not add up exactly due to rounding. Large increase in ''Other'' is due to very small size
of category.**
Source: *THE LICENSING LETTER,* © Copyright 1993 EPM Communications, Inc. Reprinted with
permission of the publisher.

About a third of all licensed products sold through retail channels in the
United States and Canada—about $22 billion in 1993—are products bearing
privately owned trademarks and brands. Many of these products are used
exclusively as promotional premiums.

organization's wilderness protection mission and to enhance loyalty within the current membership.

"The products carry our messages out into a broader marketplace," explained Rosemary Carroll, head of the organization's development office. "Less than 1 percent of the general American public can actually name an environmental group," she explained, "although awareness among the 12-million-member community of charitable donors is considerably higher."

Carroll plans to offer the merchandise to Sierra Club's 600,000 members through the organization's well-known magazine and through billing inserts for the 30,000 holders of Sierra Club's affinity credit card. "The Visa card also makes a real loyalty statement," said Carroll. "Our cardholders have chosen this affinity card above all the others in the marketplace. Both merchandise and affinity cards give people a way to express their shared values."

Issuing such affinity cards is another way that identity bonding can be encouraged. Affinity cards became popular in the mid 1980s. "Every group imaginable got together with a bank that issued a card for them," explains Deborah Sack, a consultant for MasterCard International. "There are cards for alumni, employee, military, and fraternal groups; for cause-related organizations, life-style organizations (seniors, sports), and professional associations. Everybody rushed to issue cards."

According to Sack, the affinity card is still viable for the 1990s. However, the industry is now caught up in creating co-branded cards, in which retailers or service-providers join with banks to issue their own MasterCard or Visa. The concept took off after the success of AT&T's Universal Card and, more recently, the GM MasterCard (see Chapter 6). MasterCard estimates that the opportunity for co-branded card growth is enormous. A big potential is the 711 million existing retail, gasoline-company, and telephone-company proprietary cards that account for $114 billion in annual expenditures.[4]

Social-Cause Marketing Takes Off

From its Tokyo headquarters, Toray Industries, Inc., has built a sprawling global enterprise and is a leader in the manufacture of synthetic fibers and chemical products. Like many major corporations in the textile and chemical industries, the company has become alert to its role as a corporate citizen, and it acts accordingly. It contributes actively to the arts in Europe, where it is a sponsor for Japanese Noh drama theater. And it has established an Environmental Research Center in Tokyo to develop environmental remediation and protection solutions. Toray also confronts animal-rights concerns by producing products like synthetic "deer skin" and "mink fur" to serve as substitutes for the animal products used in apparel.[5]

Such good-citizen practices are good for business, and more and more companies around the globe take measures to give back to the societies they operate in.

Whether it's old-fashioned corporate philanthropy, basic research, "green" marketing, or do-good alliances between for-profit, non-profit, and/or government organizations, social-cause marketing has become an important part of the marketing landscape in virtually all industries and all economies. In the United States, corporate spending on social causes has been increasing by 8 percent per year and is expected to top $1 billion in 1994.[6]

Michael A. Levitt, president of an association called Businesses for Social Responsibility, has said that we're witnessing "a growing movement to judge companies by their reputations as well as their products."[7] Indeed, picking suppliers based upon their social philosophies has never been more important in our lifetimes. It's a trend among both consumers and business buyers. It seems to be part and parcel of the changing social values that swept Western cultures after the worldwide recession of the early 1990s. Disillusioned with the illusory job security and conspicuous consumption that marked the 1980s, buyers in the United States, Canada, and Europe became much more interested, in the 1990s, in being part of their communities than in trying to "beat out the Joneses" with material demonstrations of success.

Hence the rise of whole new industries to match corporations with social causes. School Properties USA, for example, the brainchild of Australia native Don Baird, has parlayed what Baird calls "family marketing" into a thriving business. Baird has developed a network of grass-roots sponsorship opportunities through high school athletic associations. Participating sponsors provide year-round financial support to a given school in exchange for negotiated sponsorship rights.[8]

Innovative Marketing at Sebastian International

Creating strong identity bonds may require more than simple advertising and publicity about your decision to back a particular cause.

Innovative marketing programs can help draw attention to your effort, although they also increase its cost.

When hair-care products company Sebastian International embraced social-cause marketing, president John Sebastian Cusenza decided to build a marketing program around saving the rainforest. He knew that he'd need to do some innovative marketing to catch the attention of his retail salon network. Evidently he did something right, because five years later, Sebastian International's annual sales had doubled from $50 million to $100 million.

Sebastian's concerted "green marketing" effort demonstrates one of the more successful examples of fostering identity bonds. Company spokesperson Cathy Feliciano told us it took time to introduce distributors, salons, and consumers to the company's new concept of doing business. "But we're finding that [cause marketing] is refining the

Exhibit 5.5 Salon Sebastian Little Green Contest.

Since 1987, when president John Sebastian Cusenza decided to build its marketing programs around saving the rainforest, Sebastian International's annual sales have doubled from $50 million to $100 million.

image of the company. More and more people, when they think of the company, think, 'Oh Salon Sebastian—you're doing all that wonderful work for the environment.' If they're an aware consumer, they will choose Salon Sebastian shampoo over Prell."

The company has been able to donate more than $350,000 to the Rainforest Foundation since 1987. One of its biggest programs is a drawing contest for children called "Little Green," promoted with newsletterlike entry forms distributed at participating salons and through on-page ads donated by *Sassy* magazine. (See the contest entry form in Exhibit 5.5.) Contest winners are flown to the Amazon jungle for a tour of the rainforest, and to a special Rainforest Foundation children's concert, where they get to meet the celebrities backstage. All of this is aided by tie-in partner Hilton Hotels.

Through a separate charitable effort known as Club U.N.I.T.E. (Unity Now Is a Tomorrow for Everyone), Sebastian International, its distributors, and many of the 140,000 salons that carry the company's products have donated more than $9 million to selected charities. The program has gained more than 50,000 members, many of them salon owners. Each member contributes $10 for the company to distribute to one of several selected charities. In return, he or she receives $15 worth of Sebastian products, plus another $70 in discount offers good on future purchases.

Tying Donations to Products at Clairol

Another approach to identity bonding is to donate a portion of revenues from specific products to charitable causes. The products don't even have to be your own, as Clairol can attest. *New Woman* magazine approached the hair-care manufacturer in early 1993 with an idea for an exciting new promotion. *New Woman* proposed that Clairol raise funds for a new recording project by The Red Hot Organization, an international group that produces albums and television programs to raise money for AIDS-related research and care. (Since 1989, the organization has raised more than $7 million.) The promotion, shown in Exhibit 5.6, involved an on-pack coupon attached to Clairol haircolor products. By purchasing a product during August and September 1993 and sending in the coupon, consumers could receive a free Kathy Mattea cassette or single compact disc produced by The Red Hot Organization. The revenues from the Clairol haircolor sale were donated to The Red Hot Organization for use in producing an album called "Red Hot + Country."

Exhibit 5.6 New Woman, Clairol, and The Red Hot Organization.

A marketing alliance by publisher *New Woman* and its advertising client, Clairol, generated $200,000 for an AIDS fund-raising organization. The promotion used a novel approach—a premium incentive that linked the purchase of Clairol haircolor to the development of a country music recording featuring singer Kathy Mattea.

New Woman put the deal together because it saw a community of interest among all three organizations. The publisher produced the ad and donated space in its own magazine and in sister publications *New York Magazine, Seventeen,* and *Premiere.* Said *New Woman* marketing director Geraldine Rizzo, "My mission is to link our editorial to our clients, who are our advertisers, and to our reading audience. What we saw was that we all had a common audience—the 'mass woman.' And we all had an interest in supporting AIDS." *New Woman* wanted to support its plans to publish an article on women with AIDS. Clairol saw an opportunity to expand to the consumer market the identification of the company with AIDS relief activities that had begun in the salon division. Both companies were also attracted by the novelty of The Red Hot Organization approach, which Rizzo called "raising money by giving people a product that they want."

As this book went to press, all of the participants seemed pleased with the effort. *New Woman* received "an extensive commitment" from Clairol for 1993–1994 advertising. Clairol found a novel way to differentiate its product on retail shelves. The Red Hot Organization found a seed-money source for its next fund-raising project, the Red Hot + Country album. And, presumably, all benefited from tying their names to a cause their customers care about.

Said Brian Hanna, associate producer of the album, "This is an important new area for fund-raising that is growing rapidly. Each partner organization gets what it wants, and the consumer gets a great product. From the fund-raiser's perspective, it's very different than just begging for money."

Involving the Community at Ben & Jerry's

Vermont ice cream maker Ben & Jerry's offers another great example of tying the product to a cause. Moreover, the company has started involving needy communities directly in its business. In one case, for the new Apple Pie Frozen Yogurt, Ben & Jerry's purchases a key raw ingredient from an alcohol and drug recovery halfway house. Other line extensions with social-cause tie-ins include Wavy Gravy (proceeds are donated to a kids' camp run by the Woodstock organizer of that name), and Cherry Garcia (which donates money to the Grateful Dead Foundation).

"Partner shops" are another innovation the company has introduced in select communities. The first partner shop was established in Ithaca, New York. Another, set up in Harlem, employs men from Hark Homes, a Harlem homeless shelter. Seventy-five percent of the proceeds from the shop are also donated back to Hark Homes, which is part owner of the venture. (See Exhibit 5.7.)

For Ben & Jerry's, these activities are just natural extensions of a long tradition of social-cause marketing. Seven and a half percent of the firm's annual pretax profits (which were over $140 million in 1993) are donated to nonprofit organizations as part of a philosophy that founder Ben Cohen calls "caring capitalism." The company provides extensive support for the Children's Defense Fund and gives away ice cream to hundreds of small community groups and nonprofit activities. It also raises money for Vermont charities by charging $1

Exhibit 5.7 Ben & Jerry's Partner Shops.

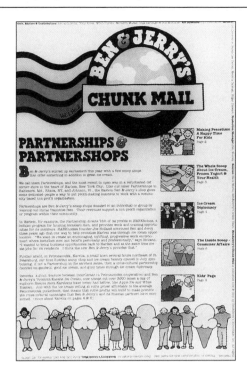

Ben & Jerry's is a leading proponent and practitioner of social-cause marketing. Among its innovations are "partner shops," which enable the company to give back to the communities where its retail outlets are established. The first partner shop was established in Ithaca, New York. Another, set up in Harlem, employs men from Hark Homes, a Harlem homeless shelter. Seventy-five percent of the proceeds from the shop are also donated back to Hark Homes, which is part owner of the venture.

---

for a tour of its Vermont headquarters. The tour, which has become the largest tourist attraction in the state, attracts more than 200,000 people a year.

Alliances Enhance Cause-Marketing Efforts

Marketing partnerships are often needed to fund cause-related marketing activities. This is because the nonprofit organizations involved with a given cause usually can't afford the exposure themselves and the for-profit businesses aren't set up to operate as charities.

That's why groups like The Red Hot Organization are finding ready markets for their services. In another Red Hot Organization project, Colorado software publisher Quark, Inc. rallied several other publishers to co-create a package of software utilities with which to raise funds. The package, called Red Hot & Publish, is really a line extension for all of the publishers in the alliance, helping each brand to build identity bonds with its prospect and customer base. The program package sells for $49. All proceeds are donated to The Red Hot Organization for AIDS research and care grants.

"All of the companies participating in Red Hot & Publish are supported by the graphic arts industry," explained Tim Gill, Quark's founder and chairman. "People in this industry have suffered enormously from the AIDS epidemic, and [this product] is an opportunity for all of us to give something back."

Well-constructed marketing alliances can reinforce the identity of each partner. This rub-off effect can really magnify the marketing muscle of small companies that team up with popular brands. Long-distance phone service packager Working Assets Funding Service discovered this power in 1993 when it tested the use of Ben & Jerry's ice cream as a premium. The package outpulled the company's control package as a lead generator. The firm chose Ben & Jerry's for several reasons, including the similarity in the two companies' customer bases and the socially responsible mission the companies share. Like its tie-in partner, Working Assets targets socially conscious U.S. consumers. It also donates 1 percent of its revenues to nonprofit organizations chosen by its subscribers.[9]

A well-chosen partnership should enhance identity bonding for both partners and for their prospects and customers. If your marketing partner has a strong identity, it may rub off on your organization. This is part of the value you're buying through the partnership.

Riding the Zeitgeist at Birkenstock

We've lingered on the topic of social-cause marketing because it is so prominent in today's environment and can help you form powerful identity bonds.

But identity bonds can be built around any product or service that evokes a strong emotional attachment. Your job as a marketer is to encourage that emotional attachment.

Paying attention to the needs of the community you sell in is key. When McDonald's largest franchiser in Indonesia opens a new restaurant, for example, he is careful to modify the fast-food menu to incorporate local tastes. And he always holds a pre-opening event for staff and their families to demonstrate to all involved that they will be associated with a respectable, wholesome establishment.

Sometimes, changing social values will turn a product or service that was previously of limited appeal into a raging sensation. That seems to be what happened to Birkenstock, a family-owned German sandal maker. After thirty years of selling its sandals in Europe and the United States, the firm suddenly found its products the rage of the West. According to Birkenstock's spokesperson, Lisa Geil, the shoes haven't changed—people have. Since 1964, when Karl Birkenstock first shook up his family's orthopedic insole business by designing a modern shoe using the comfortable Birkenstock insole, growth was slow and steady. But in the last few years, says Geil, as consumers have become more concerned with personal comfort, sales of the sandals have skyrocketed.

"There is a certain mystique about the product," she says. "It's hard to know the size of the comfort market in footwear, but since 1989, our U.S. sales have been growing by about 30 percent per year, and there has been a similar explosion worldwide. We're currently importing nearly 2 million pairs per year for the U.S. and Mexican markets."

According to Geil, it was when "antifashion" designer Marc Jacobs put his "Seattle grunge look" on the runway that things started happening. Jacobs's models were wearing Birkenstocks. Comfort became synonymous with Birkenstock for consumers across the United States and, before long, in Europe and elsewhere. Knockoffs by other fashion designers only further fueled the demand.

Marketing activities in support of the "comfort" ideal are much more aggressive in the United States than in the company's homeland. An expanding network of approximately 90 Birkenstock licensed stores augments department-store and specialty-retailer distribution. In addition to co-op advertising, point-of-purchase support, and promotions for the firm's 2,000 retailers, the firm now provides a toll-free locator service. As of Spring, 1994, the company estimates that about 10,000 callers have used the service. Each receives a product "catalog" and the names of nearby retailers that carry the firm's sandals. Although there are no immediate plans to sell direct to consumers, the

Exhibit 5.8 Birkenstock Promotion.

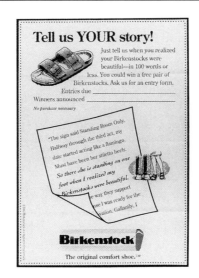

Consumers who buy Birkenstocks, wherever they reside, are certainly making a statement about themselves. The shoes don't fit the standard definition of beautiful, and yet the company's 1993 campaign has customers saying "That's when I realized my Birkenstocks were beautiful."

U.S. subsidiary has started a database through this effort and is considering how relationship programs can benefit both the brand and the retail network.

Consumers who buy Birkenstocks, wherever they reside, are certainly making a statement about themselves. The shoes don't fit the standard definition of beautiful, and yet the company's 1993 campaign has customers saying "That's when I realized my Birkenstocks were beautiful." (See Exhibit 5.8.) Women who wear Birkenstocks are rejecting the stiletto-heel discomfort of women's fashion shoes in favor of comfort and individualism. Men are expressing an attitude of ease and comfort.

Strengths and Weaknesses of Identity Bonding

The identity bond is stronger than the awareness bond alone. Where a strong identity bond exists, consumers have usually tried the product and may already be repeat users. Identity bonding can be achieved with one-way communications, yet your customers may already have an emotional attachment to your brand and, through it, a relationship with the company. They may even feel strongly enough to display their brand preference, as we saw in the discussion of branded promotional merchandise. In some cases, this can lead to brand extensions that become new revenue sources for you.

However, many of the weaknesses of awareness bonding plague the identity bond as well.

- Although customers may agree with the values, attitudes, life-style preferences, and emotions they associate with your brand or product, the bond is still relatively fragile. If a competitor overshadows your communications with a better message or a bigger budget, you can still lose your whole identity investment.

- Values that customers hold dear can and do shift without warning. Today's trendy concern may be just a fad or passing fancy, soon to be replaced by tomorrow's new cause or attitude.

- The celebrity spokesperson you select or organization you sponsor to boost your identity can always slip in the public's esteem. Whether reduced in stature by scandal or simple disinterest, your investment in an identity idol can slip away with the changing tide of public opinion.

- Because of its heavy reliance on one-way communication channels (mass-media advertising and publicity), creating identity bonding is still very expensive. It is likewise difficult to find suitable mass-media options that use every media dollar optimally. And measurement and accountability remain virtually impossible.

Critical Success Factors

To create and sustain strong identity bonds with your prospects and customers, you have to pay attention to basics. There are two related and overlapping critical success factors.

Appeal to Values and Emotions in Your Communications with the Customer

Strong consumer identification requires a strong association with values, attitudes, and emotions that your product or service, your cause, your organization, or your candidate embody.

But do make sure there is a genuine basis for the identity position you're trying to establish. While the impression a prospect or consumer has about you is partly a function of effective publicity and advertising, it is also a function of how genuinely you position your product or your company. Use the language of the people you're trying to reach and deal with the things that they care about.[10] And if you're going to engage in cause-marketing, make sure you're really prepared to provide substantial support to the causes you associate with.

Provide the Customer with a Favorable Product or Service Experience

As we discussed in Chapter 3, it is imperative that customers have a positive experience in every aspect of their dealings with your organization. The identity bond is directly affected by your company's public persona and reputation, by the performance of your products and consumers' ease of access to services and support, and by every interaction your customers have with your staff or your representatives.

The importance of the experience factor may account for Palo Alto software publisher Intuit Corporation's ability to corner the market for personal accounting software a few years back. The company's intensive attention to detail has paid off in customers who are so loyal to the company's accounting product, Quicken, that they have ignored retailers' efforts to switch them to competitive offerings.[11]

It also explains how the U.S. baseball industry brought criticism on itself in the last few years by ignoring fans in favor of profits. Baseball is a national pastime, the stuff of boyhood dreams, small-town allegiances, and endless family outings. But at the major league level, baseball is big business and increasingly out of reach of the average American. One fan of the sport estimated that he will spend $5,000 each on his sons' activities as baseball fans and another $10,000 on his own behalf over a lifetime. Add to that the expenses for memorabilia and he estimates his family's lifetime value as consumers of the sport at roughly $50,000. If this fan's family bears any resemblance to the norm, that's a lot of future revenue potential for the industry.

Yet the industry has missed the importance of that future potential. Baseball's bitter lesson is a sad story of powerful customer loyalty that has been abused. The sport has been losing fans at an alarming rate in recent years as its image has suffered. Spiraling ticket prices, restrictive television access, and frequent team moves have made the game increasingly inaccessible. Frank Dell-Apa of Public Citizen, a consumer-watch organization in Washington, D.C., writes "Americans are becoming less rhapsodic about their sports, and more aware of the cold impersonality of big business. Owners justify the maximizing of profit because they say that sports is business, or sports is entertainment. But sports is also sports, as much a manifestation of culture as dance or music. As sports becomes increasingly perverted by greed, its fabric is ripped apart and few of the values it should embody are left."[12]

Making Room for the Unexpected

There is always an element of the unexpected in marketing. And nowhere is it more noticeable than in identity bonding. As we noted earlier, there are times when a corporate logo becomes a fashion statement. It may or may not indicate product loyalty. But it sure gets your brand out there!

A case in point. Parisians, ever fashion-conscious, have gone wild over *télécartes*, the little plastic cards used in place of coins in the nation's public telephones. Since 1986, the cards have carried advertising by companies like IBM, Air France, Grundig, and Ford Motor Company. By 1993, more than 1,500 designs had been produced and more than 300 million of the cards have been sold. Many are just scooped up into collections unused, increasing their value as collectibles.

Savvy marketers have fueled this collectible craze by creating special limited series to display specific products or services. That was Ford Motor Company's strategy when it issued 1,000 cards for its dealers as a promotion for a special Fiesta automotive model. The cards, costing $16 each, are today worth about $30 as collector's items.[13]

This collectibles craze isn't limited to French *télécartistes*, either. Around the world, 150 countries and 200 phone companies had issued cards by early 1991. "Fusellatilists," as the card collectors are called by some, number around a million in Japan. And Americans are entering the act, too.[14]

An unexpected consumer craze such as this actually provides great opportunities for creating awareness and for building on your purposeful efforts to create identity bonds. We suggest that it's not always relevant whether an identity bond is a fashion fad or a loyalty statement. The more your brand is seen in the hands of customers, the more you build the potential for bonding at higher levels.

Recap and Where-To

The identity bond is a powerful base upon which higher-level bonds can be created. The consumer identifies with your product, your service, or your company. Treat this loyalty with respect and you have the basis for a long-term relationship.

Identity bonding is stronger than awareness bonding because it reflects the consumer's perception that he or she shares the values, attitudes, and life-style preferences embodied by your product or service, your organization, your cause, or your candidate. It involves a strong emotional attachment. And although no direct interaction may have occurred between you, your customer is already more involved in a relationship.

Giving your customers merchandise that bears your logo may help to enhance identity bonding. Cause marketing, through alliances and brand extensions, is another technique. Celebrity endorsements can be very powerful, too. But the core requirements are that your communications appeal to your consumers' values and emotions and reflect your genuine position in the marketplace. Underlying this is the ever-present need to provide the consumer with an excellent experience of your products, services, and staff.

The identity bond is still fairly vulnerable to weakening and breakage due to outside forces: competitive maneuvers, bad publicity, and so forth. This is because it is based on a one-way communication from advertiser to consumer. There is, as yet, no relationship between the advertiser and a named individual who can express preferences and feelings directly to the advertiser. In the next chapter, we'll see how this situation changes when you introduce the all-important element of dialogue into the system.

Checklist

1. What are the predominant values and concerns of your target markets?

2. In what ways do the people in these markets usually express those values and concerns? By the products they buy? By what they read? By the causes they support? By their heroes or the way they behave?

3. Is there any attribute of your organization's culture, mission, or leadership that genuinely fits those values?

4. Is there anything inherent in the nature of your product or service, your candidate, or your cause, that would appeal to these values?

5. Is your product, service, company, candidate, or cause positioned in the mind of your customers and constituents to appeal to these values? If not, can it be repositioned?

6. Are your customers proud to use your product or service or to support your candidate or cause? Is there a human need that is fulfilled by doing so, one that goes beyond the utilitarian value of what you're offering in the marketplace?

7. Are you providing ways for your customers to publicly show or express their attachment to your product? If not, how might you do so?

8. Can your product or service message be strengthened by relating it to a cause that your audience cares deeply about? What are your competitors doing in this area?

9. Are there marketing partners who would help communicate your values to your audience? Who are they and what values do they convey? What might the nature of a partnering relationship be? Celebrity endorsement? Co-sponsorship? Brand-name licensing? What relationship would best demonstrate to your audience the depth of your concern? How could you measure the benefit you would receive from a partnering agreement?

Chapter 6

Relationship Bonding

Bird's-Eye View

This is the first level of bonding in which there is a true dialogue between consumer and marketer. It is built around a direct exchange of benefits between them, an exchange that can go far beyond basic transactions. Albert the Advertiser may give one or more intangible benefits (information, recognition) and tangible rewards (discounts, extra product, or credits towards future purchases). Charles the Customer gives a stream of information about his or her interests and requirements, as well as repeat business.

Dialogue requires a database and some form of media to communicate one-to-one with the customer. The database powers your outbound communications and receives all response from prospects, customers, or supporters. Relationship bonding is characterized first and foremost by this continuous, closed-loop communication system.

The relationship bond can be very durable. The combination of recognition, rewards, and continuity encourages loyalty because customers have a vested interest. Their loyalty may, in fact, be so great that they regard competitive communications with disdain. But the price for such loyalty is high. No organization can expect to achieve it without making a significant long-term commitment and adopting an information-driven marketing strategy.

Loyalty marketing programs have mushroomed, making their way into virtually every major business category from department stores and other retailers to banks, newspapers, and packaged-goods companies.

Gary Levin, *Advertising Age*[1]

Advertising creates customers, but once you get them, what are you doing to keep them?

Bruce Bolger, director, Premium Incentive Show
as quoted in *The New York Times*[2]

For a quick picture of what relationship bonding is all about, just think about the frequent-flier programs you belong to. Most people with the means to travel consider frequent-flier rewards in every airfare purchase. For many, opportunities to earn frequent-flier miles also color choices about which credit card, telephone-calling card, hotel, or rental car to use. Indeed, a whole cottage industry of software vendors and publications has sprung up just to help travelers keep track of the ever-evolving mileage-related offers. And few remember the time, scarcely a dozen years ago, when there were no rewards for flying with a particular airline, and purchases were based on price, flight schedule, in-flight amenities, or the newness of the aircraft.

The airline frequent-flier programs—membership programs offering "free" mileage rewards and special services for loyal customers— were introduced in the early 1980s, creating a whole new class of marketing programs known as "freqency marketing" or "frequent-purchaser programs." These programs have become almost a requirement for being a participant in the industry, whose product has become a commodity.[3] Frequent-flier programs are now offered by carriers around the world.

Frequency-marketing programs build relationship bonds because they involve The Three D's discussed in Chapter 2: Dialogue, Database, and Direct Media. These three elements are prerequisites to higher-level bonding because they enable you to form one-to-one relationships with your customers or supporters. When you do that, you start operating miles above awareness bonding or identity bonding. Relationship bonding is what enables you to *keep* your constituents once you have them.

An Exchange of Benefits

The relationship bond involves a much greater interaction with customers than either the awareness or the identity bond. Prospects and

Exhibit 6.1 Albert and Charles: The Relationship Bond.

The relationship bond involves a much greater interaction with customers than either the awareness or the identity bond. Prospects and customers are no longer unknown. When relationship bonds form, prospects and customers are actively involved in the relationship with the marketer.

customers are no longer unknown, passive recipients of your communications. You now know who they are from your marketing database, and you can use this information to conduct an interactive dialogue with them using direct media. (See Exhibit 6.1.)

When relationship bonds form, prospects and customers are actively involved in their relationship with the marketer. It is dialogue that makes this possible. The dialogue permits a direct *exchange* of benefits—benefits that often go beyond delivery of your basic product or service.

Benefits to the Customer

Ideally, the outbound benefits—those you are offering to your constituents—will involve a tangible benefit program that includes three interrelated components:

- *Recognition* of the individual's status as a preferred customer or donor or supporter. This might include some combination of prestige (as in VIP frequent-flier clubs), dedicated communications channels (a members-only hotline), special treatment by your personnel, special services, or special purchasing options.

- Some type of tangible *reward.* Rewards should be something of value that your constituents get each time they buy your product or service, donate funds to your cause, or invest their time on behalf of your candidate. Most often, rewards are given in the form of reduced prices on future purchases or totally free products or services (your own or those of a marketing partner who wants to reach your customers). They can be earned by accumulating something—coupons, points, or miles—each time a purchase is made or a donation given.

- A frequently overlooked, but critical component, is *continuity.* A structural requirement for the reward component of relationship-marketing programs, continuity creates a cumulative reward system. Customers accumulate credits toward a reward in a way that makes each purchase more valuable than the one before because it puts the customer closer to a pre-defined point-accumulation goal. Continuity is enhanced by progressive awards that multiply the value of purchases after certain accumulation levels are reached.

We'll look at these critical components in more detail later in this chapter.

Customer benefits can also include intangible benefits such as information, entertainment, or education. Nestlé U.S.A., for example, is using information to get new mothers to try its infant formula. The program, called the Carnation Special Delivery Club, was launched in September of 1992. It offers new mothers regular mailings of infant-care information geared to the stage of their pregnancy or the age of their newborn. They can also call a specialist toll-free for answers to their questions about the benefits of breast-feeding, infant formula use, or about baby care in general.

Advertised in print and in 60-second TV spots, the campaign generates an average of 6,000 to 7,000 responses a month. By summer 1993, more than a million women had responded to the program, and Nestlé's share of the market had increased from about 2.5 percent to 8.5 percent.

Nestlé's Al Multary explained that the company wants to position itself as a provider of information and uses multiple bonding levels to do so. "We want to work with the mother and the family and help them understand what nutrition is. We use advertising for general awareness and to identify individuals that we can then begin a dialogue with. Then we use the database and direct marketing to provide nutrition information, product promotions, and special offers of relevant products. The elements all have to work together."

Many marketers combine both tangible and intangible benefits to build relationship bonds. Such multitiered benefit strategies offer even more powerful bonding possibilities.

Burger King, for example, uses a combination of recognition, entertainment, education, and discounts to make its 4-million-member Burger King Kids Club appeal to both kids *and* their parents. The club's mascots are a bunch of likeable multi-ethnic cartoon characters, from the disabled boy, "Wheels," to the Afro-American environmentalist, "Jaws." They appear repeatedly in the company's advertising and marketing materials. Kids joining the club receive a welcome kit replete with a membership card and guide and various goodies. (See Exhibit 6.2.) Membership benefits include bring-in offers designed to build traffic at Burger King's 6,100 U.S. restaurant locations. But many program elements are designed to promote education and encourage club members to interact with parents or other kids. For example:

- A pen-pal club that matches up Burger King Kids Club members and gives them special stationery and pens (including an invisible ink pen), and tips on letter writing.

- Three age-targeted magazines containing stories, puzzles, cartoons, write-ins, and other activities that invite interaction between kids, their parents, and Burger King. The magazines contain some paid advertisements that help Burger King defray the cost of the 3-million-issue mailings.

- The Burgers n' Books Reading Incentive program, which encourages kids to read. Upon submitting their completed reading list to the club, they are rewarded with a free Kids Club meal.

- A 24-hour-a-day toll-free hotline for parents and kids to call with questions or complaints about the program.

Burger King's member program is expanding rapidly to the company's 1,163 other retail locations around the world. By early 1994, Burger King Kids Clubs were operating in 25 countries outside the U.S., including Canada, Mexico, the United Kingdom, and selected locations in Eastern Europe and Asia. In each case, the program's marketing elements are modified to suit local market needs.

Exhibit 6.2 Burger King Kids Club.

Program elements in the Burger King Kids Club are designed to educate and entertain club members and to encourage them to interact with parents or other kids. They also sell a lot of burgers and fries. The program is expanding rapidly around the world. By early 1994, Burger King Kids Clubs were operating in 25 countries outside the United States, including Canada, Mexico, the United Kingdom, and selected locations in Eastern Europe and Asia. In each case, the program's marketing elements are modified to suit local market needs.

Benefits to the Marketer

What benefits can the marketer expect to get in the relationship exchange? If you have designed a program with all of the key benefits in place—recognition, rewards, and continuity—and have adequate support with database, dialogue, and direct media, you'll get an ever-richer bank of knowledge about the people who are attracted to your product or service, your cause, or your candidate. This is knowledge

Exhibit 6.2 *cont.*

you can use to deepen their loyalty further, to increase sales or contributions, and to find and attract other people like them. Every contact you have with them is an opportunity to interact—to learn more about their needs, their likes, their dislikes, and how they regard you.

So the Carnation Special Delivery Club helps Nestlé's infant-formula division to build market awareness and market share while it creates a database of potential customers. The database is a critical marketing tool in a product category where the target consumer is changing every month. Knowing the names and interests of mothers with young families can also help Nestlé identify cross-selling opportunities for other Nestlé products.

Burger King also collects information every time a Kids Club member or parent reponds to a club activity. Moreover, the club extends the child's connection with Burger King beyond the 20 minutes spent in the restaurant, says company spokesperson Michael Evans. "We want to capture the hearts and minds of kids and keep them until they're 60," he says. There's a shorter-term payoff, too. Sales of Burger

King Kids Meals have grown threefold since the club was launched in January 1990.[4]

Competing on Value-Added Benefits

The value-added benefits that relationship-bonding programs offer to customers often become key competitive tools as well.

The grand-daddy of present-day frequent-purchaser programs (also known as "frequency" programs) is the American Airlines AAdvantage Program. This program gave American an immediate advantage in the marketplace when it was launched—one that was tough for competitors to overcome.

According to senior vice president Michael Gunn, the airline's decision to launch the club in the early 1980s came in the wake of deregulation and fuel shortages that jacked up airfares and opened the field to upstart airlines like People's Express. In the newly competitive skyscape, American wanted to make sure that it kept its best customers in the American hangar. For some time, it had been providing extra services to 250,000 of its most frequent fliers through a recognition program called Very Important Traveler (VIT). But the program was "cumbersome to handle," said Gunn.

So when development of its SABRE on-line-reservation system was complete, the company took advantage of the technology by launching a rewards-based club. Gunn explained, "We wanted to launch the program, grow it fast, and communicate directly with our members while saving on [general] advertising."[5]

Although American's announcement caught the entire industry by surprise, United managed to assemble a competitive response within 10 days, one-upping American by offering a 5,000-mile enrollment bonus.[6] In short order, all of the major carriers followed suit.

Such swift competitive responses are now standard for the industry. Within one three-week period between September and October 1992, for example, every major U.S. airline came out with a special mileage bonus promotion. What was notable about this competitive skirmish was that *none* of the competitors' full-page ads in major media once mentioned *anything* about their services. Only their new frequent-flier reward promotions were mentioned.

This demonstrates an important maxim for developing relationship bonds: *If you can't compete by selling the product, sell the value-added benefit!*

In the airline industry, the value-added benefit of private money (mileage rewards) has become a key basis upon which the airlines compete. You can expect to see a similar phenomenon anytime a product or service becomes a commodity, and frequency-marketing programs become a primary competitive battleground.

Consultant Stevan A. Grosvald, writing for *Frequent Flyer* magazine, has compared the airlines's promotional use of frequent-flier programs to retail use of special sales and other promotions. He noted that although U.S. airlines "gave away" the equivalent of more than 7 million round-trip flights in 1991 and owed passengers more than 20 million flight miles, the economic impact of these rewards is figured into the airlines's pricing and capacity strategies. "Free" passengers, he says, account for only 4 to 6 percent of a carrier's capacity. And the programs *do* impact loyalty.[7]

"Frequent-flyer programs are not flights of fancy, but credible economic vehicles aimed at inducing you to concentrate your flying on one carrier," he writes. They address "an airline's need to build long-

Exhibit 6.3 Competing on Value-Added Benefits.

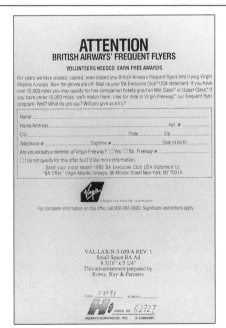

When products become commodities, you can compete on the value-added benefits of a relationship-building program. In this ad from May 1993, Virgin Atlantic Airways used its frequent-flier program for conquest marketing, offering customers of arch-rival British Airways who held more than 10,000 miles in the British Airways program free companion tickets on Virgin Air.

term relationships by offering a combination of special services, benefits, and customer recognition."[8]

Grosvald confirms that frequent-flier programs are an important
factor in determining preference when two competing airlines can
get you to your destination in approximately the same time period.
Members of frequent-flier programs, especially those close to an
award, will often wait an hour or two for a flight on their preferred
airline, even though a competitor has a more convenient service. "It's
exactly that type of activity that contributes to the incremental revenue generated by these programs," he concludes.

The airline industry's global embrace of frequent-purchaser programs is a good example of "the battle of the database."[9] When products become commodities, database-driven programs can become a
key—and sometimes the only—means of achieving competitive differ-
entiation. In such cases, frequent-purchase programs can be valuable
for conquest marketing, as the Virgin Atlantic Airways advertisement
in Exhibit 6.3 demonstrates.

To date, no airline in the United States has been able to match
American Airlines's frequent-flier membership, probably because of
a combination of American's aggressive membership recruitment and
the principle that the advertiser that gets there first usually wins the
most. At 18 million members, American has captured just about every
American flier in the United States in its database, frequent or otherwise. Insiders report that the program has saved the company more
than $100 million on mass-media advertising.[10]

Make Your Frequency Program a Profit Center

Any organization wanting to design a reward program to encourage
customer loyalty must figure out how to make the reward program
pay for itself. Programs that are designed as profit centers are likely
to endure because they add measurably to the bottom line.

Despite the financial problems plaguing the airline industry, for example, frequent-flier programs are clearly here to stay. According to Jeff
Blyskal, writing for *Worth* magazine's May 1994 issue, the key to these
programs' longevity is that they contribute to the bottom line through
partners (hotels, car-rental companies, long-distance carriers, and others
who buy miles for 1 to 2 cents each) and through breakage (the fact
that 30 percent of miles awarded will never be used).

A Strong Bond Takes a Big Commitment

Once you achieve a relationship bond with a customer or supporter, you can breathe a little easier. Relationship bonding is much stronger than awareness or identity bonding. Competitors will find it harder to entice loyal constituents from you because you are recognizing and rewarding your customers' patronage based on information obtained in your ongoing dialogue with them.

That is the strength of the relationship bond. Your customers or supporters have a good reason to stay in touch with you. They have tried your product or service, or membership in your organization, and have been at least satisfied—and hopefully genuinely delighted—with the experience. If you have structured a good relationship-building program, you are continually recognizing their interests and giving them relevant benefits that are too valuable to give up. These benefits give the relationship greater value than that contained in the product or service itself. Your customers, therefore, have a stake in maintaining communications.

The strength of the relationship bond is not without a price. Achieving this level of bonding takes a big commitment to a long-term strategy that may not have immediate payoffs. The benefits of this strategy may not be intuitively obvious to everyone in your organization, especially when compared with tactical programs that promise favorable short-term impact on the bottom line. And the concept of relationship marketing is often attacked because of the big investments involved in building, maintaining, and using databases.[11]

Al Multary of Nestlé U.S.A. spoke to us of the need for someone within an organization to champion the database-marketing approach. "We [the infant-formula division] were pioneers partly because our market dictated it and our product is conducive to it. Now people at Nestlé are beginning to understand its importance. People have to break out of the thinking that this is just a promotional tool and start thinking about it as a new element in the marketing mix."

When allocating marketing budgets, it is not advisable to view relationship-bonding programs as completely alternate activities to awareness- or identity-bonding programs. Remember that customer bonding works as a system: awareness supports identity and both support relationship bonding. The stronger your image in the marketplace, the more people will be aware of your organization or what you offer, and the easier it will be to create relationship bonds. To be successful, your relationship program will probably need the power of mass advertising to support your relationship-building efforts.

The truth is that few organizations approach information-driven marketing with such a systematic, top-down strategic perspective. Instead of viewing the marketing database as the core of the company's advertising, marketing, and promotion activities (as discussed in Chapter 2), it is often seen as just one component in the mix. The result is sadly predictable. Lacking a strategic vision that values actionable customer information, loyalty programs are viewed as a sideline, and primary emphasis is given to awareness advertising and promotion.

A recent report on Saab Cars U.S.A. illustrates this point. In its first test of direct response to sell cars to U.S. consumers, the firm generated $62 million in incremental sales on an outlay of less than $2 million. That's a return of over 3,000 percent! But Saab Cars budgeted $25 to $30 million for mainstream advertising in 1993 and only $2 million for its direct programs. Based on this out-of-balance budget allocation, it appears that Saab has not yet developed an information-based marketing vision for its U.S. operations.[12]

To effect really powerful relationship bonds, organizations must work holistically, approaching every element of the marketing mix as a tactic empowered by, and responsive to, the information contained in the customer database. This is the information-driven marketing approach we discussed in Chapter 2. As we noted there, it takes a top-down commitment and ongoing attention from senior management. Without clear vision and total commitment to long-term relationship building, the impact of many programs is diminished by competing in-house interests. For example, the in-house data-processing department that insists, beyond any reasonable justification, that it can handle the demands of information-driven marketing programs can actually delay implementation. It can also multiply the cost of your efforts as compared to better-equipped service bureaus. Or you may face resistance from external suppliers such as advertising agencies eager to continue their complete control of your advertising dollars.

Critical Success Factors

As we mentioned earlier in the chapter, any marketing program that intends to build long-term relationships with constituents must include three critical components: recognition, rewards, and continuity. Let's look now at each of these elements in detail.

Recognition

The desire to gain individual recognition—just for being a customer or supporter or for completing a given achievement—is a powerful motivator. Successful fund-raisers are particularly adept at building such recognition into appeals or member benefits to increase response. (Membership cards, donor certificates, thank-you letters, surveys, and invitations to special facilities or fund-raising events are some of the fundraiser's tools. All provide valuable recognition opportunities.)

Recognition can be used in various ways to build relationship bonds. Let's look at a few examples.

Recognizing achievement. Recognition for achievement is featured in an innovative new program from Saucony, a United States manufacturer of athletic footwear.

To increase Saucony's presence in the enormous market of American walkers (70 million strong), the company launched the Saucony Walking Club in 1993. The program is targeted to women walkers, the largest segment of the market. Recruitment was done through print ads in *Walking* magazine and a direct mailing of 100,000 invitations to readers of *Prevention, Walking,* and other publications. The requirement? Just purchase a pair of Saucony walking shoes at an authorized retailer and complete a twelve-question enrollment form.

While enrolling, each member chooses from three information tracks—cardiovascular health, weight loss, or overall fitness—and decides on a goal. The resulting dialogue is built around her selection and her goal, with rewards for every milestone achieved. Saucony sends each member a kit, including a forty-page booklet with customized walking workouts and tips and a quarterly newsletter geared to her interests. Most interesting of all, however, is the logbook she receives. She uses it to track her progress towards her stated goal. When she reaches a milestone, she sends in the logbook and receives awards and recognition from the club. (See Exhibit 6.4.)

This innovative, interactive approach also lets Saucony track when members are due for a new pair of shoes. But program manager Donna Coskren points out that the program's intent is "long-term provision of education and information, not high-pressure salesmanship." Sau-

Exhibit 6.4 Recognizing Your Customers' Achievements.

Saucony's 1993 launch of the Saucony Walking Club was promoted through *Walking* magazine (38 percent response), direct mail (17 percent response), and in-store materials at 400 athletic footwear retailers (43 percent response). Virtually every member who signed up in 1993 switched from another brand. In early 1994, Saucony was readying a second program in cooperation with Lady Footlocker.

cony is hoping for 15,000 to 30,000 enrollments by the end of 1994, which would make the program comparable to Saucony's 30,000 member runner's club, Extra Mile Club. While she wouldn't reveal the actual number of members gained by early 1994, Coskren indicated that 99 percent had switched from another brand and that the program may have helped to account for a 25 percent increase in walking shoe sales for 1993.

Acknowledging the importance of retail support, a second program was being readied for launch as we went to print, a joint effort with Lady Footlocker, the biggest women's specialty retail chain in the United States.

Recognizing status. Recognition of special status has long been a popular appeal in mass advertising for big-ticket consumer items and in fund-raising appeals to big-dollar donors. But it is equally powerful as a tool for creating enduring relationship bonds. Used in this context, special-status recognition says "You're one of my very best customers" or "You can be part of my inner circle of supporters."

Air France's Club 2000 shows how popular, and powerful, such a program can be. The members of this by-invitation club have dramatically increased their number of flights with Air France at a time when overall passenger miles were declining (and despite the fact that membership carries absolutely no purchase obligations). The program, which was launched in 1990 in response to aggressive competition from European and U.S. airlines, is based specifically on status and recognition. Its goal, according to Rapp & Collins/Piment, the Parisian agency that supports it, is to develop customer loyalty. Bérengère Malin, Air France account manager for Rapp & Collins/ Piment, says that only French citizens with high position or stature— such as CEOs, cabinet ministers, or famous members of the arts— are invited to join the club. Names are suggested by travel agents. Members are notified of their acceptance into the club and asked to complete a brief enrollment form that asks for information about their

Exhibit 6.5 Air France's Club 2000 Recognizes Status.

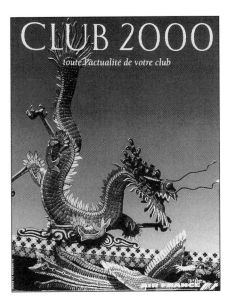

The premise of Air France's Club 2000, like other VIP clubs, is that membership both recognizes and confers status and privilege, thereby creating brand loyalty and gaining influential brand advocates for the airline.

interests and the names and ages of family members. Each receives a membership card and the name of his or her designated Air France representative. Benefits of Club 2000 membership include guaranteed reservations, deep discounts on third-party services, access to private business planes and airport facilities, and invitations to special events based on each member's interests. (See Exhibit 6.5.)

So successful is this club as a gauge of status that people long to belong to it. Membership has more than tripled to 7,000 since 1990.

But Air France hasn't overlooked loyal customers who cannot earn such privileged status. When it launched Club 2000, it also launched a frequent-purchase program called Service Plus for its most frequent fliers. This club contains two tiers geared to the number of air miles flown in a year and it grants each tier a unique set of benefits similar to, but less valuable than, those of Club 2000. Membership in Service Plus has grown from 33,000 to 43,000 since 1990. (See Exhibit 6.6).

(In 1992, the airline also nodded to the new realities of the European market by launching a traditional rewards-oriented frequent-flier

Exhibit 6.6 Air France Service Plus.

Air France Service Plus recognizes its best customers—those who fly more than 35,000 miles per year—by bestowing automatic membership in one of its Service Plus recognition and reward programs.

program called Fréquence Plus. Members of the other Air France clubs are automatically enrolled in this mileage-earning program.)

Although few airlines have a VIP club like Club 2000, most of the major U.S. and European programs offer elite-level status for very frequent fliers, rewarding them for their patronage with higher mileage awards than other frequent-fliers receive. According to Stevan Grosvald, these programs "recognize the financial worth of these most frequent customers," offering them "extraordinary extra benefits, service, and enhanced recognition." The average frequent-flier member may fly between nine and twelve flight segments a year, while premium-level members fly twenty, thirty, forty, or more, so earning their loyalty is very valuable. "Once a traveler obtains premium-level credentials and begins enjoying the rich benefits that come with those credentials, it is extremely difficult for a competitive airline to woo that traveler away from his or her existing program," he explains.[13]

Recent reports indicate that other airlines are looking for ways to get more mileage out of their elite-level programs. American Airlines's Michael Gunn said that "there are opportunities for more specialized recognition" for Gold-level members (flying 25,000 miles per year) and Platinum-level members (flying 50,000 miles per year). "We can look at our platinum members and further enhance our bond with them," he explained.[14] British Airways has been experimenting with enhancing the personalized services offered to its Executive Club travelers by adding personalization to the check-in process.[15] Refining reward structures in this way is an ongoing process and is made possible by customer dialogue.

Recognizing information needs.   At its most basic, recognition simply acknowledges and responds to the unique needs and interests of each individual. Such recognition can move a prospective or actual customer, donor, or supporter from being a passive recipient of your communications to being an active participant in an interactive relationship with you.

Nestlé U.S. does this by making sure each member of the Carnation Special Delivery Club receives information and offers uniquely suited to her stage of pregnancy or her newborn's development. If she is eight months pregnant, for example, she'll get information on her own nutritional needs and third-party offers for relevant products such as a breast pump, diapers, or an infant car seat. When her baby is one month old, she'll get information about breast-feeding. At seven months, the focus might be on feeding her baby solid foods.

Using information to recognize customers' individual needs was also the rationale behind DowElanco's development of a marketing database. The system, conceived and developed by the company's French subsidiary in Valbonne, went live in early 1992. Known as "Matilde" (Method for Approaching Territorial Information through a Logical Database), the system helps the company meet the disparate information needs of the French dealers and farmers who buy its crop-protection products. This has given the company an important edge in a highly competitive marketplace.

Designed to aid the firm in its marketing, Matilde is available to company salespeople and selected dealers who connect with Valbonne using their personal computers. In addition to managing order transactions electronically, these users can also request that a specific informational or promotional campaign be mailed to

Exhibit 6.7 DowElanco Mailing.

DowElanco salespeople in France notify headquarters electronically of the names of customers who should receive specific direct-mail campaigns. Customer communications are now precisely targeted to the specific needs of each customer. Both response rates and profits have improved. This personalized mailing on a new fungicide included a mailback request for a detailed report on the product's performance in the individual customer's exact location.

prospects and customers whom they name. (See Exhibit 6.7.) The result: Customer communications are now precisely targeted to the specific needs of each customer. Both response rates and profits have improved.

Matilde was the brainchild of DowElanco France market research and direct marketing manager Jean-Claude Guémas, who explained that 12,000 customers are now in the database. "The system gives the firm a unique edge in the agrichemical industry," he said. "The key to success for manufacturers is to speed the response to parasite attacks. At DowElanco, our strategic goal was to gain an advantage by mastering marketing information from the field."

Matilde helps the company track field activity and target marketing programs by region based on usage patterns. It also enables the company to sensitize dealers to market opportunities and to stimulate purchases at the end of the supply chain.

Not long after we spoke with Mr. Guémas, DowElanco's U.S. headquarters in Indianapolis reported that it was building a similar centralized database system. The vendor designing the system described it as a tool to make "recommendations for marketing programs more relevant" and to help DowElanco create "dialogue relationships."[16]

To some degree, the DowElanco effort may seem like little more than crafty marketing. But in the context of an overheated marketing climate, most customers appreciate receiving timely, relevant sales messages. Such messages indicate to the customer that the marketer understands his or her needs and won't waste time with irrelevant drivel.

Recognition alone is seldom enough.   One final thought on recognition programs: *Don't expect recognition alone to do the job.* Consumers are accustomed to shopping for deals, and they have come to expect rewards. Just look at the beating the American Express (Amex) charge card has been taking. At the same time that retailers and service establishments have been rebelling against the card issuer's high fees, many long-term cardholders have been switching to new credit cards that are accepted at more locations, offer lower fees, and have tangible rewards to boot. The number of outstanding Amex cards dropped 4.5 percent between 1992 and 1993, and merchant fees are dropping, too, in response to competitive pressures.[17]

One colleague who recently terminated her thirteen-year relationship with American Express put it this way: "Why should I pay $55 a year for the 'distinction' of being an Amex cardholder when I can get a lot more for my money with a revolving-balance, co-branded card from one of the airlines?" She added that American Express's attempts to win her back have only alienated her further. Instead of asking her why she was canceling her account, the company sent her repeated appeals that focused on the status and "privileges" of membership. "What privileges?" she said. "I pay a lot for them, and they're not as good as I can get from my airline card."

Rewards

As we saw earlier with Carnation Special Delivery Club and the Burger King Kids Club, intangible rewards based on recognition— such as information, entertainment, or education—can be powerful tools in relationship bonding. But adding tangible rewards through a point-accumulation program can add materially to a program's success. (This is especially true when the reward systems are structured with continuity, as we'll see shortly.)

Marketers in virtually every industry are experimenting with such rewards for customer loyalty. The U.S. hotel industry was the first to jump into frequency programs shortly after the airlines proved the concept in the early 1980s. By the late 1980s, the U.S. retail industry was exploring how to develop target-marketing programs using scanning technology, in-store interactive couponing, and smart cards. The entertainment industry—from newspapers to radio stations— has begun segmenting customers into database-driven clubs of all shapes and sizes. From banking to pharmaceuticals, everyone is building databases. And everywhere you look—the world over—commercial enterprises and nonprofit organizations are seeking partners with whom they can expand the added-value rewards they offer to their best customers. (See the discussion of "Dollar Doublers" in Chapter 2.)

One of the most interesting examples of this trend is the co-branding occurring in the U.S. credit-card business. In recent years, major U.S. firms like AT&T, Sears, General Motors (GM), General Electric (GE), and GTE have launched their own general-purpose credit cards. Most of these cards have attracted significant followings by:

1. Offering lower interest rates and annual fees than traditional bank cards.

2. Offering special discounts on the issuer's goods and services, and/or

3. Offering discounts on the goods and services of participating partners.

Collectively, such nonbank credit cards have taken over one-quarter of the general-purpose credit card market, posing a major threat to the banking industry.[18] (The only bank-issued cards that are showing strong growth these days are cards co-branded by a bank and a major airline, which award cardholders with airline miles based on purchase volumes. These lucrative affinity cards generate revenues averaging $13,000 per account per year.)[19]

According to Anne Moore, president of Atlanta research firm Synergistics, the credit card business is seeing a rapid rise in frequency marketing because "consumers are looking for value and a good deal." She credits the Sears Discover card, with its 1 percent rebate, as the trend starter.[20] AT&T was the next big innovator, launching its Universal Card in 1988 with no annual fee for charter cardholders and a 10 percent discount to all cardholders on all AT&T long-distance calls charged to the card. So successful was this launch that AT&T quickly became the second-largest card issued in U.S. history (behind Citicorp.)[21]

But the September 1992 launch of the GM MasterCard surpassed even AT&T's launch records. GM signed up more than a million new members per month for the first three months. By May 1993, GM had more than nine million cardholders who had collectively charged several billion dollars on their cards. What's more, they had purchased more than 100,000 GM cars and trucks. And the really slick trick of the GM card is the high value of the reward structure. Five percent of every dollar charged on the card is rebated (up to a $500 annual cap) if you buy a GM car or truck (purchases from GM partners enabled cardholders to bypass the cap by rewarding 10 percent rebates plus selected discounts). GM Gold MasterCard holders get similar benefits plus a $1,000 per year earnings cap. Clearly, the GM card is serving both new-customer conquest and customer-retention functions for GM and its partners.[22] (See Exhibit 6.8.)

A spate of other co-branded cards have recently hit the U.S. market:

- Apple Computer, Contiki Tours, Carnival Cruise Lines, and Shell have been among the many companies introducing co-branded Visa or MasterCard credit cards that give volume-based credits toward purchases of the sponsoring company's goods or services.[23]

- GE's Reward MasterCard offers discounts and rebates on products from GE and partners like Waldenbooks, Toys R Us, and Hertz.[24]

Exhibit 6.8 General Motors Offers Co-Branded Credit Card.

The really slick trick of the GM card is the high value of its reward structure. Five percent of every dollar charged on the card is rebated (up to $500 annual cap) if you buy a GM car or truck. Within eight to nine months of the card's launch, GM was crediting it with sales of 17,000 vehicles, and it had attracted numerous tie-in partners.

- The GTE MasterCard offers 10 percent discounts on GTE call-ing-card calls, with a maximum savings of $50. Discounts are also extended to services purchased with the card from third-party partners in the travel industry.[25]

- Ford Motor Company unveiled MasterCard and Visa co-branded cards in February 1993 that are quite similar to the GM MasterCard.[26]

- Intuit, a personal-finance software company in Menlo Park, California, introduced its own Visa credit card in September 1992. While it does not offer any cumulative awards or discounts, the card is available only to Intuit customers and is specifically designed to help them automate their credit card expense accounting.

There are two key requirements for a reward program to be effective with customers:

Rewards must be easy to understand and easy to earn. Marketers sometimes create such elaborate reward schemes that consumers have difficulty following them. Consumers expect marketers to place some restrictions and caveats on rewards and accept them as the tradeoff for getting a good deal. But they don't appreciate marketers who impose gratuitous rules or set hurdles that are too high for them to jump.

By the same token, it is possible to design overly rich reward structures that give away the store! Arby's Inc. of Miami discovered that during a recent test of its new frequent-diner incentive program. The program electronically tracks member purchases through smart cards and rewards club members with food prizes and coupons. In test programs launched in four cities, Arby's experimented with the reward structure and quickly discovered that points are easier to manage than other systems. In test cities where rewards could be earned simply for visiting the restaurant, explained marketing director Dave Shannon, "We were giving free meals to someone who came in four times and bought four cups of coffee. The initial rules made it a pretty rich program."[27] The lesson: Rewards should be easy to earn. But be careful not to make them *too* easy.

Rewards must be consumer oriented and easy to use. The 1993 withdrawal of Air Miles from the United States illustrates the importance of these points. Air Miles was the co-sponsored continuity promotion run by Boston-based Loyalty Management Group, the now defunct affiliate of U.K.-based Air Miles International. The firm signed up 45 national sponsors and 150 local sponsors—major firms like Time Warner, General Cinema, and AT&T. Each company designed its own program to encourage consumer usage. But all shared a common reward structure—mileage credits good toward air travel, administered through Air Miles.

According to Air Miles International chairman, Keith Miles, one of the critical factors in the program's demise in the United States was that it wasn't set up to be sufficiently easy for consumers to participate, and to do so frequently. He contrasted the U.S. operation with Canada's, where Air Miles has enrolled over 20 percent of households and is fully electronic. Canadian consumers carry magstripe membership cards that are swiped at point-of-sale by participating sponsors.

In the United States, consumers had to assemble reams of documenta-
tion and mail it all in after their purchase in order to claim any award
at all. Moreover, says Miles, there were too few retailers involved
with the program, making it difficult for consumers to earn points.[28]

When Rewards are Mostly Promotional

So far, our discussion of rewards has focused on programs structured
with simple continuity, which means that the value of the rewards,
while cumulative, does not magnify with subsequent purchases. (See
the discussion of continuity on pages 141 through 144.) But many
companies give awards without leading to continuity. These are often
database-driven promotions rather than long-term loyalty builders.
They may help the marketer acquire a database. They often serve
promotional objectives quite well. But they seldom build long-term
loyalty.

A spate of major promotions from U.S. tobacco companies illustrates this point. The R.J. Reynolds Tobacco Company started the
current round with its Camel Cash program in 1991. A dizzying array
of merchandise festooned with the Joe Camel image became available
for purchase with "Camel Cash," private money included with each
pack of Camel cigarettes. R.J. Reynolds attributes its 1992 market
share stability to the successful catalog promotion, which continued
throughout 1993.[29] A company spokesperson said that the catalog was
very effective in attracting smokers of competitive brands.[30]

Philip Morris followed Reynolds's lead in January 1993 with a promotion called the Marlboro Adventure Team. The company positioned the campaign's intent as conquest marketing, saying that the
30,000 adult smokers who switch brands daily represent $10 million
a year to tobacco companies.[31] Proof-of-purchase "Adventure Team
Miles" were packaged with each pack of Marlboros. Smokers could
exchange them for camping gear, clothing, lighters, and other merchandise from the Official Gear catalog. As with R.J. Reynolds's private money, Adventure Team Miles coupons require customers to fill
in information about themselves. Those that were sent via direct mail
were preprinted with the customer's name.

R.J. Reynolds tried a similar promotion for its Winston brand with
the May 1993 launch of Winston Weekends. However, this program
was not renewed.

As we saw in Chapter 4, these promotions provide smokers with an opportunity to display the logos of their favorite brands—to express their identity bonds publicly. They also helped the tobacco companies to amass databases with the names, addresses, and smoking habits of adult Americans. While widely considered to be the costliest promotions ever undertaken by the industry, the ability to target smoking consumers evidently was a prize worth paying dearly for. While such programs have the "feel" of relationship programs, they are really extended promotions. Take them away, and sales may well return to pre-promotion levels. No doubt this is one reason Philip Morris chose to launch the Marlboro Country Store promotion when its highly successful Marlboro Miles program ended in 1993.

Continuity

What we mean by continuity is *structuring your program so that each purchase the customer makes magnifies the value of the next.* In other words, you create a reward structure that enhances the customer's incentive for repeat purchases and multiplies the importance of each transaction.

Continuity by this definition is the critical edge that separates a relationship-building activity from a sales promotion aimed simply at moving product off the shelves.

Our usage of the term "continuity" is also different from traditional direct-marketing usage, which refers to a specific type of program that sells a series of products with a single promotion.[32]

The airline frequency programs have truly mastered continuity. The more you fly, the more miles you earn. But the first award levels are quite high, so you have to do lots of flying to reach them. (You can accelerate your mileage earning by using co-branded airline credit cards and by patronizing frequent-flier partners such as hotels, rental-car companies, long-distance phone service companies, and others.) Several of the frequent-stay hotel programs incorporate continuity in their reward structure, too.

Few other programs that we've seen have mastered continuity, however. We are not aware of any business-to-business marketers or fund-raisers who've seriously attempted it. It is possible to have continuity without building a relationship. Think of all the "Buy Three, Get One Free"-type deals you've seen. These should not be confused with long-term continuity. When they are used within the context of a frequent-flier or other frequent-purchase program we think of them as promotions within a relationship program. As such, they are good examples of how you can use a long-term relationship program tactically to reach short-term sales goals.

Managing a reward program can be complex and expensive. Many companies interested in frequency marketing opt for simpler solutions, such as that devised by Neiman Marcus. Its InCircle frequent-shopper club, launched in 1984, rewards members who spend $3,000 or more in a calendar year with high-ticket awards like a ten-day vacation in the French Riviera (along with other benefits, such as special member shopping events, publications, mailings, and a toll-free hotline). Each dollar spent in any of the company's twenty stores earns one point good toward the awards. But accumulated points do not carry over from year to year. This supposedly encourages members who are close to the $3,000 threshold by early December to boost their holiday spending. But we wonder about all the other shoppers—people who might have gone on a shopping binge right after Christmas or when they get their tax refund in the spring.

Neiman Marcus won't reveal any actual results of the program. But its creator, Bernie Feiwus, indicated that the program has met the company's primary goals: (1) to reward its best customers for their loyalty and (2) to encourage customers to consolidate their fashion purchases with Neiman Marcus rather than shopping at two or three competing stores. "There is no doubt that InCircle has increased our share of the market in a market with declining sales," said Feiwus. And to illustrate the value of reward points to his customers, he added, "Points are disputed in divorce cases. They're left in settlements. And not too long ago, we witnessed two sisters battling over their deceased mother's points."[33]

Building continuity into your program may take some effort and some trial and error. Waldenbooks has been grappling with how to improve this aspect of its Waldenbooks Preferred Reader Club. In place since 1990, the club is unique in the bookstore industry because it gives members both a straight 10 percent discount on every item in any of the chain's 1,275 stores and a reward of one point for every dollar spent. When a member accumulates 100 points, Waldenbooks issues a coupon worth $5 towards any Waldenbooks purchase. The program tracks each member's purchases and sends segmented mailings based on prior spending patterns. So, if you buy a lot of mysteries, you're apt to get a special mailer with promotions for new releases in that category. While the program is chiefly designed to increase store traffic, members are given the option of purchasing by mail.

Members must pay $10 a year to earn these privileges, and the coupons carry over from year to year. Marketing vice president Steven Morvay believes the program has given Waldenbooks a decided advantage in the industry. The closest competitor is B. Dalton's Booksavers program, which gives members a straight 10 percent discount on in-store purchases (and also imposes a $10 annual fee).

Morvay told us he wants to add incentives that will encourage increased participation in the Waldenbooks program. "We want to give people a way to strive for higher rewards by accumulating more points," he explained. "Under the current system, people who spend $1,000 with us really get no more than those who spend $100. We're trying to do some predictive modeling to determine what share of the customers' book purchases are being done at Waldenbooks and whether they would respond to higher awards. We want to get them to make more of a commitment to buy more books with us."

For now, says Morvay, the Waldenbooks Preferred Reader Club is meetings its objective of serving higher-spending customers. Its 3.5 million members account for almost a third of the chain's total sales.

We can readily understand why Waldenbooks might decide against a reward system that offers progressively greater rewards as dollar-level purchases advance. It might not enhance loyalty among book buyers, and profit margins—slim enough in this business—could suffer. But applying other components of the customer bonding system could help them develop other solutions. For example, they might position their $5 coupons as private money, applicable to purchases of goods and services by marketing partners eager to reach the Waldenbooks audience. To enhance the value of their reward system, they could also make their coupons transferable to friends and family, or exchangeable as gift certificates, encouraging advocacy bonding and generating new business.

Retail franchise chain Egghead Software is another company whose frequency program lacks the continuity element. Launched in April 1992, CUE (Customer Updates and Eggstras) has done a bang-up job of tracking sales and paying attention to customers. CUE members sign on free in any Egghead store and earn an immediate 5 percent discount on all purchases. Based on information they provide about themselves and their computer usage upon enrollment, they receive segmented mailings and quarterly newsletters geared to their interests. (See Exhibit 6.9.)

Exhibit 6.9 Recognition, Rewards, No Continuity.

Launched in April 1992, CUE (Customer Updates and Eggstras), has done a bang-up job of tracking sales and paying attention to customers. But its reward structure has no continuity incentive to keep customers buying more from Egghead Software stores. It is primarily a discount program.

Egghead obviously sees CUE as an important weapon in a fiercely competitive industry. The program offers excellent recognition of each customer's information needs and a promotional incentive to increase sales. But its reward structure lacks a critical continuity component. It is primarily a discount program. How much more valuable CUE could be if it carried some means for keeping Egghead customers from migrating to other retailers or direct-mail vendors. That's what can happen when you construct a program that includes all three aspects of relationship bonding: recognition, reward, and continuity.

Recap and Where-To

Relationship bonding occurs when Albert the Advertiser opens up opportunities for an ongoing relationship with Charles the Customer. The relationship is based upon interaction and dialogue and is powered by a database and facilitated by direct media.

This foundation permits an exchange of benefits. Albert the Advertiser gains an ever richer understanding of the needs and preferences of his customers and supporters. Charles the Customer receives recognition as an individual and tangible rewards, preferably structured in such a way that they become increasingly difficult for him to give up.

The relationship bond is much stronger than awareness or identity bonds. It is less susceptible to dislocation by competitive activities or changes in the marketing environment. Effective marketing at this level requires a commitment from senior management to information-driven marketing and a willingness to make the necessary investments. The up-front costs of database building and usage are great, and it may be some time before you can prove the viability of this approach with incremental revenues.

Relationship bonding requires that you build three elements into your program: (1) recognition of the customer's loyalty, (2) rewards, and (3) continuity (so the customer has an ever-increasing incentive to maintain the relationship).

In the next chapter, we'll look at what happens when you ascend the customer bonding scale and foster bonds *among* your constituents.

Checklist

1. Have you established relationship bonds with your customers? Through recognition? Rewards? Continuity?

2. Are you using a database, direct media, and dialogue?

3. Are you running a frequent-buyer program of any sort?

4. What are your competitors doing to create relationship bonds? What impact do their activities have on your current success in the marketplace? What impact could their relationship-bonding activities have on your future potential in the marketplace?

5. What do you recognize your best customers for? Their "achievements" as buyers of your product, their status, or their information needs? How do you recognize them? With better deals on products or services? With information and education? With exclusive rewards for frequent purchases? What are your specific objectives in doing this? Are you meeting them? If not, why not?

6. How can you create or modify a reward structure to encourage the customer behavior you desire? (Remember, you can use tangible or intangible rewards, or some combination of both.)

7. How can you make each customer transaction add to the cumulative value of the relationship for the customer?

8. Should you be using "private money" in your reward program, if you aren't already?

9. Could marketing partners add value to the program and make it profitable for you? What would be the requirements for a good marketing partner? How would they be involved? If you're already working with marketing partners, how could you increase the value of the alliance?

10. What kinds of direct media (newsletters, magazines, catalogs, audiotapes, videotapes, fax publications, and so forth) should you be using to create two-way communications with your customers? Which of these have you already tried? Could you make better uses of direct media?

11. How can you use other media to deliver rewards and create dialogue?

12. Do you have the organizational backing or authority to undertake a relationship-bonding program? Who in your organization can champion the effort? What obstacles will you or they have to overcome?

13. Which arguments will be most persuasive in convincing your management that long-term loyalty building is necessary to your organization?

14. If you must deliver short-term payoffs to get management approval of your relationship-bonding efforts, how will you do so? What are the risks that adding a short-term focus will damage the integrity of the relationship bonds you are trying to build with your customers?

15. How can you support your relationship-bonding program with other degrees in the customer bonding system?

16. How can you keep competitors from copying your program?

Chapter 7

Community Bonding

Bird's-Eye View

Some marketers have figured out how to encourage the inclusive process that we call community bonding. At this level, your customers or supporters are bonding (1) with your brand, be it a product, service, candidate, or organization; and (2) with other people who share their interests and whom they find through their involvement with you. This bond involves a high degree of loyalty, and it is therefore a valuable asset to the organization that can create it. Indeed, it often serves as a springboard to the very highest bonding level, advocacy bonding. When customers or supporters come together because of their common interest in your brand, it generally indicates that the brand has become central to their life-style interests. Indeed, life-style–related activities and events are critical success factors for this level of bonding.

Relationships at this level are highly interactive. Direct promotion is an appropriate communication vehicle, but mass media generally plays little or no role and may even detract from the participants' sense that they are part of an exclusive community.

Community. A social group sharing common characteristics or interests and perceived or perceiving itself as distinct in some respect from the larger society within which it exists.

Webster's Encyclopedic Unabridged Dictionary
of the English Language[1]

Human beings are highly social creatures. Most of us have strong needs for affiliation, which we fulfill by joining communities of various sorts. Be it by joining a motorcycle club, a religious congregation, the county chess league, or a national political organization, many of us like to get actively involved with others who share our interests.

And therein lies the secret of the community bond: *When you offer a product, a service, or a cause that gives people a reason and a means for forming (or joining) a community, they often respond wholeheartedly and develop great loyalty to that community and to the product or service.* They may not even need any encouragement or help from you. If your product, service, or cause becomes an integral part of their life-style—and particularly if it supports some of their recreational, social, or career needs—it can become a catalyst, spurring them to form relationships with like-minded others.

Forming Communities of Interest

Our ideas about this level of bonding began to gel a couple of years back when we passed what looked like a city of aluminum cocoons shining in the sun next to an Ohio interstate. At first we thought we were witnessing a new kind of construction. But we later learned that it was Silver City, the international rally of the Wally Byam Caravan Club International, whose 14,000 members are all owners of Airstream trailers and motor homes. Their annual rally, complete with cooking classes, games, craft fairs, entertainment, and trailer-travel seminars, is the crowning event of a busy schedule of local and regional gatherings and caravans throughout North America. The club is run completely by members, with some financial support from the Airstream manufacturer. Its mission? Fun and fellowship.

You can find similar communities clustered around many kinds of activities. The common theme is that those interests are integral to the consumer's life-style.

Leisure and Recreation

Recreational activities—from biking to race-car driving to video-game playing—are natural community creators, and many brand-name manufacturers have established clubs to help their brands become central to their customers' life-styles. Most, like Harley David-son's 220,000-member club, HOG (Harley Owner's Group), are run completely by the manufacturer (with support from dealers, in Har-ley's case) to encourage customers around the globe to integrate the product into their life-styles. Others, like the Wally Byam Caravan Club, for owners of Airstream trailers and motor homes, are largely member managed, but receive funding and other support from the manufacturer.[2] Regardless, the communities commonly rally around events of some sort, to which the manufacturer usually sends generous contingents of staff, merchandise, information, giveaways, and other goodies.

Business Communities

Brand-related communities are common in business, too, bringing interested users together to share tips and resources for getting the most from their chosen brand.

Among the better known brand-related professional clubs are those that involve computer usage. Larger computer manufacturers like International Business Machines (IBM) and Digital Equipment Cor-poration (DEC) have supported their customers for years with user groups like DECUS (Digital Equipment Corporation Users Group) or IBM's "Guide," "Share," or "Common." Typically, the manufac-turers create separate groups or subgroups of users according to their level of function in the customer organization. So you would find, for example, separate user groups for senior executives and computer programmers. And within each group, users are encouraged to seg-ment themselves further around highly specialized fields of interest.

Smaller business-to-business firms use this technique heavily, too. Sonic Air, a $52 million provider of logistics and distribution outsourc-ing services, warehouses crucial replacement parts for high-tech equipment in a global network of 46 warehouses. According to vice president of marketing, Hal Rabin, the company focuses heavily on increasing the value of existing customers. Among its activities are semiannual forums that gather together groups of key customers for two-to-three day working sessions in resort locations. "The forums give both Sonic Air and our customers a chance to bring up issues and work them out," Rabin explained. "We also ask customers to share their business vision with us, so we can learn how to be of maximum value to them."

Trade fairs have long functioned as community forums, too. These product-oriented gatherings let marketers meet with customers, suppliers, middlemen, and influential industry figures. European trade fairs, which trace their roots all the way back to the guild gatherings of the Middle Ages, are particularly sophisticated and influential, and participation in them is mandatory for anyone seriously contending for market position.

Technology as a Life-style

Similar user groups have sprung up around personal computers, video games, and other technological products. Members of these groups can attend local gatherings and converse with fellow aficionados of their favorite brand. They participate in diverse information exchanges to solve product problems and share software and ideas. The groups let them stay in touch—in person, electronically, by mail, and by phone—with other "techno-niks" who are users of the same brand.

Technology as a Community Builder

Computer technology has spawned a whole new way for people to congregate around shared interests without ever leaving their home or office. With a personal computer and a modem, it's now possible to join electronic conferences or browse through electronic mail discussions on almost any subject you can imagine, and with people from all over the globe.

As the much touted "information superhighway" in the United States is developed, and high-bandwidth gateways permit greater and greater information exchange globally, the communities of interest available to electronic users will continue to expand exponentially. Currently, most sellers of computer-related equipment, software, or services operate their own on-line networks or bulletin boards. Community- and political-interest forums are growing at a rapid rate. Professional interest groups, dating services, collectors' exchanges . . . . if you can name it, you can probably find it in the world of the on-line computer.

Among the three major U.S. on-line services that currently promote electronic interest groups to the public at large there are already literally hundreds of organized on-line communities on topics as diverse as parenting and diabetes management. Prodigy boasts 850 bulletin board topics, in which readers post at least 100,000 notes per day. In late 1993, CompuServe was supporting 600 on-line "forums," which they define as "mini-communities where people with a common interest gather electronically to share." Fast-growing America Online doesn't keep track of the number of user forums among its 500,000 subscribers, but indicated that the number grows daily.[3]

So far, relatively few forums are centered on specific products. Most of these are still related to computer hardware or software, according to on-line services spokespeople.

Industry experts say that the next major growth area for on-line service sales will be among nonprofessional, home-computer users who currently account for less than 5 percent of worldwide information-service sales of $10.1 billion.[4] So the phenomenon of on-line communities has only just begun, according to Chris Elwell, editor of the annual study from which these figures are cited. "It's really the first stages of the global village vision starting to come through," he explained. "On-line networks are breaking down barriers of space and time and letting people with common interests get together. Mostly it's happening today in communities that have something to do with computer hardware and software. But as people become more familiar with technology and get used to using it as a tool in their everyday lives, it will be used more and more as a tool for communing."[5]

Concerned Citizens' Communities

Still other communities form around issues or causes—such as saving the Amazon rainforests from deforestation, promoting inner-city development, assisting impoverished children, improving the lot of an oppressed group of people, or supporting a particular political candidate in a run for office.

In the United States, cause-related activities are almost always sponsored by nonprofit organizations. Many of these have been community builders from their inception, relying on volunteers and members to find and recruit others just like themselves into the organization's activities. Others simply use donor funds to support organizations of hired professionals who actively work on the issue or cause. Although much fund-raising literature stresses the idea that the would-be donor belongs to a select community of people who care about the issue or cause, too many of these groups never actualize the power of this implicit community bond. They would do well to create more bonding opportunities for their supporters by galvanizing their members into grass-roots activities.

The Powerful Whammy of the Communal Bond

Customers or supporters who form a community bond around your brand, product, service, candidate, cause, or organization are usually *extremely* loyal. Your competitors will be hard-pressed to shake their allegiance.

Think about it. When people get together to share their use of your product or service or to jointly support your cause, they are really putting their brand loyalty out there for others to see and judge. If they're willing to do that, they are often willing to be advocates as well, meaning that they will sell others on the benefits of your offering (See Chapter 8). And, in general, the more they engage in brand-related community activities, the more their loyalty deepens. Such a bond is very strong. Breaking the product bond also means breaking the social bonds that tie together the customer community.

There are several characteristics of this level of bonding that account for its strength. They are also critical success factors for marketers wishing to create community bonds among their constituents:

1. Community bonding occurs in connection with life-style–related events or activities.
2. Community bonding is highly involving by nature.
3. When community bonding occurs around a product, service, cause, or candidate, rallying customers or supporters around shared life-style interests.

Life-Style-Related Events or Activities

The opportunity to interact with others around a common interest is a powerful attractor for many people. So if you can create an event or activity that gives people a chance to indulge their interest—together—you've got the basis for creating community bonds. Depending upon how you structure it, you could be giving them multiple benefits: social contact, education about using the product, special privileges that recognize their loyalty to your product, and so forth. If your customers or supporters value these benefits, they will not want to give them up.

Courting the Motor Home Crowd

Earlier we spoke of our experience with the Wally Byam Caravan Club. Actually, the recreational vehicle (RV) industry is rich with examples of community bonding. Although the term RV encompasses many different kinds of products—from nonmotorized tow trailers to luxury motor homes—most people who buy them share a common interest. They are into a certain RV life-style. They may be retired "snowbirds" following fair weather back and forth. They may be weekend budget campers or once-a-year vacationers. They may take to the road every chance they get. But they all have strong associations between their RV ownership and a definite life-style experience. For many, sharing the experience with like-minded RVers is half the fun.

Wally Byam, creator of the silver Airstream tow trailers, launched the earliest RV club, The Wally Byam Caravan Club, in the mid-1950s. It established a model that was followed in 1965 by motor-home manufacturer Travco. The model relied heavily on gatherings of owners—rallies and caravans—organized with the aid and financial support of the manufacturer. Said Warren MacKenzie, who headed the Travco Club several years later, "I think in the beginning most of the manufacturers realized that the loyalty that was developing from owners in the Airstream club could not be overlooked."

Today, there are more than thirty manufacturer-sponsored RV clubs in the industry, plus clubs organized by the publishers of *Trailer Life* and *Motorhome Life* and by the Family Motor Coach Association.[6] The manufacturers' clubs actually compete with private RV travel companies that also organize tours and caravans.

MacKenzie now works for Foretravel, Inc., a manufacturer of luxury motor homes, as assistant to the president, and formerly headed an organization of industry clubs. He spends a good part of his year on the road with the 2,300 members of the Foretravel Club. He noted that the common interest that draws club owners to manufacturer events is the fact that they own the same kind of vehicle. "It's a whole psychological study in customer bonding," he commented. "We know it is there and that it's important. It develops a loyalty to the product. That's why we put in such strong support."

While many of the clubs are run partially by members, all receive support from the manufacturers. Said MacKenzie, "Our whole motivation in supporting the club is to develop a continuing loyalty to the product and to the company. We can almost pinpoint the percentage of sales that can be credited towards the club and the support of the club. We know that it works if you do a good job."

According to Tom Walworth, who researches the industry for trade publication *RV News*, almost every major manufacturer has a club for owners of its vehicles. Many maintain designated areas at campgrounds for their club members, and a few even run club-specific parks. Most of these clubs are heavily supported by the manufacturers, although they are sometimes run as separate organizations and overseen by member management boards.[7]

Winnebago Industries was among the first motor-home manufacturers to develop an owner's club in 1970. Winnebago homes had been on the market for about three years at that time and, with 11,000 coaches on North American roadways, the company was eager to encourage customers to use and enjoy the product. "We wanted to encourage people to use the Winnebago motor homes to start out on a new way of life. The club helps our typical customer get the most out of motor home living," said Mike Anderson, general manager for the Winnebago-Itasca Travelers Club (WIT).

Today, there are over a quarter million Winnebago coaches on the road, and the club has grown to a network of 11,000 owners organized into 250 local WIT chapters and state clubs. Club members attend caravans and rallies throughout the continental United States and Canada. They receive a monthly magazine and a range of benefits such as road service, insurance, trip routing, product discounts, and mail-forwarding while on the road. And about 4,000 owners (in 1,600 coaches) convene annually in Forest City, Iowa, home of Winnebago Industries, for a Grand National Rally.

Although the club does not pay for itself, it does account for almost 20 percent of the company's total annual motor-home sales (1993 Winnebago-Itasca revenues were almost $327 million, up from $45 million in 1970). Winnebago holds its second-place share position in the marketplace and is even gaining, thanks to aggressive acquisitions through the 1980s and a solid reputation with its customers.

"Our customer loyalty is partly due to the club," says Anderson. "And also to our product, which gives a lot of bang for the buck. It is possible that people would switch brands more if we didn't have WIT. Most people trade up their coach every five years or so." Ac-

Exhibit 7.1 Recreational Vehicles: Natural Community-Builders.

Winnebago's Grand National Rally draws upwards of 4,000 motor home owners a year for product-related fun, education, and fellowship. The new Winnebago Motorsport Club is using more conventional event sponsorship to gain share of mind and appeal to a younger crowd.

cording to Anderson, many WIT members first joined the club when it started. In fact, he said, most people only leave WIT if they have to stop using motor homes due to sickness or some other circumstance.

In 1993, Winnebago moved outside its owner community to build awareness, identity, and community with a younger audience, again through events. The new effort is Winnebago's sponsorship of NASCAR races under the name Winnebago Motorsports. Motorsport members sit in a special section of the NASCAR racing pit, meet with celebrity spokesmen Dale Ernhard and Kenny Schrader, attend special functions in a Winnebago hospitality tent, and take home Winnebago Motorsport memorabilia. (See Exhibit 7.1.)

Advertised both through mass media and the WIT magazine, the Motorsport promotion has generated excitement among WIT members as well. "We're signing up fifty members per week," said Anderson. "We'll definitely be doing some more of these sponsorships. It's a great way to increase awareness for Winnebago."

"Multilogue" Is Essential to Community Bonding

Dialogue between the marketer and customers or prospects is crucial at higher levels of customer bonding. When encouraging community bonds, the marketer carries out a direct dialogue with each individual constituent by providing information, incentives, and brand-related rewards, and gathering feedback through some form of direct communication (surveys, telemarketing, and so forth).

But at this level, two new dimensions are added to the basic dialogue concept we discussed in earlier chapters:

1. The interactions are now likely to be conducted face-to-face.

2. Interactions move beyond basic dialogue between Albert the Advertiser and Charles the Customer. Now interaction becomes a "multilogue," including communications between Charles and Albert and between Charles and other customers or supporters. (See Exhibit 7.2.) The marketing job is much more complex, too. You must now foster communications directly with constituents and among customers as well.

The "Saloning" of America

According to futurist Faith Popcorn, Americans are "cocooning" in the 1990s, drawing inward to home and family for a sense of comfort

Exhibit 7.2 Albert and Charles and Friend: The Community Bond.

Interactions move beyond basic dialogue between Albert the Advertiser and Charles the Customer. Now interaction becomes a "multilogue," including communications between Charles and Albert and between Charles and other customers or supporters.

and satisfaction. And the "socialized cocooners," explains Popcorn, want to bring society home with them.[8]

Maybe she's onto something. Or maybe it's more that the constant mediation of information through television news and advertising has created a hunger for direct discourse with others. Whatever the reason, a phenomenon is afoot that many praise as the rebirth of discussion. And at its center is *Utne Reader*, a bimonthly magazine popular with U.S. baby boomers for its bright, easily digestible recaps of progressive topics from the nation's alternative presses.

With the launch in 1991 of its Utne Reader Neighborhood Salon Association, this small publisher started a community-bonding phenomenon that has taken the country by storm. Thanks to an innovative matchmaker program, people all over America are gathering in each other's living rooms to talk. About what? You name it. From the isolation of modern living to how to start an organic garden, *Utne Reader*'s readers are connecting through dialogue with each other. They're bringing friends and strangers to meet their fellow "salonistas." And oh, by the way, they're staying in touch with the magazine that helped them to find each other, sending in group pictures and reports on where they meet and what they discuss. Initially, this feedback was published in a standalone newsletter mailed to the people participating in these "salons." Recently, *Utne Reader* began a section on salons in the magazine itself, along with occasional ads to recruit new members (See Exhibit 7.3).

The Utne Reader Neighborhood Salon Association was launched with a cover story on salons in the March/April 1991 issue. The 18-page article series was called: "Salons: How to revive the lost art of conversation and start a revolution in your living room." At its end, a small on-page ad asked a simple question: "Shall we salon?" More than 8,000 readers responded, far more than the magazine expected, and its newly appointed "salon-keeper" scrambled to match the respondents up into small groups clustered by zip code.

Exhibit 7.3 *Utne Reader* Creates 3,000 Neighborhood Salons.

The mission of the Neighborhood Salon Association, says *Utne Reader*'s editor-in-chief Eric Utne, is "to help salon participants reinhabit their neighborhoods and fully participate in the life of their communities, and to revitalize democracy through vigorous discussion and debate." The program has sparked a community revival among literate, "cocooning" Americans.

By summer 1993, the known Neighborhood Salons numbered more than 300 and the total qualified members more than 13,000. (The program instituted a $12 lifetime fee in March 1992 to help cover its administrative costs and to formalize the membership list; but another 7,000 people have contacted the company since the 1991 launch, and they may still be saloning on their own.) The matching of salon members is now handled using sophisticated mapping software.

Upon joining the Neighborhood Salon Association, each member receives a list with the names and phone numbers of twenty-five or so members in the member's area. New members also receive a handbook called "The Salon-keeper's Companion," offering tips and insights for people willing to host salons in their homes. The publisher provides periodic updates on salon activities in the magazine, with ideas and messages from other salons across the country.

In short, subscribers, newsstand readers, and their friends, colleagues, and family all can become part of a community facilitated by *Utne Reader*.

But according to Griff Wigley, Utne Reader Neighborhood Salon Association "salon-keeper," Utne takes a hands-off approach to the communities it helps to create to protect the integrity of the relationships. "We want each salon participant to view this as 'good for me, for my neighborhood, for the community, for the planet,'" he said. "Indirectly, we get some association with that, because we've had a lot of media attention. But it's important that people know this is not a top-down, orchestrated thing. We just kind of throw the seeds out there and offer enough structure to help it get going. After that, it is really citizen-driven."

Utne correlated salon membership with subscriber renewal rates and new subscriptions in 1993. While overall renewal rates for non-salon members were 53 percent, salon member renewals were running 81 percent. The *salonistas* also donated magazine subscriptions (as Christmas or other occasion gifts) at a higher rate than non*salonistas*, says Wigley. But despite the company's insistence, we doubt it is coincidental that the publication's circulation soared from 30,000 to 305,000 between the launch of the salon effort in 1991 and the end of 1993. Could it not also be that community and advocacy bonding are at work here?

According to Wigley, the salon program grew out of the magazine's mission to "raise the level of understanding and dialogue about important political and cultural issues. Of course," he added, "we aren't shy about being capitalists and wanting to make a profit, and we are proud of our renewal rate." The program has also helped *Utne Reader* sell ad space by demonstrating the unusually "committed, involved relationship" between the magazine and its readers, added Wigley.

The magazine also gets input from the salons about issues its readers care about. "The salons help us tap into the current zeitgeist," said publisher Craig Neal. "They give us a feel for what's really going on in the communities. . . ."[9]

Utne declines the many suitors offering cross-promotion proposals targeted to Utne's salon members. "We don't sell our salon list," said Wigley. "Research shows us that people hate to be targeted, but they do like to choose. We are feeling our way on offering new services to the salon group. But we'll be judicious about it, and offer primarily salon-related activities, because we have a kind of social contract with them." Among the recent innovations are on-line salons. And Utne is eagerly encouraging newspapers, radio, and TV stations who are interested in creating their own salons.

Brand Integral to Life-Style

By now you appreciate that community bonding helps customers participate in activities that are somehow integral to their life-style interests. You may be asking yourself how your product or service or candidate might fit into the model and whether there are limits to this concept.

Products that have only a tangential relationship to life-style may not seem, at first blush, to lend themselves to community bonding, even though they might be "integral" to life. But this is not a hard and fast principle. Would you be inspired to join a community of fellows to commune over a bar of soap? Well, if you're a new mother, you might be interested in attending a seminar or joining a club that is sponsored by a soap company. That is, if it offered useful information on caring for your infant or an opportunity to meet with other new mothers. And, it's not that difficult to imagine a group of beer drinkers getting together around their favorite brew.

Holiday Inn Gets Business Travelers Out in Their Spare Time

You might think that getting frequent business travelers to go back out on the road on a weekend would be next to impossible. But maybe you haven't heard about how Holiday Inn does precisely that!

Exhibit 7.4 Holiday Inn Customers Convene.

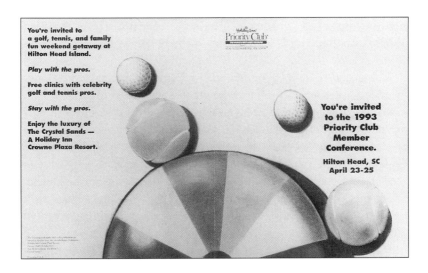

Holiday Inn's member conferences in the United States are sold out weeks in advance. The conferences are considered one of the benefits of membership in the chain's frequent-stay program, Priority Club. They are offered at below cost and shower attention and perks on attendees.

Twice a year since 1989, the Atlanta-based mega-hotel chain has enticed five hundred to one thousand of its most frequent guests to bring themselves and their families out to a resort property for a weekend of hobnobbing, recreation, and roundtable discussions with hotel management. These conferences are considered one of the benefits of membership in the chain's frequent-stay program, Priority Club. They are offered at below cost and shower attention and perks on attendees. (See Exhibit 7.4.) (Holiday Inn also plans to develop international member conferences down the line in support of its expanding Priority Club, according to global frequency marketing director, Kathy Howe.)

The April 1993 conference at Holiday Inn's new Crowne Plaza Resort on Hilton Head Island featured the first ever Priority Club Classic golf and tennis tournaments. Also offered were clinics with professional golf and tennis players, plus sea sports, bicycling, and area tours for the family. And, of course, plenty of opportunity to schmooze with fellow club members and company management.

"These conferences are so popular that they are sold out well in advance," said Ken Pierce, vice president of frequency marketing for Holiday Inn. "What we try to do is to provide a value to our customers that they just can't get somewhere else. It's the opportunity to meet and talk firsthand with some of our celebrity speakers and with Holiday Inn management."

Pierce said that the programs have definitely deepened customer loyalty. Customers get a lot of personal attention, and Holiday Inn management encourages them to use the event to give the company direct feedback on their needs. "During the conference we'll ask some of our members to come to meetings and focus groups with us," he explained. "They stand in line! We do offer an incentive to come to those meetings—typically club points—because we're getting a benefit from their participation. But most members tell me they'd do it for free. They welcome the opportunity to share feelings and ideas with us."

Pierce added that many of the individuals attending these conferences stay in touch with him afterwards, calling or writing with ideas and competitive information. "They're helping us do our job, and I don't believe it's in a self-serving manner," he explained. "They just believe in what we're trying to do."

Outside of the conferences, the hotel chain has established some regional advisory boards among its 3.8 million members. However, most other club communications occur in one-on-one contacts between Priority Club members and the hotel—through the mail and through direct contact with the chain's employees. Employee awareness and support for the frequent-stay program is a priority for club management, which provided intensive training to 15,000 front desk representatives in North America plus 1,000 franchise owners and 1,500 general managers. A similar training effort was launched when the program expanded its scope to include international properties in 1993.

The member conference is just one of the important ways in which Holiday Inn differentiates its club from the programs offered by Hilton, Marriott, and ITT Sheraton. Together with other competitive differentiators, it has helped to make Holiday Inn's program the largest in the industry. In fact, it's interesting to note that the Holiday Inn story demonstrates how all levels of the customer bonding framework can work together to produce strong consumer bonds.

- Awareness. This takes into account the sheer size of the brand. (Holiday Inn has 1,450 locations in the United States and 1,800 worldwide; its main competitors have closer to 200.) Awareness for Holiday Inn is supported by ongoing awareness advertising (40 percent of the total marketing budget). Unaided brand awareness in the United States is 99 percent (97 to 98 percent overseas), and 100 percent among Priority Club members. And awareness for the Priority Club program itself is 36 percent, eight points higher than the nearest competitive program.

- Identity. Priority Club members feel a strong loyalty toward their club, according to Pierce, spending 60 percent of their nights on the road with Holiday Inn. (Holiday Inn Hotels offer about 10 percent of the available room nights for sale in the United States.) Members of the club's very frequent-traveler segment, Priority Plus, spend 70 percent of their room nights at Holiday Inn properties. In fact, said Pierce, most report that they only go elsewhere when the location they want is full or is not served by a conveniently located Holiday Inn.

- Relationship. The chain places heavy emphasis on relationship building through newsletters, employee interaction, and conference activities. These marketing elements are complemented by continuity-building point-based awards for member stays and for promotional offers. Recently-added airline mileage rewards are expected to enhance the popularity of the program.[10]

- Community. No other frequent-stay club has attempted to create community bonds by gathering its members together like Priority Club. Holiday Inn builds each conference around life-style activities and incorporates plenty of opportunity for dialogue, both among customers and with company management.

- Advocacy. Priority Club encourages its members to refer others. This is done by offering bonus points to members who refer friends and through promotional offers that give awards and discounts. Referral recruitments netted 12,000 new members in 1992 (4 percent of the total increase in membership for the period) and were bringing in an average of 1,000 new memberships per month in 1993.

Getting to Success

We've seen that a life-style connection, three-way interactivity, and an event or group gathering are critical success factors for marketers wishing to encourage community bonding. But there are a couple of other things you should consider as important requirements, too. Let's take a look at them before we move on.

Have the Right Attitude

The first requirement is a light hand and a wholesome attitude. The community bond is strong, but your role in the communal relationship can be sensitive. When your customers meet with others to share their interest in your offering, they are exposing their brand affiliations for public scrutiny. Any attempt by you to elicit endorsements or sell on your behalf could be considered out of place. It is, in any case, probably quite unnecessary. Let your customers spontaneously share their brand interests and you will automatically reap the indirect benefits of their ever-increasing loyalty. Just bring them together to enjoy their common interest.

Facilitate Communication

The second requirement is that you be a facilitator of community bonding. Your role is to help your constituents find each other, offering a means for them to communicate amongst themselves as well as with you.

Different communities require different degrees of support. *Utne Reader* just had to help readers find each other and then step back and let the community direct itself. Winnebago and other RV clubs take a little more active role—organizing and managing a year-round schedule of events and coordinating an extensive network of local subgroups. Holiday Inn, on the other hand, completely orchestrates and manages its program.

Connect the Event with Your Brand

If you buy a motorcycle but have no one to ride with, you may not feel like using it much after the initial thrill wears off. But if you belong to the Harley Owner's Group, you have friends to ride with every day and in every part of the country, as well as gatherings and events to participate in anytime you feel like it.

Event sponsors often fail to make the connection between the consumer's life style and the brand, according to Jim Crimmins, executive director of strategic planning and research at DDB Needham World-wide in Chicago. In an interview with *Advertising Age* in June 1993, Crimmins said that most events are just media-buying opportunities and are wasted because the sponsors fail to help the consumer connect their product to his or her life-style.

"One of the biggest mistakes sponsors make is assuming the visibility they get by contracting with the event is worth much. It rarely is worth much of anything," he was quoted as saying. "If the sponsor wants to make the link with an event, he has to do it himself. The brand has to . . . tell people, I'm bringing you this event, and you should think of me this way because of this sponsorship."[11]

We agree with this statement as far as it goes. But Crimmins believes that such a connection is accomplished through promotions, public relations, in-store merchandising, advertising, and direct response. We disagree. Those are just communication vehicles. We would include opportunities for attendees to tell us who they are and something about themselves, for database-building purposes. (Remember the information-driven marketing model in Chapter 2?)

The real way to help consumers make the connection is to make sure your brand or cause really has a role to play in their lives in the first place. If you've made the right connection yourself between what you're offering and how your consumers can use it in their lives, you are then in a position to build meaningful communities and events around it.

Long-term Commitment

Another key requirement for success in community bonding is a long-term orientation. Again, customer bonding can have short-term pay-offs, but only if your overall orientation is long-term.

Customers want to know that you're not just making a show to grab their attention. They're used to that behavior and can spot it a mile away. Nothing is a bigger turnoff for consumers in this overmarketed age than feigned altruism. It's okay to admit that creating the community is good for you, but you have to prove that you're going to be behind it for them, too. And that means being committed to your community-bonding program for the long haul.

This is the other great failing that Crimmins points to in most event sponsorships. "If you're associated with the Olympics, the Indianapolis 500, or whatever, the fans of those properties are impressed by the

sponsorship for long periods of time, not merely [during the event],"
he said. "But [marketers] wait for the event itself to make their sponsorship known and have a very short time to enjoy that connection."

Have Strong Support at Lower Levels of Customer Bonding

We mentioned earlier that Holiday Inn spends up to 40 percent of
its annual marketing budget on awareness advertising (see Chapter
4). Another 10 to 20 percent is dedicated to promotional advertising
and the remainder to relationship marketing. Such allocations reflect
an understanding that all of the elements in the customer bonding
framework rely on each other.

"There is a certain baseline you have to achieve to get your message
across. We have found that our image advertising to the market segment that our relationship programs are placed with has greater impact," said vice president Ken Pierce. "Of all our market segments,
our Priority Club members typically have the most positive image of
our brand. And we have learned from them that we have to tend to the
relationship, too. We can't just bribe them with award promotions."

Recap and Where-To

Community bonding lifts your relationship with customers, prospects,
and supporters to a new level by creating opportunities for interactive,
three-way communication—between you and your constituents, and
among your constituents themselves.

This bond is much stronger than lower-level bonds, but it is also
much more complex to create and manage. It is generally event-driven
and revolves around life-style interests. It is highly interactive—often
relying on face-to-face contact between you and your constituents.
You must be sensitive to your role as a facilitator and not attempt to
overlay your own selling agenda upon the community. Your role is
primarily to bring like-minded individuals together and give them a
means for sharing their interest in your brand. You must also stay
behind the effort for the long-haul and support it with effective bonding at the lower levels of awareness, identity, and relationship.

Because your customers are putting their allegiances out there for
others to see and judge, community bonding is closely allied to advocacy bonding and often serves as a springboard to this highest bonding
step. We'll examine the nature of that highest of customer bonding
levels in the next chapter.

Checklist

1. What life-style connections might your customers, donors, or supporters make with your brand, your product or service, or your organization?

2. If there is no obvious existing life-style relationship, could you create one? Which aspects of your marketing programs or your product or service might lend themselves to being shared with others?

3. Are there existing events that you can link to your brand, cause, or candidate? How could you do that in a way that could bring your customers or supporters together?

4. Could you win stronger bonds by creating your own events?

5. What should your role be in these events? How much control should you retain over the community, and how should you use this control?

6. What are your competitors doing to create community bonds? What impact is this having (or might it have) on your market situation? How could you defend yourself from competitive community-bonding programs?

7. How will you measure the impact of what you do to create community bonds? Can qualitative measurements suffice?

8. Can you get the necessary management support to engage in this activity for the long-term?

9. What might competitors do to copy *your* activity? What impact would this have on your program? How can you minimize this impact?

Chapter 8

Advocacy Bonding

Bird's-Eye View

Advocacy bonding is another way of describing what direct marketers call "buyer-get-a-buyer," fund-raisers call "member-get-a-member," salespeople call "referral selling," and Madison Avenue calls "word-of-mouth advertising." It is one of the oldest, most effective ways to gain new business and strengthen your relationship with your customers. But it's amazing how few marketers take advantage of it.

Customers, donors, or supporters who are willing to advocate your product or service, cause, or candidate are your very best salespeople. They are willing to state their allegiance publicly, indicating the highest level of customer loyalty.

Advocacy bonding with your existing customers can happen without any action by you. But some marketers have discovered that formalizing advocacy can pay big rewards. To realize these rewards, you will need:

1. A way to empower customers to contact new prospects.
2. An incentive to do so. But be careful—customers already advocating your brand may be offended by a "bribe."
3. Commitment and care. You are tapping a powerful vein of loyalty. Treat it with sensitivity and respect.

Personal influence describes the effect of statements made by one person on another's attitude or probability of purchase. Consumers consult each other for opinions about new products and brands, and the advice of others can strongly influence buying behavior.

Philip Kotler and Gary Armstrong[1]

When customers become advocates for your product, your service, your candidate, or your cause, you have achieved a relationship of great closeness and trust. (See Exhibit 8.1.) This is the most valued and sought-after level of bonding, where word-of-mouth advertising flourishes. And, with a database, you can take steps to encourage it and keep track of it.

It always surprises us how few companies take advantage of the opportunity to ask customers for referrals. Indeed, in researching this book and many articles, we have asked quite a few companies about their policies in this area:

- Many organizations seem to recognize that their customers are their best advocates, but prefer to just let referrals come spontaneously rather than actively seek them.

- Some do approach customers for referrals on a regular basis, usually in a very straightforward manner. Holiday Inn, for example, has been generating about 1,000 new Priority Club members in a month this way. And our discussions with Ross Perot's United We Stand America organization lead us to believe that he has gathered several million members through referrals in a matter of months.[2]

- As we'll see shortly, one company we spoke with tried soliciting referrals only to get its hands slapped by loyal customers who preferred to see the moneys invested in the referral effort go to product development or customer service. We'll address how you can avoid such results in *your* program in our discussion of critical success factors.

Perhaps organizations hesitate to ask for referrals because they don't want to offend. It is true that your customers or supporters may well be advocating your products right now, without any effort on your part. But you may be missing an important marketing opportunity by being passive. If your customers are satisfied with their experience of your brand and your organization, they may be willing to share their satisfaction publicly. And that can give you a tremendous marketing boost.

Exhibit 8.1 Charles and Friend Demonstrating Advocacy Bonding.

When customers become advocates for your product, your service, your candidate, or your cause, you have achieved a relationship of great closeness and trust. This is the most valued and sought-after level of bonding, where word-of-mouth advertising flourishes.

Referrals tend to produce highly qualified prospects who are already disposed to hear your message favorably. As marketing guru Philip Kotler points out in the most recent edition of his classic marketing text, the most effective information sources for consumers tend to be personal. "Commercial sources normally *inform* the buyer," he writes. "But personal sources *legitimize* or *evaluate* products for the buyer."[3]

Because of the legitimizing quality of the referral process, the job of converting referred prospects into customers will be easier and more profitable than converting other prospects. With a strong referral program in place, you can reduce the amount of prospecting you have to do through direct-response and mass-media advertising. And your actual selling cycle with each prospect may be shorter and your conversion rate higher.

When your customers, or even your prospects, are willing to advocate your brand to their friends, relatives, and acquaintances, their loyalty is strong and durable. If you are already using database-driven marketing, you can create opportunities to find these customers and tap into their loyalty.

All Customers Can Be Advocates

MCI Communications Corporation's 1991 launch of the MCI Friends and Family discount calling program was a stroke of marketing genius. It is a discount scheme, and the discount is an incentive for customers—old and new—to become advocates.

Customers and prospects for MCI's long-distance telephone calling service are invited by mail, by telemarketing, and by mass-media advertising, to create their own MCI-based long-distance Calling Circle by naming friends or relatives whom they regularly call to become members. Each nominee who agrees to become, or is already, an MCI long-distance customer is eligible to create his or her own Calling Circle. This person, and anyone who agrees to join his or her Calling Circle, gets a 20 percent discount on all calls they place to each other via MCI. Sign-up is easy—each new Friends and Family customer simply fills in a form, naming Calling Circle candidates, and can add to the list at any time. MCI contacts each Friends and Family candidate so named and invites him or her to join.

The hook is the 20 percent discount. The twist is the fact that, in the course of deciding whether to join, the prospect is also deciding whether his or her *friend* or *relative* gets that discount. Imagine if MCI calls you and says that your brother nominated you for his calling circle. They tell you he will get 20 percent off on his calls to you if you switch to MCI, and what's more, *you'll* get 20 percent off, plus the chance to create your own Calling Circle. You'd think twice about saying "No," wouldn't you?

Friends and Family has been so successful that MCI has gained four share points worth almost $1.5 billion in revenue. (The company's share increased from 15 to 19 percent, mostly at the expense of market leader AT&T.[4]) This increase was achieved despite a mammoth disadvantage in marketing budgets (MCI put all of its 1990 and 1991 long-distance advertising budgets [$50 million and $100 million, respectively] behind the launch of the Friends and Family program. AT&T's total advertising budget was 20 times that amount.)

MCI was able to put the program into effect because it had a database advantage: with access to direct billing information about each customer, it could monitor call volumes. Even with 65 percent of the market, AT&T has not been able to implement a similar program because it has had to rely on the Baby Bells for billings. Sprint, with 10 percent of the market, launched a much more limited discount program in mid-1992, offering a 20 percent discount on calls to whatever single number the customer dialed most.

MCI Friends and Family marketing director Cari Sanborn also attributed the lack of direct copycat programs to the expense. "It is an expensive program," she said. "But if you are the underdog trying to work your way up, it is a natural for gaining marketshare. Because it lets you offer something to your existing base as well as to new customers. It helps us get new customers and also to keep our loyal customers."

Sanborn pointed out that the MCI Friends and Family program also provides an important basis for the company's image and is used for both awareness and promotional advertising. "Just about anything on the air except our new 1–800–COLLECT is specifically talking about Friends and Family in some way," she said. A noteworthy 1992 example was a TV spot filmed at a customer's wedding, with MCI chairman Bert Roberts in attendance. The voiceover read the groom's letter of gratitude for allowing him and his fiancé to stay in touch while she was away at college. In 1993, aggressive promotional campaigns were built around Friends and Family promotions, including tie-in offers from family-oriented partners and free-call deals. The company also broke a new ad campaign showing the Star Trek cast reuniting through their Friends and Family Calling Circle. MCI also uses the program to cross-sell new services such as Friends Around the World, Friends & Family 800 Services, and a new Friends and Family Calling Card. (See Exhibit 8.2.)

Friends and Family will remain the cornerstone of MCI's consumer marketing, said Sanborn. "Friends and Family customers are good quality customers," she explained. "They stay with us longer, spend more, and save more than if they were just straight MCI customers. The key benefit to us is that every time someone joins, we get a list of names we can call in their behalf. We have found that those campaigns work much better than just standard cold-calling techniques."

Exhibit 8.2 MCI Friends & Family.

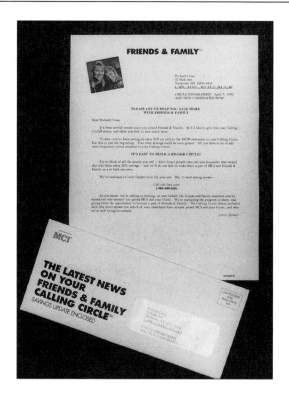

A Competitive Advantage

The advocacy bond is the strongest of all the customer bonds in our system. Constituents with whom you have developed this bond are almost universally dedicated to your brand or your organization. They have formed a positive impression and are willing to share it.

If you are practicing the customer bonding system and support buyer-get-a-buyer programs with incentives, your customer champions can give you a tremendous advantage in the marketplace. If you have an advocacy program in place, the chances are that you are also supporting customer relationships at other levels in the customer bonding model, too, so that awareness, identity, relationship, and perhaps even community bonds have been formed.

Of course, advocacy bonding can occur without your knowledge, too. Supporters or customers may try what you offer and like it enough to tell others about it. But this can be difficult to track.

Exhibit 8.2 *Cont.*

MCI keeps in touch with current Friends and Family customers, offering them new services and ongoing opportunities to name new recruits for their Friends and Family Calling Circle. The program earned the company four market-share points, worth almost $1.5 billion in revenue.

Attempts to formalize advocacy bonding sometimes backfire, too, as Intuit, a Menlo Park, CA company, discovered. One of the fastest-growing software companies in the United States, Intuit has built a devoted following for its personal and business financial software, Quicken, by relying heavily on customer referrals. Said founder and president Scott Cook, "We have hundreds of thousands of salespeople. They are our customers."[5]

The bulk of the million copies of Quicken that Intuit sells each year come from referrals by current customers, according to an Intuit executive we spoke with in 1993. She noted that the company calls its customers "apostles" and sees its mission as making customers "feel so good about the product that they'll go and tell five friends to buy it."

"The heart of Intuit's customer bonding comes from this attitude," she explained. "And the most important element of that is the product. Intuit researches every aspect of its products with customers."

But when Intuit tried a formal promotion to solicit customer referrals, the results were "disastrous," said this spokeperson. "It was the worst promotion we've ever done," she said. "We got back more upset letters on that promotion than anything else since I've been here. Customers said, 'You don't need to pay us or give us anything to recommend your product. You just need to keep building a great product. Why don't you put this money into delivering better customer support, better product, lower prices? If you do those things, we'll keep recommending your product.'"

The company also tried offering a discount to any friend a customer recommended. That also backfired. Explained Intuit, "The feedback was, 'Quicken is already a value. Why are you giving this new person an even better deal?' I believe our installed-base users want to be treated special, but not when it's not needed."

The Intuit lesson is an important one for the customer bonding practitioner. The process of a customer recommending your product to a prospect may be its own reward, and all you have to do to make it happen is to simply ask customers to make referrals. Test your advocacy program to determine how customers will respond and whether an incentive is appropriate. Customers may simply be flattered by the request and satisfied that they are doing the right thing by introducing a friend to an excellent product or service.

Critical Success Factors

There are three critical success factors for advocacy bonding: excellent follow-through, incentives, and empowerment.

Excellent Follow-through

Regardless of the method you use to elicit recommendations, you should demonstrate sensitivity to and respect for your customer's role.

For one thing, be careful not to abuse the privacy of your customers or the people they refer to you. Through the referral process, they are making their relationship with your brand publicly visible. They are, therefore, taking a risk that their trust in you is well-placed. They expect you to follow through responsibly and conscientiously and not to offend the prospect with a hard sell or with discourteous selling practices. They also expect that you will offer the people they refer the same level of product or service quality that they have experienced.

Incentives

Incentives can be very helpful in any formal advocacy program. A "hard incentive" provides customers or supporters with a tangible reward for referrals. MCI built its Friends and Family program around the 20 percent long-distance calling discount. And a local investment consultant we know recently expanded his prospect database by 20 percent just by offering a free 15-week subscription to *Forbes* in return for referrals from his newsletter readers.

"Soft incentives" can work, too. Direct-response printer Solar Additions of Greenwich, NY simply offered to send a Thanksgiving Day card to two friends that each customer named and that generated about $250,000 in incremental sales.[6]

But as Intuit's example demonstrated, very loyal customers will sometimes balk at incentives. Intuit's most vocal customers spoke loudly, telling the company to focus on delivering quality product and service. They rejected incentive-based advocacy initiatives. This points to the importance of testing your advocacy program in focus groups or in small trials before rolling it out in the marketplace.

Empowerment

Although we saved it for last, empowerment may well be the most critical success factor for marketers wanting to create advocacy bonding. Often, customers or supporters would willingly refer others but lack a convenient means and the stimulus to do so. This is easily solved when you practice information-driven marketing. With a simple response device, you can invite customers to make referrals. It is a basic form of dialogue and a time-honored element in many direct-marketing programs.

When you empower your customers or supporters to become advocates, you invite them to participate fully in the implicit partnership between you and them. You are tapping and deepening existing loyalty in a way that benefits both you and your customers. You are making your customers "insiders," partners in a special pact. They may delight in your products and services and in the opportunity to share them with others. And as long as you ask them to refer people they know are interested in what you can do, the people they bring to you will automatically be insiders, too.

Les Editions Play Bac, a fast-growing publisher of educational products for French youngsters, discovered the importance of this last point

Exhibit 8.3 Testing the Advocacy Concept.

When French publisher Les Editions Play Bac launched a novel specialty catalog of children's items in the fall of 1993, 10 percent of the 60,000 names in the initial test were referrals from an existing network of parents who had served on focus groups in the development of the catalog.

when it launched its new catalog of educational children's toys, *Bien Joué*, in late 1993. (See Exhibit 8.3.) Director Jean Luc Colonna D'Istria built a significant test population for the first 60,000 catalog drop. Ten percent of the test mailing went to names referred by a network of parents who had served on focus groups in the development of the catalog. D'Istria, who mailed the catalog to these referrals with a personalized letter explaining who had referred them, found that only 4 percent of these individuals responded, compared to 5 and 6 percent for rented names and 25 percent for the parents in the Play Bac test network.

"We will have to be more specific in future about the kinds of referrals we desire," he concluded. "Four percent response on our referred names is a good response, but I believe that criteria were too broad. To be a friend of a friend is not enough if you don't have kids yourself or are not a mail-order buyer already."

D'Istria remains committed to gathering referrals for his specialty catalog, and he is gathering one to three referral names apiece from every catalog buyer, thanks to a referral request on the catalog's order form. He is also an active practitioner of other aspects of the customer bonding system, generating awareness and identity through publicity efforts and building relationships and community through an active network of parents who help him select and test catalog products and review the design of the catalog.

Putting It All Together

Ross Perot's political organization, United We Stand America (UWSA) is doing a remarkable job of high-level customer bonding. Only in this case, the "customers" are citizens who support Perot's positions on reforming American politics. (See Exhibit 8.4.)

Mr. Perot's organization has a long history of political activism.[7] But it burst onto the 1992 electoral scene in the United States with the heady force of a hurricane. This is partly explained by the nation's economic and social troubles, which have weakened traditional party affiliations and angered many voters. But it is also a function of UWSA's skill in organizing. When Perot won nine million votes in the 1992 presidential election, he did so by applying modern marketing technology to create awareness, relationships, community, and advocacy.

We spoke with state and headquarters UWSA officials to find out how the organization has been building and organizing its membership since March 1993, when Perot announced his latest membership drive. (To be a member, you now have to pay a $15 fee.) While no one at UWSA would divulge actual membership size, we believe it was already several million by late summer 1993. On the day after Perot made his televised membership appeal, 65,000 people called his toll-free number to join.[8] Since then, he has bought additional infomercial time on several occasions, as well as print ads in both major media and local media. UWSA sponsors rallies at three or four locations every weekend (with membership applications on every chair) and conducts a steady, purposeful organizational campaign to build membership on a state-by-state basis.

In Washington state, for example, a strong Perot support base existed even before the March announcement. Like many of the state

Exhibit 8.4 Creating Political Advocates.

Ross Perot's organization continues to recruit members through all levels of the customer bonding model. Advertising and publicity, rallies, door-to-door canvassing, home infomercial-watch parties, and direct-response are all techniques that are put to good use.

operations of UWSA, this one began in the spring of 1992, with the petition drive that put Perot's name on the presidential primary ballot in Washington state. Of the 50,000 people who signed that original petition in early 1992, 40,000 had joined the "new" UWSA when we spoke with state director Connie Smith in late August, 1993.

"The group is marked by its activism," said Smith, "part of which extends to signing up other members. We all realize Mr. Perot is the catalyst that got us going. But UWSA is successful in Washington because we don't tell the members what to do. We have many levels of organization, but the core are our 'issue teams.' They work on a local level on things they care about. And if the headquarters needs a letter-writing campaign started, they're right there to help."

Smith recounted an example of a local team that formed a working group of concerned citizens to cut over $1 million from the county budget. They then produced a video about the effort and, at their own expense, sent it to UWSA chapters around the state. The video was publicized through the state organization's sophisticated telecommunications network, which is used both for recruitment and for member communications. The network has been financed completely by volunteer contributions. It includes broadcast fax (for top-down communications to about seventy core officers), interactive fax retrieval for members, voice-mail (for information and polling), electronic bulletin-boards, and a private newspaper. (See Exhibit 8.5.)

Exhibit 8.5 Techno-Politics in Action.

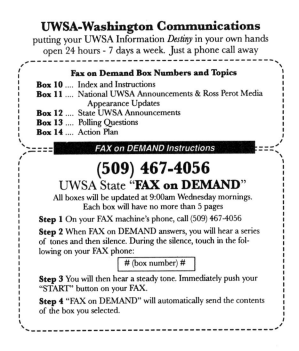

In Washington state, UWSA members have paid for a sophisticated telecommunications network out of their own pockets. It includes broadcast fax (for top-down communications to about 70 core officers), interactive fax retrieval for members, voice-mail (for information and polling), electronic bulletin-boards, and a private newspaper.

The Seattle chapter created a television talk show that was so popular it wound up getting a regular slot on the local public television station. The show has become a must-appear-on for politicians all the way up to Washington's governor.

On the other side of the country, Maryland's state director Joan Vinson has a tougher organizing challenge. Maryland is a strongly Democratic state, and membership remains small. When we spoke with Ms. Vinson in late August 1993, she was about to launch a membership drive. "You have to think outside the box," she said. "We're going to be using every means you can think of." Among the ideas she mentioned were fax and telephone trees, telemarketing, a program to encourage each current member to get five more members, and automotive giveaways that would prominently display the UWSA toll-free number. "We have a relatively small budget," she said, noting that state budgets are proportional to membership. "But we have been asking members to stuff literature into all of their outgoing personal mail and bills. We have booths at every gathering you can think of. We're on college campuses signing people up. We have a speaker's bureau. And we have small businesses displaying the brochure on countertops and delivering it with pizzas."

To aid in such recruitment efforts, the national organization has created a new catalog of giveaway promotional items. It spreads the word from one area to another when a particular membership-drive technique is successful and acts as a clearinghouse of information for the state organizations.

While it's impossible to gauge accurately the numbers of recruits UWSA has gained through one-on-one referrals, that form of grassroots advocacy is a critical component in the UWSA strategy. And when there is a call from headquarters for a letter-writing campaign or for support at a rally, supporters use the occasion to pull more people into the organization. Indeed, one way to gauge the strength of Perot's strategy is in the turnouts UWSA commands at political events and for political activism. After launching a UWSA direct-mail campaign on the Clinton administration budget that requested that recipients to sign a protest form, UWSA received 12.5 million signatures.

We have spent considerable time talking with politicians and political party representatives about the need to revamp their approach to politics. So far, established parties seem surprisingly uninterested in Perot's accomplishments. Or, if they are aware of the competitive threat his activities pose to them, they are simply standing by waiting to see if it will stand the test of time. With the loyal and active membership he is creating in UWSA, Perot could be a powerful force to contend with for years to come.

Recap and Where-To

At the advocacy-bonding level, customers or supporters take up your offer, your product, or your cause, and spread the word on your behalf. They are dedicated to your brand or organization and become, in effect, your best salespeople. Word-of-mouth, the most powerful form of advertising, flourishes. Advocacy bonding, then, is the ultimate relationship between Charles the Customer and Albert the Advertiser.

Of course, you may not always know when customers or supporters are making referrals. And, occasionally, loyal customers will resist your attempts to formalize the advocacy bond with a member-get-a-member or buyer-get-a-buyer program. But many organizations should try to take advantage of this powerful bond. It requires a means to empower customers to make referrals, an incentive for them to do so, and excellent follow-through so that their trust will not be betrayed.

Checklist

1. Are your customers referring you to their friends or family or colleagues already? What is motivating them? How can you motivate others to do the same?

2. Can you improve the effectiveness of the referral process by providing incentives? What is it about your product or service that would make customers eager to recommend it? Can you modify or change your product or service in a way that would make recommending it irresistible?

3. What specific incentives can be used to encourage your customers to recommend your product or service?

4. Do you have a special referral handling process? How can you ensure that referrals are handled properly throughout your organization to protect and enhance customer loyalty? Do your em-

ployees understand the importance of the referral process? Can they create a regular system for encouraging referrals?

5. How can you ensure that you qualify referrals sufficiently to prevent an unwieldy and unproductive sales conversion effort? What are the key qualifiers? What makes a referral a sure-fire buyer?

6. What resistance do you think you will run into if you ask for referrals, either within your own organization or among your customer base? How can you test out your expectations? And if it's true that resistance is there, how can you overcome it?

PART III

How to Achieve Successful Customer Bonding

Chapter 9

A Quick Review

Bird's-Eye View

Let's pause a moment now to review what we've covered. A good grasp of the system's basics will help you move forward and build your own customer bonding solutions. It will also help you sell your own fresh marketing ideas to the rest of your organization. Our goal is to enable you to tap the range and power of the system and develop your own ideas for applying it to your own unique situation.

One might say that all the important new directions in management thought are marketing-oriented.

Alexander Hiam, *Closing the Quality Gap*[1]

We first developed the customer bonding system because of our work with Fortune 500 organizations, nonprofits, and political groups struggling to bring information-age marketing techniques and technologies into image- and promotion-driven advertising and marketing programs. Over and over we saw the newer strategic approach of targeted, relationship-oriented marketing clash with traditional image advertising. We also saw too many database-driven marketing programs that treated customers or donors as faceless targets, barraging them with unwelcome mail and telephone solicitations. Very few marketers have grasped the real opportunities presented by information technologies and the importance of using them in ways that delight customers rather than alienating them.

Today, there is growing recognition among opinion leaders in business that, as markets mature and competition intensifies, only breakthrough efforts will find, win, and keep loyal customers. The same is true for nonprofit organizations vying for the support and loyalty of a finite number of interested citizens. Political candidates and groups, and even government agencies, would do well to study these ideas, too, as they vie for the resources to effect changes in the land.

Many organizations have already invested heavily in total quality management (TQM) concepts and customer service towards this end. And, thankfully, many are also trying to develop customer databases in a responsible manner so that they can master the kind of individualized, relationship-based marketing we've discussed throughout this book.

Unfortunately, entrenched interests are still apt to resist these trends—often in subtle ways—and are too often discovered to be jealously guarding hard-won budget lines and spheres of influence. We hope that the customer bonding framework will be seen by all as a means for bringing existing approaches together with new approaches in a way that serves the interests of your organization and your customers, donors, or supporters.

Reviewing the System

This chapter, Chapter 10, and our Epilogue will help you brainstorm your own customer bonding ideas and figure out how to implement them. First, let's briefly review the basics of the customer bonding system. The five degrees were summarized with the help of the now-familiar Albert and Charles in Exhibit 3.2 and in chart form in Exhibit 3.3. For a more thorough review, you may want to go back and re-read Chapters 2 and 3.

As you've seen throughout this book, the customer bonding system provides a framework for profitable marketing. It focuses all of your marketing activities on serving one overriding goal: to build long-term relationships by earning the greatest possible loyalty. It works because it meets the needs of both marketers, who face increasing competitive markets and fragmented media, and consumers, many of whom want to get past marketing hype to find quality products and services and fair treatment at reasonable prices.

The system defines five levels of loyalty bonds between marketers and customers:

Awareness

Marketers gain share of mind among prospects and customers, generally through one-way monologue (image advertising, public relations, direct-response promotions, or event sponsorship). At this level of bonding, you establish recognition and image for your product or service, your candidate, or your cause, but your relationship with prospects and customers is fragile and easily disrupted by competitive activities or other external interference. Critical success factors at this level are the repetition, reach, and creativity of your communications to your chosen markets.

Identity

Prospects and customers identify with values or feelings that they see embodied by your product or service. One external manifestation of this may be their willingness to display your logo or name—on hats, sweaters, lapel pins, campaign buttons, and so forth. No direct interaction is required to create such a bond. You can encourage identity bonding by emphasizing the organizational and product-inherent values in your marketing messages and programs, by using celebrities or spokespeople who embody those values, and/or by supporting a cause that your customers care deeply about. But, as in awareness bonding, the bond is vulnerable to disruptions. Critical success factors are the nature of your communications (you should appeal to values and emotions) and the customers' satisfactory experience of your company and brand.

Relationship

Now the database must come into the picture, enabling you to move from mass marketing to interactive dialogue with individual constituents via direct media. This bond involves a direct exchange of benefits between you and your prospects and customers. It is considerably stronger than earlier levels because your customers now have an investment in their relationship with you that's costly to break. Customers may even come to regard competitive communications with disdain. Critical success factors are: recognition of each consumer as an individual, rewards for interaction (which give the customer a vested interest in maintaining communications with you), and long-term continuity in your reward system.

Community

Here you empower prospects and/or customers to form relationships with each other around their common interest in your product or service. This bond is extremely durable. To break it, competitors must actually disrupt social ties among friends, colleagues, or family. Mass media generally plays little or no role, although savvy marketers will recognize news opportunities arising from customer gatherings. The key is the creation of events or some gathering of groups of customers around life-style interests related to your brand.

Advocacy

The highest form of bonding, advocacy occurs when customers refer others to your product or service. This can and does happen independent of any marketing activity. But it can also be encouraged with incentives and by empowering customers, donors, or supporters to involve others with your product, cause, or candidate. Loyalty is at its highest level here and so is the risk if you don't work *with* your customer champions, or are cavalier about the loyalty inherent in this level.

Using Information-Driven Marketing

As we discussed in Chapter 2, your ability to use the complete customer bonding system will depend upon your command of a marketing database. This is the database of information about prospects and customers—created and constantly replenished from sources such as incoming calls to your sales- and customer-service departments, from product-registration cards, from replies to survey or promotional offers, and the like. All of this information becomes a critical strategic asset, the Information Core that informs and drives virtually all of your marketing strategies and activities. (See Exhibit 2.3.)

Your customer information is constantly in motion. We call this "Datamotion." When you use your existing data to determine marketing plans, data moves outward from the information core to impact the marketplace. Every time you make contact with an individual in your universe and record his or her response, you supply fresh data to the information core, which enables you to refine future marketing efforts.

Building your strategies and activities upon this core enables you to develop a powerful, dynamic approach to all of your markets, as depicted in Exhibit 2.4, the Information-Driven Marketing Model. The strategies you develop for building customer loyalty—awareness, identity, relationship, community, or advocacy bonding—determine the specific program tactics to be used. And ideally, every tactic will be guided by your analysis of the customer data in your database, the Information Core. Wherever possible, your tactical marketing programs—publicity, relationship programs, direct marketing, general advertising, sales promotion, point-of-purchase—should also be designed to capture new data with which to refresh your knowledge of the marketplace.

As the bottom level of Exhibit 2.4 shows, the data in the information core supports a range of applications. See pages 31–32 for a review of these applications.

Getting Started

In the next chapter, we present some fictitious case studies to show you how different companies might leverage their unique situations to apply customer bonding and to encourage your creative thinking about your own situation. Below is a summary checklist to help you make a quick sketch of your customer bonding opportunities. We urge you, however, to use the detailed checklists at the end of each chapter in this book to prepare a thorough assessment and plan. The Epilogue will show you how.

Customer Bonding Strategy Checklist

1. Have your customer bonding goals been clearly stated? Are they consistent with core corporate strategies? With customer service strategies?

2. Does the program have wide corporate support and involvement? Do all the elements of the program enhance your organization's image?

3. Does the program have broad customer appeal while maintaining special features for targeted sub-groups?

4. Is the program difficult for competitors to copy?

5. Have you made allowances for the program to constantly evolve and improve?

6. Are you treating your customer bonding program as a new product with its own business plan? Its own profit requirements? Its own objective measures of success?

Awareness Questions

1. Can you strengthen awareness bonds by using techniques and media channels new to your organization?

2. Is your message repeated often enough to adequately increase share-of-mind?

3. Do the awareness components of your program do double duty by supporting relationship-building components?

4. Does your awareness-building program include direct-response media that will help build your database?

5. If promotions are part of the program, do they help add names and specific information about prospects and customers to the database?

6. Do point-of-sale displays support awareness of the program while encouraging customer interaction?

Identity Questions

1. What values do you believe your prospects and customers hold dear? What attributes of your product or organization appeal to these values?

2. Are your customers especially proud to use your product or service? What is it about your product that appeals to their pride? Does your product positioning reflect these values and emotions? Is it reflected in your advertising and promotion? In your customer-bonding program?

3. Would your customers be proud to display your logo? Have you made it possible for them to do so?

4. Are there specific causes that your customers support with which you could associate your product or organization?

5. Can you create your own cause-oriented program that would appeal to your customers' values?

Relationship Questions

1. Are rewards easy to earn and is the program easy to understand?

2. Does the reward structure have defined reward levels (targets)?

3. Are rewards based on purchases alone or are there special rewards for customers who have displayed their loyalty over a long period of time?

4. Are rewards greater for using your more profitable products?

5. Does the reward program involve just the individual, or the whole family?

6. Are rewards immediate (i.e., discounts for members at the cash register), or are they delayed by requiring an accumulation of points, miles, or other private currency? Are there expiration dates for rewards or can they be carried indefinitely on the customer's account?

7. Does the reward structure include recognition (i.e., status) rewards such as special on-site treatment, entertainment, or access to special or priviledged information?

8. Is there a variety of rewards that appeal to a broad range of customers?

9. Is there a way to use your "private money" rewards at marketing partner locations?

10. What portion of rewards do you think will never be used (i.e., what are your "breakage" expectations)?

11. Does your reward structure encourage continuity (i.e., does it work in a way that makes each successive purchase more valuable than the last)? Are rewards progressively more valuable (i.e., the more the customer purchases, the more valuable the reward)?

12. Have you included opportunities for dialogue throughout your program? Do all your communications, whether through the mail or face-to-face, provide useful information for your database that will guide future program development? Do your plans include private media to communicate with your members/customers?

13. Do your reward and recognition systems deliver on the promise of the program? Can you delight your customers by exceeding the promise of the program?

14. Is it possible to leverage the effect of your program by involving marketing partners who are interested in reaching the same customers you serve? Are there potential partners who are serving a market you would like to reach? Can partners help share the cost of the program by purchasing rewards from you to give to their loyal customers? Can partners help make your customers more loyal by promoting purchases and increasing awareness of your product? Can partners help you introduce variety into your program by providing rewards?

15. Are you planning to use new communication technologies such as fax-on-demand, selective binding, interactive voice response, interactive television, and on-line networks to reduce costs and to increase the level of personalization in your program?

Community Questions

1. Does your product fit into the lifestyle or workstyle of your customers? Does your program get your organization involved with customers' life-styles and/or work-styles?

2. What attributes of your organization or product can your customers share with others? Have you used these attributes to bring customers together for socializing, sharing, and learning?

3. Are you using events, on-line services, interactive voice response systems and other communication technologies to help one customer to communicate with another?

4. Is it necessary to create your own events to bring customers together, or can you "piggyback" on events sponsored by others (i.e., can you create an event within an event)? Can you do both? Can these events be used to support other levels of bonding by creating a newsworthy event that will help increase awareness and make others want to attend next time? Are your customers encouraged to invite their friends and colleagues to attend to help with advocacy bonding?

Advocacy Questions

1. Have you provided an incentive for your customers to recruit other customers for you? Is the incentive financial or does it involve a simple thank-you or other encouragement that facilitates recruitment?

2. Have you provided an opportunity for your customers to allow friends and colleagues to sample your product or service?

3. Have you provided a fool-proof system to follow up on referrals?

4. Have you empowered your customers to give something of value from you to prospective customers?

Chapter 10

Three Sample Strategies

Bird's-Eye View

Frameworks, guidelines, and checklists are all well and good. But without a creative orientation and an expansive approach to your unique situation, even the best models won't enhance your organization's growth potential. This chapter will help you turn on the creative juices. It illustrates the customer bonding system in action in three hypothetical businesses. Our goal is to give you insight into the range and power of this system and ideas on how to apply it to your own unique situation.

Everything should be made as simple as possible, but not simpler.
                                                            Albert Einstein

The power of the customer bonding system described in this book is its flexibility. Depending upon the unique characteristics of your business and your industry, you can focus your attention on one or two bonding levels or create a comprehensive strategy for all of them. You can emphasize a particular technique or experiment with many.

But the one thing we hope you will now do is evaluate every marketing decision in the context of customer loyalty. Ask yourself, How can I use loyalty marketing to turn my prospects into customers and my customers into repeat customers who will stay with my brand for the long-term?

The optimal use of the customer bonding system is to create a coordinated marketing strategy that uses a core of customer information to maximize customer loyalty. In this chapter, we will explore the use of customer bonding in three different situations, in order to give you a sense of how to use it in your own unique situation. In our first example, we examine customer-bonding strategies for magazine publishers, who face the challenge of marketing to readers as well as advertisers. For our second example, we create a relationship-marketing program "Downhill Dudes" for a ficitious ski resort. Our third example puts bonding to work for an anonymous business-to-business service company. As you read through these scenarios, try to draw forth the underlying ideas that might apply to your own industry and your organization's unique place within it.

Double-Edged Bonding for a Magazine Publisher

The fact that magazine publishers already own a database of readers gives them a powerful advantage over other marketers. But they also face a big challenge in that they have two diverse groups of customers: readers who must be persuaded to subscribe, and advertisers who must be persuaded to buy ad space. Most publishers structure separate marketing functions for these audiences and try to reach on optimal balance between circulation levels and advertising rates. The customer bonding system can be used to create a synergistic marketing strategy that builds loyalty with both audiences.

Awareness

Image advertising is seldom part of a subscription-acquisition marketing strategy. However, savvy publishers do know how to economically establish image and name recognition for their publications in order to attract advertisers, to maintain top-of-mind awareness among potential subscribers, and even to help launch products carrying the magazine's "brand name."

One approach is to package editorial material into syndicated newspaper columns, radio shows, and television news features. The latter are either conventional short-form features or full length (half- to one-hour) entertainment and talk shows. Some publishers have been producing such shows for years. *Consumer Reports* magazine, for example, has a nationally syndicated radio show, newspaper column, and television show. *Money* magazine provides special radio reports, as does *Mother Earth News*. *Playboy* has its own cable network to carry its material. *National Geographic* magazine has its own syndicated television program. Time, Inc. publications *Entertainment Weekly*, *People*, *Time*, and *Life* all participate in a daily half-hour show called "Entertainment News Television." Hachette Publications' *Elle* magazine is planning its own TV show.

The key to success with such programming efforts is that they are not infomercials, but true, high-quality editorial ventures. They attract viewers, and as the programs are heard or seen week-in and week-out, the exposure enhances name recognition and awareness of the sponsoring publications, helping to establish them as household names. These efforts can even become profit centers: radio, television stations, and newspapers will often pay for strong programs, issuing scrip applicable to advertising space or time slots.

Innovative publishers are developing other twists to get free media exposure:

- Book publisher Houghton Mifflin got its *American Heritage Dictionary* named the official research source for the popular television show, "Jeopardy." Packages of other Houghton Mifflin reference books are awarded on the show as prizes to contestants, building even more awareness.

- To encourage free publicity, *The New Yorker* company hand-delivers copies of its weekly magazine every Sunday evening to reporters, editors, media executives, business leaders, and government officials.

- More magazines are using general advertising. *Newsweek* magazine credits its awareness-building print and outdoor ads for its successful eclipse of competitor *Time*'s ad-page production in 1993.

Identity

Achieving identity bonding is fairly easy for magazine publishers, since most magazines are highly targeted to fit the life-style preferences of specific readers and to appeal to their values and interests. A little ingenuity can create dozens of opportunities for building on this strength to increase brand loyalty *and* create revenues from branded product sales.

Several publishers are experimenting with this. Yankee Publishing offers memorabilia sporting *The Farmer's Almanac* logo. The American Girls Collection of books uses dolls (starting at over $80 apiece) to bring to life the heroines featured in its books. Celebrity endorsements can also foster identity among subscribers, enhancing the emotional and life-style links that characterize identity bonding. A strong endorsement that is well-matched to the publication can create identity bonds with advertisers, too.

Relationship

Magazine publishers have what other marketers crave: a regular, ongoing one-to-one relationship with customers. Many nonpublishers go to great lengths to create this, launching their own private periodicals in order to reliably deliver their message to their target audience.

But relationship bonding—and information-driven marketing—require a *dialogue* between the marketer and the customer. Dialogue can help publishers improve the product and become smarter marketers. Readership surveys fulfill this function admirably, while also increasing readership and renewal rates. *Consumer Reports*, for example, does double-duty with its annual questionnaire. Not only does the questionnaire provide invaluable data for some of the periodical's most popular editorial features, but survey respondents are excellent donor prospects and are among the magazine's most loyal subscribers.

As we saw in Chapter 6, the relationship bond also grows when marketers *recognize* their customers as individuals. Selective-binding technology, which enables publishers to print multiple versions of a publication simultaneously, can help them do this. Combined with a database, selective bonding can be used to customize editorial product and advertising pages, subscriber-by-subscriber. (The convergence of selective binding and subscription-driven database-marketing technologies—along with growing interest in relationship marketing among publishers— has also created new management imperatives. It behooves publishers to coordinate the strategies and activities of their editorial, advertising, circulation, and production functions. The resulting synergy can lead to ever more profitable information-based marketing activities.)

Another key to building relationship bonds is offering *rewards* to loyal customers. But the choice of reward is very important. Straight discounts simply cut into renewal revenues and diminish profit margins. And free magazine subscriptions would just go to readers who already have a subscription. Most publishers therefore turn to merchandise premiums: books, audiotapes, videotapes, or other products related to the interests of their readers.

But more imaginative rewards are possible. For example, cooperative programs with advertisers can create strong bonds that support both circulation and advertising goals. Subscribers can be given identification cards to present for special deals when buying from advertisers. This enables advertisers to readily measure response to their advertising campaigns, and it gives publishers new information about subscribers—information they can use to help advertisers form their own relationship-marketing programs.

Community

Publishers have a natural line into customer life-style interests. They also have the database with which to invite readers to participate in life-style-related events. But very few take advantage of such opportunities.

Among consumer magazines, *Utne Reader* is the most notable exception. This compendium of the alternative press has created an unusual community of readers and nonreaders through its Neighborhood Salon Association. As we saw in Chapter 7, as many as 20,000 readers have responded to this program since its launch in 1991, and at least 12,000 readers are presently meeting in more than 300 discussion salons in homes, coffee houses, community halls, and vacation spots. *Utne "salonistas"* are even chatting it up through electronic mail over on-line services!

Business-to-business periodicals such as *Inc., Folio, Target Marketing,* and *Adweek* promote community bonds through revenue-generating seminar or convention franchises. Gathering groups of subscribers and nonsubscribers together for education and debate on industry topics builds both community and awareness and creates much appreciated awareness-building opportunities for advertisers.

Advocacy

With all the one-on-one marketing advantages that a circulation database offers, creating advocacy bonds should be a breeze. Any publication worth its salt has a well-developed gift program, but many could go further. For example, the subscription gift could include a sampling of ancillary products produced by the publisher or its advertisers or other marketing partners. The keys to success are offering a strong *incentive* for referrals and *empowering* subscribers by letting them share this benefit with friends, family, and colleagues.

A Ski Resort Grooms Its Marketing

Any business involved with entertainment and recreation has many interesting opportunities to employ virtually all of the bond-building techniques discussed in this book. This discussion will center on a fictitious ski resort to illustrate just how the system might be applied.

Skiers can be tough to please, in part because they come in so many varieties. As in other sports, skiing attracts lots of "experientials"—those venturesome folks who choose their residences, occupations, and recreation based on their love of variety and challenge.[1] Often young males, these skiers have been the mainstay of the sport, but their numbers are gradually declining as a percentage of the total skiing population. And because the individuals in this group love variety, they come and go as easily as good powder snow. Getting them to stick to a particular resort is the marketer's greatest challenge.

At the other end of the spectrum are less adventurous skiers, many of whom prefer to return again and again to experiences and places that are proven, comfortable, and familiar. Loyalty-building programs can go far to attract and retain these customers, while offering enticements to the other, more restless skiers to return more frequently to a resort. Moreover, information-driven loyalty programs can help ski resorts pump up off-season sales volume, create new revenue streams through cross-selling, and forge powerful marketing alliances with area merchants.

Awareness

Ski resorts typically rely heavily on image advertising to create awareness bonds and attract new customers. But most campaigns are one-way monologues that just emphasize the experience, challenge, or fun of the sport through short-term promotions.

Loyalty building could begin right here, in the resort's mass-marketing efforts, if a customer database guides media and creative strategies and if the advertising is used to support loyalty programs. At the same time, the resort needs a fail-safe system for receiving and recording inquiries, for converting inquires into orders, and for collecting demographic and transaction data on every customer. For example, a well-maintained database can correlate purchasing behavior with geographic proximity of the skier's residence, identifying skiers who tend to buy package tours, who tend to be day-trippers, or who stay for a couple of nights on weekends. It can also reveal areas that abound with students, singles, or families. All of this information can be used to determine what type of advertising messages to run in each region and via which media. It could also be used in concert with selective binding to target print ads to focus on narrow niches in ski-buff magazines.

Identity

Skiers, like many sports enthusiasts, often strongly identify with the clothing and equipment they use, and are proud to display the manufacturer's logo. The skier's choice of a brand can be just a fashion statement, but it often reflects directly on the skier's view of his or her status in the sport and concern for safety, quality, and functionality. A savvy ski resort marketer can turn the resort logo into a loyalty badge, encouraging skiers to display "their" ski area with pins, window and bumper stickers, clothing, and accessories. This will be particularly effective if it's part of a larger relationship-bonding program.

What's more, the resort that understands the power of the identity bond will position itself to appeal to the values of its audience by how it acts, not just what it says. Skiers who value healthy life-styles, for example, will be drawn to areas that feature healthy foods rather than the fried fast-food services found at many resorts. Those companies that grasp this principle also understand another: Today, *marketing* is the message! It's not just what you say that counts, but what you do.

Relationship

Frequency-marketing programs that recognize and reward repeat business are naturals for ski areas. Such programs reward skiers for the volume of business transacted at resort-owned properties, capturing each transaction in the customer's database record. They provide a powerful magnet to pull customers back again and again, even customers who otherwise like to roam to different resorts. And every contact with every skier provides data that resort management can use to better target future services and communications.

Let's create such a program for a fictitious ski resort. We'll call the program the "Downhill Dudes Club." Members can accrue points for purchases of lift tickets, lodging, lessons, equipment rental, and clothing. And we can fine-tune the reward structure, like a pair of skis, to fit the needs of our various audiences. For package vacation buyers, who might respond to rewards that offset the high cost of travel packages, we might offer twenty-five or fifty "Downhill Dollars" for every $500 spent at the resort. These Dudes can spend their private money however they wish at the resort. Day-trippers might prefer to accumulate rewards based on days skied rather than dollars spent. Weekenders might prefer to add a day or two to the usual visit. Careful testing will reveal the optimal reward structures.

With a good foundation of database-driven awareness, the program can also include marketing partners, thereby expanding the loyalty-marketing power of the resort. Just imagine your reach and retention capabilities if restaurants and hotels in a 25-mile radius of your resort accept, and offer, Downhill Dollars tied exclusively to the Downhill Dudes Club. What a way to attract and lock in competitors' skiers! And what a way to use relationship bonding to attract new business and hold onto existing customers! Perhaps most importantly, the sponsoring ski resort can sell Downhill Dollars to marketing partners, just as airlines sell miles to car-rental agencies. Revenues from such sales can turn the relationship-bonding program into a profit center for the ski resort.

Community

Our ski resort is a natural for community bonding, which typically requires face-to-face gatherings of customers based on a shared life-style interest. Special facilities can be designated for patrons to congregate and meet each other. And special events of all sorts—competitions, festivals, clinics, and trade fairs—can draw people to the resort, even during the off-season or periods of poor snow conditions.

Marketing partners—local merchants, ski apparel and equipment manufacturers, and ski-magazine publishers—will readily see the value of participating as sponsors of these events. And offering members of the Downhill Dudes Club their own exclusive gatherings—or exclusive treatment during public events—adds recognition and reward benefits to club membership.

Advocacy

Advocacy bonds are formed when customers are given incentives or are empowered to recruit business for you. So a key goal would be to get every Downhill Dude (or Dudette) to recruit one or more friends, relatives, or colleagues to membership in the club. Since the vast majority of skiers partake of the sport in couples, families, or other groups, encouraging referrals should be easy. Making Downhill Dollars transferable would empower members to share the benefits of club membership with others. Or you could limit the transferability of the scrip for use during certain seasons and days of the week. You could even create a market for Downhill Dollars, such as the one that existed for airline travel awards (but watch out for competitors buying up your rewards and using them in counter-promotions). What a way to get attention for your ski area and your relationship program!

Broaden Your Business-to-Business Marketing

Business-to-business marketers operate in a world apart from consumer marketers. Business customers are often experts about what they are buying. The value of each sale may reach into six figures or more. And the universe of potential buyers may be very small and highly specialized.

Face-to-face selling is often a prerequisite for establishing a relationship with a business buyer, but up-to-date information about the last customer contact is crucial for maintaining a professional relationship. Moreover, the seller may have to know the buyer's business quite well to make the sale—as is the case when the medical equipment salesperson helps a surgeon use the new medical equipment right in the operating room. Or it may be that in order to sell the product, the business-to-business supplier has to provide ancillary and value-added services. Some office furniture companies, for example, provide space planning with the purchase of desks and file cabinets in order to differentiate themselves from their competitors.

Despite these differences, the business-to-business marketer faces many of the same motivational factors that contribute to strong customer bonds in consumer-goods marketing. Business-to-business customers most decidedly make value judgments about products, services, and vendors based on what they hear through their network or in the press (identity), and are relieved when they can establish relationships with vendors they know they can trust. Most are very active information-seekers and attend professional gatherings of many sorts to learn about techniques, services, and products that can help them be successful. Also, referrals are more key in business-to-business settings, perhaps, than in any other.

Database-driven marketing in the business-to-business arena is on the rise. More than 90 percent of business-to-business marketers use their databases for customer retention and new customer acquisition.[2] Most use it for making specific promotional offers, but management and tracking experiences vary widely. Most of the business-to-business marketers we talked with in preparing this book were not yet very sophisticated about marketing usage of the customer database.

Let's look at how a specific business-to-business marketer takes advantage of the business buyer's strong motivation to develop seller-buyer relationships. In this example, we put the customer-bonding system into action for a well-established, but anonymous, computer-service company.

Awareness

The function of awareness advertising for the business-to-business marketer is the same as it is for any other marketer. It is where you gain the customer's attention or, as advertisers refer to it, capture share of mind. Awareness bonding is the first stop on the way to higher levels of customer bonding.

Awareness bonding activity by business-to-business marketers is often limited to advertisements in appropriate trade publications, booths at trade shows, lead-generating direct-response programs, and perhaps some publicity. For the most part, these are product-driven rather than customer-focused efforts.

In the case of our computer service bureau, the product consists of a bundle of customized computer services that differ from customer to customer. One approach to creating awareness is to promote the idea that the company sells "solutions" as a way of suggesting that each customer's problems are approached and solved individually.

But just selling solutions may be tough. To succeed, the product must be made concrete and understandable, even to a novice buyer. Awareness-bonding efforts must be accompanied by direct-response devices so that our company can follow up with a relationship-building program that establishes a dialogue with the prospect.

Identity

To be effective at establishing an identity bond, the service bureau must project the image that appeals to the mind-set, values, and emotions of business decision makers. These are often highly successful, progressive people. They want to be seen as on the cutting edge; as leaders, innovators. And they want their organizations to be regarded as growing and profitable. They probably are striving to be, if they aren't already, the biggest and most acclaimed in their industries. These are all concepts that achievement-oriented managers identify with and want for their own companies and their own careers.

To establish identity bonds with these buyers, it is important to stress that our service bureau has this standing, too, and is geared to helping its customers achieve best-of-class status. But words alone may not be enough. Deeds count, too. One way to demonstrate the company's actual accomplishments is to provide an impressive client list. Business buyers derive a security from the knowledge that other companies they admire are also clients and users of the firm's services. An impressive client list serves the same function in this context as a celebrity endorsement in the consumer-products arena. Computer services may be just too mundane, too much of a commodity, for the customer to identify with strongly, but name a few companies that the prospect would like to associate with, and you've got the beginning of a strong identity bond.

The potential for identity bonding doesn't end there, however.

Our savvy service bureau understands that customers and prospects love to participate in industry award programs. So every year it sponsors leadership awards in partnership with an industry trade association or trade publisher. Such partnership brings prestige to our service bureau, not to mention publicity and identification with industry leaders. It's also a good way for our service bureau to stay informed on what industry leaders are doing and to give them reason to be in touch with the best in their target audience. (Note: Even a small company without a prestigious client list can catch attention and create identity with an idea like this. Extra resources might come from linking up with marketing partners.)

Relationship

Providing rewards and recognition for loyal patronage is tricky business for the computer service bureau. Rewards that might be acceptable in the consumer marketing environment could be considered by corporate purchasers as having exerted improper influence over the corporate buying decision. (Think of companies that claim ownership of frequent flier awards given to employees while carrying out company business!) Under these conditions, how does our service bureau establish a legitimate relationship bond with prospects and customers that endures?

The answer for many lies in creating relationship bonds based on information exchange. It's not surprising that business-to-business suppliers from IBM down to the local office supply store have magazines and newsletters offering helpful information on how to run your business better or advance up the corporate ladder. Federal Express has two such private media: one aimed at the office clerk who may well decide which overnight carrier to use, and the other to top business executives.

For our computer-service bureau, we would suggest an all-purpose information tool that services a wide variety of interests very economically, while positioning the company as a user of new, efficient communications technology. It is a combination fax-newsletter and fax-on-demand information service.

Here's how it would work. The monthly faxletter, as we'll call it here, contains important industry news as well as news about our service bureau's product offerings. Feature stories are summations of longer stories. The full-length stories are available simply by calling a special 800 number that leads the caller into an information library. The library contains original how-to articles, case studies, and important features selected from trade publications (with the permission of those publications, of course).

Each time a customer or prospect calls the fax number for free information, the information is sent, along with a feedback device (a questionnaire or poll). Any information that is gleaned from monitoring when customers call and for what materials, and from their replies to survey questions, gives the company valuable information for the customer database (the marketing information core). That information can help the marketing staff determine the effectiveness of the communications going out. It also can help the sales staff determine which prospects or customers might need personal follow-up.

Meanwhile the same technology that serves up the monthly faxletter also carries special announcements. Using the customer database, these can be customized to target only relevant information for each category of customer (by position, by industry, and so forth). For example, the marketing director might get one version of the faxletter while the chief financial officer may get another. The packaged-goods manufacturers will certainly get a different version of the faxletter than that sent to a retailer. And the political fund-raiser gets something different altogether. All of these varied organizations—and more— could be service-bureau customers, but each has different concerns and different computer-service requirements.

Information is an excellent way to build bonds, but it may not go far enough. So, while our service bureau is taking care of prospect and client information needs, it could also serve up tangible rewards for repeat business. For example, it could offer Database Dollars as rebates based on each customer's volume of purchases in a year. Customers could elect to receive a small percentage of yearly expenditures directly back at the end of the year, or could have the service bureau donate a larger amount to a charity of their choosing.

Community

Community-building activities flourish in the business-to-business world. We recently spoke at a customer-service conference at which the organizer had thoughtfully devised a system for helping attendees find communities of interest when seeking a table for the luncheon banquet. The system made it easier for everyone to find people of like industry background and interest to network with during lunch.

People from manufacturing sat with colleagues from other manufacturing businesses. Retailers sat with retailers. If you chose to be a renegade service-industry person and sit with the communications people, you could do that, too. In this way, the conference organizer practiced community bonding. It not only organized the conference; it facilitated the participation of everyone who came.

Many companies we know of have annual client conferences. Some sponsor highly regarded client training sessions. Others have rotating client advisory boards and regional roundtables. Such forums give key clients an opportunity to meet and bond with each other. One of our favorites in this category is the leading consumer credit company in France, Paris-based Cetelem. Cetelem sponsors a popular marketing tour every two years for their clients only. These tours have taken participants to the United States, to Canada, or to locations in the Far East. Hundreds of participants willingly pay the equivalent of thousands of dollars to join the highly regarded tour each October because it brings them face-to-face with executives and opinion leaders at leading corporations and institutions in these locations. Attempts by competitors to imitate this success by organizing getaways at resort locations have failed, we are told. Business leaders these days are more interested in information than junkets.

Our service bureau, of course, sponsors its own annual client conferences in each of the major industries it supports—fund raising, retail, automotive, financial services, and so forth. It considers these gatherings crucial investments in face-to-face relationship building and dialogue with customers. But our heroic firm plans to one-up these expensive and time-consuming sessions with quarterly telephone chat-lines featuring leading lights from the database-marketing industry. And as the technology develops and installations are in place, they plan to contract with Kinko's, the national chain of office service stores, to use their closed-circuit television studios for interactive, national roundtables featuring panels of experts called together just to answer client questions. These sessions, in conjunction with the fax-on-demand newsletter, reinforce our service bureau's high-tech image.

Advocacy

To foster advocacy, our service bureau swings its doors open to people selected and referred by its clients, granting them free attendance at some of its informational client conferences. It is also evaluating the use of on-line electronic roundtable audio seminars to achieve this purpose cost effectively. Such efforts empower prospects to share in some of the information benefits normally reserved for clients.

Another advocacy effort is implemented through a periodic promotional offer. Each promotion offers a specific incentive to clients willing to make qualified referrals. In one case, the service bureau donated money to a charity of the client's choice for every referral. In another, the referring company was given an opportunity to use the service bureau's services to run a joint mailing with the referred prospect.

Formal advocacy efforts are still fairly new for our service bureau, but they are generating much excitement. We expect to see many new ideas tested in the months ahead.

Recap and Where-To

We could go on making up customer bonding scenarios for you. It's a fun and rewarding mental exercise. But now it's time to make up some of your own. The examples in this chapter are by no means all-inclusive. In every case, other approaches could be tried. That's the beauty of customer bonding. It offers a strategic framework, a set of objectives within which every marketing tool can be applied to maximum advantage.

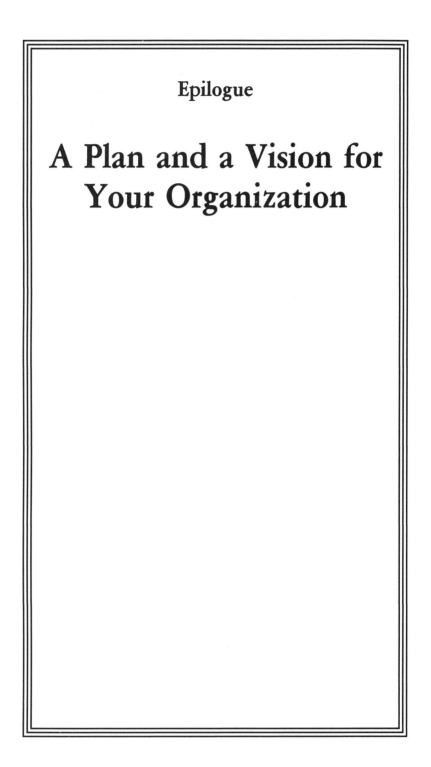

Epilogue

A Plan and a Vision for Your Organization

From the moment we started writing this book, our vision has been to excite you about our new, customer-focused, strategic approach to your marketing program. Our goal is to help you achieve a lasting competitive advantage by showing you how to make every marketing move build customer loyalty.

The picture is now complete except for one key thing: direction on what to do next. That is how we will end this book.

As we've stated before, we have found many examples around the world of companies running innovative customer bonding programs at one or two levels of the system. They are committed to building customer loyalty, and they recognize that building such loyalty is an ongoing, long-term process that requires continual enhancements.

But we have found no company to date that has developed a complete program, with customer bonding activities at every level of the system: awareness, identity, relationship, community, and advocacy. We hope you will become the leaders and innovators who will do so.

To help you get your creative juices flowing we developed three examples of systematic approaches to customer bonding in Chapter 10. They should give you an idea of what a complete program could look like. But your situation is unique. No other company has the same combination of customers, products and services, resources (including both internal and marketplace infrastructure resources), and competition that you do. So now it is up to you to find your own ways to apply our system to create lasting bonds with your customers and constituents.

What exactly should you do now? Assess where you are, plan where you'd like to be, benchmark your ideas, overcome any obstacles, and then make it happen!

Phase I. Assess and Plan

First, you'll need to assess your customer bonding needs and resources. The end result of this assessment will be a written plan. Writing out a plan will help you appreciate the power of the customer bonding system. It will also help you convey the power of the system throughout your organization and to your outside agencies and consultants.

Your assessment and planning should, at a minimum, cover the following key areas:

Identify Current Realities

You first want to establish a starting point from which to lay your plans. The keys here will be honesty, open-mindedness, and the support of your management as you do this assessment.

Acknowledge even unpalatable truths about the way you and your staff and agencies have approached marketing and customer relationships in the past. If something didn't work well before, and the organization has forever after dismissed it from the current consideration set, revisit it. Ask yourself why it didn't work and whether it could be improved upon and tried again. Virtually every program we discussed in the book—from Saucony Athletic Shoes' Walking Club to Holiday Inn's Priority Club to Waldenbooks Preferred Reader Program—has moved through difficult periods of retrenchment and redefinition. Don't be too quick to proclaim something dead forever because it failed once.

Ideally, the inventory will be conducted with the involvement and support of every department that contacts customers: general advertising, direct marketing, publicity, sales, order administration, and customer service. All can provide valuable input on current realities and make contributions to your plan. Moreover, all should be involved in the planning and eventual implementation of customer bonding programs to ensure enthusiastic support across the organization.

If you're working in a medium-sized or large organization, you will need to create a team with an adequate budget to conduct this assessment. (The team will also be invaluable in developing the plan.) One way to organize this is as a "skunkworks" project. A skunkworks is a team with a mandate to do the best possible job, in the simplest way, at the cheapest cost, and in the quickest time. Alternatively, you might use the matrix management approach. This involves creating a team of key people from every department that has a role to play in the eventual outcome of a project, but which is organized without regard for hierarchies and "normal" reporting channels. Whichever model is most appropriate in your organization, make sure that the team has adequate leadership and is empowered to gather the necessary information and to charge other company functions with a commitment to customer bonding.

Your assessment may require formal or informal market research in the form of surveys, interviews, or focus groups. It will certainly require a thorough evaluation of the marketing infrastructure available to you: media, communications approaches, technologies, and so forth.

Specifically, your inventory should cover the questions included as checklists at the end of chapters 1 through 9. That means you should organize your evaluation around the following headings:

The Big Market Picture: Your market strengths and weaknesses; your competitors' strengths and weaknesses; the marketing infrastructure available to you, including media, technologies, and consumer readiness for each.

Awareness: Current awareness levels for your brand, product, or service, and for that of your competitors. How big is your awareness-creation effort and how well is it working? What avenues haven't you explored yet? How vulnerable is your awareness bond to outside influences such as competitors' advertising and publicity, negative public information, or other market forces?

Identity: What values and emotions do your customers associate with your brand, product, or service? How strong is this bond?

Relationship: Do you or your competitors have any relationship programs in place today? How well are they working as a means for creating lasting customer bonds? Do you have a customer database? If so, how well is it serving your current needs? Your growth needs?

Community: Do you or your competitors have any community-bonding programs in place today? How well are they working? Are there media, event, or life-style opportunities you have not exploited for creating or strengthening communities of interest around your products?

Advocacy: To what extent are your best customers referring new prospects to you today? If you don't know, how could you find out? What avenues exist for encouraging customer referrals in the future? How could you determine whether your customers would like to be asked for referrals? What are your competitors doing in this area?

Define Marketplace Objectives

Once you have taken stock of your situation, you will have to spell out specific objectives for your program. These will guide you in making sensible decisions and getting effective support from management, staff, and any external service companies you may hire.

Start with your big-picture objectives, and don't be afraid to think big. Just because you're number ten in the marketplace now doesn't mean you couldn't become number three, or better. It takes bold vision to break through tough competition.

State objectives in terms of time frames, too, so you will have measurable milestones. And be realistic about the need to place long-term loyalty-building at the top of your list. You will no doubt be under a lot of pressure to make your programs produce short-term results. Some of your customer bonding programs may, in fact, do so. But if you can't get your management to understand the long-term benefits of investing in customer loyalty, you could end up with a series of sales promotions rather than a customer bonding system.

Develop Your Plan

By the time you've completed your assessment and defined your objectives, ideas will probably be popping up all over for customer bonding programs. If not, see if you and your team can come up with fresh ideas in brainstorming sessions. Or you may want to hire professionals to run idea-generating workshops with you.

However you approach idea generation, try to do it with an open mind. Have fun with it. Let your imagination run wild. Afterwards, you can cull the ideas that seem most doable with the objectives, resources, and time frames you have available.

Your plan should ideally define specific customer bonding programs for each level of customer bonding. At this stage, they will be broad-brush outlines only. Later you can write a specific plan for each program. You may have to develop one program first, get it going, and then return to develop another.

In making such determinations, look for ways to make every program do double duty. For example, if you're starting with an awareness-building publicity campaign, can you include a reply component so that you can start building a database? Many business-to-business companies do this by creating a study or report and then announcing key findings through press releases, with a phone or fax number to call to get a free copy. Consumer marketers might accomplish the same goal by including in their advertising or direct-mail promotions 800 numbers or offers to join a club, attend an event, sign-up for a reward, obtain a sample, and so on.

Be sure that your plan identifies specific objectives for each program and milestones for measurements, but be realistic. Some programs will be long-term in nature and difficult to measure.

You may want to define an overarching communications theme to include in all of your programs. This is not always appropriate, however. As we've seen, some themes don't translate well from one market segment to another or from one geographic market to another.

A key task that many organizations forget to cover in their planning is training and incentives for their own people. A great bonding idea can fail if your own employees or the people in your distribution channel don't know about it or aren't enthusiastic about supporting it. How can you empower them to take appropriate action to fulfill the customer bonding mandate? And how can you train them on the customer bonding concept to make sure that everyone in the organization spots bonding opportunities and acts upon them?

Phase II. Benchmark and Test

After completing your assessment and planning, you will need to test out your customer bonding plans before implementing them. This step is crucial. It will enable you to refine your ideas and develop detailed plans for your program before you roll out to the market at large. It may even reveal that your program is wrong and prevent costly public errors later.

There are a number of ways to try out your ideas at this stage. You may want to start with customer focus groups to get feedback on one or another element of your program plan. If it just doesn't excite your customers, don't blame them for their stupidity—as we have seen managers do. Clearly identify the troublesome parts and fix them if you can. If you can't, go back to the well for a better idea.

Once you have a good idea of your program's direction, you may want to benchmark it, either formally or informally, with other companies' customer bonding programs. Benchmarking grew out of the total quality management movement and is increasingly being applied in marketing. It is defined by the American Productivity and Quality Center as "the process of continuously comparing and measuring an organization against business leaders anywhere in the world to gain information that will help an organization improve its performance."

Benchmarking will help you appreciate what you yourself can accomplish and will also help you to fine-tune your strategy. It gives you a privileged look below the surface of another company's marketing image and communications. You may be able to find companies associated with your own industry to benchmark with, or you may have to look to other categories entirely. You can benchmark your entire program or just pieces of it. You can even benchmark against several companies if that makes sense and you have the time and resources to do so.

Phase III. What You Need To Get Where You're Going

Before you roll out your customer bonding system, take time to identify any obstacles that might keep you from getting where you want to go, and develop a plan to overcome them.

For example, if you are not accustomed to building awareness but recognize the need to do so, you need to seek out effective, breakthrough vehicles that you can afford.

Conversely, if you currently rely heavily upon awareness advertising and wish to go beyond it to develop a relationship program that rewards loyal customers, you will need to develop a database and a means of keeping it fresh and up-to-date. That means you will need to establish dialogue with your customers in ways you may not have experienced before.

If you have never thought about the power of having your customers identify with the values inherent in your product or service, or how to make every customer really love you, you may have to reach a new conceptual and communications ground to give your product, service, or company a new image. Think about what you can do to make your customers truly admire you, your company, and your product.

Or, if you see benefits in creating community among your customers, but have no obvious means to do so, you will need to create and support an event or life-style activity to sustain community involvement.

Phase IV. Just Do It!

Once you have accurately defined your situation, made a plan, tested it, and identified ways to overcome any obstacles, you're ready to get rolling.

As you get going, you'll continually discover new tools and tricks to improve your customer bonding skills. Media or technologies may emerge that—though new to you or your marketplace—could offer powerful ways to strengthen bonds with your customers.

You'll probably discover, as have many companies before you, that building and using customer databases effectively can get pretty complex and quite expensive. Starting and maintaining one-to-one relationships is a powerful loyalty strategy, but it is not cheap. Take care to build good reporting and accountability systems into your database marketing system, so that you can act quickly if a given program isn't producing optimal results.

The process of customer bonding will be one of continual refinement and improvement. The marketplace changes daily. Even with major successes under your belt, you can never afford to rest on your laurels. With good management and reporting systems, proper staff training, and careful planning, you may never again have to go through the kind of massive overhaul that may be required at the outset of your customer bonding effort. You will be in a position to detect market shifts and adjust incrementally to them.

A Vision for You

With a healthy dose of inquisitiveness and the willingness to ask yourself "what if . . . ?", you can master customer bonding in no time. As we said at the outset of the book, you are probably doing some customer bonding activities already. By now, you probably have a lot of ideas on how you could do more such activities and do them better.

If there is any one thing to be gained from the system we prescribe, it's to allow information given to you by your customers to guide your marketing decisions. Not everything you plan will work, and your customers will be the first to tell you. Good! That's the whole point of information-driven marketing and the whole reason for getting close to your customers with the customer bonding system.

Moving from a product orientation to a customer-focused orientation is not easy and may be resisted by those who have an interest in the status quo. But, the beauty of the customer bonding system, as you can now attest, is that it is based on common sense and is refreshingly easy to appreciate. If anything, it speaks to the basic needs and wants of people in whatever role they are playing—as your customers, your constituents, your employees, or your audience. It incorporates the best ideas of leading marketers and, properly executed, its feedback and dialogue mechanisms will always keep you abreast of changing market conditions. It is a strategy you can count on for the long haul.

In this millenial era, as the information age radically shifts the way we all live our daily lives around the globe, marketers can never sleep. There is always a new challenge to be answered in the marketplace or a new opportunity to be uncovered and exploited. Our vision for you is that you will be masterful in your marketing activities. That means that you will gain and keep the edge in your chosen markets by focusing all of your activities on building customer loyalty. You will become wizards at breaking through commercial clutter because you will have a deeper understanding than anyone else in your market of what such loyalty requires. You will earn the trust, admiration, and support of an ever-expanding base of customers. And you will have a permanent and ever-improving system for staying in touch with your market.

Checklist

If you have been using our checklists throughout, you already have a very good outline for your customer bonding plan. We have just five more questions, one for each level of bonding. We think they will get to the core of the challenge that lies ahead of you.

1. **Awareness Bonding.** How can you make marketing your message?

2. **Identity Bonding.** How can you make your customers really love you?

3. **Relationship Bonding.** How can you get intimate with your customers?

4. **Community Bonding.** How can you become part of your customers' lives?

5. **Advocacy Bonding.** How can you help every customer be your champion?

In closing, we ask that you stay in touch with us to keep us abreast of your customer bonding progress. Perhaps we can even report your experiences with the system in our next publication. Our fax number and addresses are printed at the end of the book. Thank you very much for joining us in this important project.

Notes

Acknowledgments

1. Rapp, Stan and Tom Collins. *MaxiMarketing*. New York: McGraw-Hill, 1987.
2. Rapp, Stan and Tom Collins. *The Great Marketing Turnaround: The Age of the Individual—and How to Profit From It*. Englewood Cliffs, NJ: Prentice-Hall, 1990.
3. Rapp, Stan and Tom Collins. *Beyond MaxiMarketing: The New Power of Caring and Daring*. New York: McGraw-Hill, 1994.
4. Cross, Richard. "The Five Degrees of Customer Bonding." *Direct Marketing* (October 1992): 33.

Introduction

1. Database marketing is most advanced in the United States and Canada, where use of customer data for targeted marketing is more accepted than in Europe or Asia. Nevertheless, database usage is growing abroad, particularly in the United Kingdom, France, and Japan. In certain Middle East and South American economies, lists of consumers or business customers are sparse, but targeted marketing is expected to grow as these economies continue their expansion.

   In the United States, Canada, and the United Kingdom, the following reports seem to confirm the rise of database programs linked to direct-response print, radio, and broadcast advertising, as well as direct mail:
   - In "The Year Ahead" (*Direct*, December 1993:29), the editors reported that more than 50 percent of the 3,100 U.S. direct marketers they polled expected to increase the size of their marketing database in 1994 on average by a factor of 30 percent.
   - McCann-Erickson's senior vice president for forecasting, Robert Coen, conducts an annual survey of advertising expenditures. While he does not track database usage, his "1980–1993 Estimated Annual U.S. Advertising Expenditures" reveals

223

steadily slowing growth in mass media and steady gains by
direct-mail since 1980, suggesting the potential for database
growth.

- Over 55 percent of Canadian direct-response agencies polled
  for a 1993 study believed that database marketing offers the
  most potential for growth (*Canadian Direct Marketing News*,
  January 1993).

- In the United Kingdom more than two-thirds of the respondents to a Direct Marketing Information Services survey
  reported that they have a marketing database (*DM News*, September 27, 1993:28).

- "The 14th Annual Survey of Promotional Practices," Donnelley
  Marketing, Inc. (Stamford, CT), found that database marketing is increasingly part of the packaged-goods marketing mix.

- Respondents to Myers Reports' "Survey on Marketing Effectiveness & Media Accountability" branded direct mail highest
  among available targeted media in its ability to target specific
  audiences. Respondents included client/brand product managers, agency and media directors, and client advertising and
  marketing managers (*Target Marketing*, January 1993:52).

- Chicago-based promotional tracking service Summary Scan!
  found that since 1989 U.S. shampoo and conditioner ads have
  been heavily laden with database-building devices (Hume,
  Scott. "Sweepstakes grow with coupons." *Advertising Age* [De-
  cember 7, 1992]: 28).

2. Kotler, Philip and Gary Armstrong. *Introduction to Marketing:
   Third Edition*. Englewood Cliffs, NJ: Prentice-Hall, 1994.

3. As we'll discuss in Chapter 2, the philosophical footings of traditional image advertising remain focused on creating and supporting a product image, while database marketing is leapfrogging
   into targeted information-highway potentialities.

4. Bharadwaj, Sundar G., P. Rajan Varadarajan, & John Fahy.
   "Sustainable Competitive Advantage in Services Industries: A
   Conceptual Model and Research Propositions," *Journal of Mar-
   keting*, 57 (October 1993): 83.

Chapter 1

1. Stuart Ewen, quoted in an interview by Mark Dery entitled "Op-
   positional Cultures," *Adbusters* (Summer/Fall 1992):59. A media

historian, Dr. Ewen is among the growing number of scholars and consumerists arguing for an American cultural policy to replace what is seen as a rigid nonpolicy driven by the marketing imperatives of American conglomerates.

2. See note 1 above.

3. Stern, Aimee L. "Courting Consumer Loyalty With the Feel-Good Bond." *The New York Times* (January 19, 1993): 10.

4. *Worldwide Insider's Report.* New York: McCann-Erickson Worldwide, December 1993.

5. In 1994, U.S. advertising expenditures are forecast at $138 billion, according to McCann-Erickson's *Worldwide Insider's Report* (December 1993). The U.S. population is roughly 248.7 million.

6. *United States Postal Service Direct Marketing Guide to Canada.* Alexandria, VA: Braddock Communication, Inc., 1992.

7. "How Uncluttered Are Their Mailboxes?" Postal Direct Mail Services, 1992 Rank Order of Items Per Year, as reported in *Target Marketing*, (September 1992):40.

8. "Advertising Everywhere." *Consumer Reports* (December 1992): 19.

9. The number of products increased from 25,855 in 1989 to 30,000 in 1990, as reported in *FMI Speaks*, published by Food Marketing Institute, Washington, D.C. (May 1992). However, growth stalled at around 30,000 between 1990 and 1993, as reported in *FMI Speaks* (May 1994).

10. Space Marketing Inc. (SMI) sold Columbia Pictures the right to put Arnold Schwarzenegger's *Last Action Hero* on the side of the first "space billboard," a rocket that unfortunately never left the launch pad in 1993. Undaunted, the firm is actively seeking commercial sponsors from all over the world to underwrite the launch of a mile-long environmental platform that would monitor the earth's atmosphere. The platform, scheduled for a mid-1994 launch, would carry a mylar screen that would be visible two or three times a day and would disintegrate after fourteen to twenty days. The screen would contain an environmental symbol that the sponsors could use on their marketing materials.

11. Magazine and newsletter citations from Gale Lists; newspapers from Newspaper Association of America.

12. Magazines that carry advertising, listed by Standard Rate and Data Service as of March 2, 1994.

13. "World Advertising Expenditures." Starch/INRA/Hooper, New York.

14. Angelo, Jean Marie. "1992 Printing and Distribution Trends." *Folio* (May 1, 1992): 74.

15. See note 14 above.

16. See note 4 above.

17. Source: Spokesperson for Cable TV Advertising Bureau.

18. See note 13 above.

19. Hume, Scott. "Coupons set record, but pace slows." *Advertising Age* (February 1, 1993): 25.

20. Egol, Len, "Is Couponing Growth Flagging?" *Direct* (March 1994): 13.

21. See note 4 above.

22. *The Friday Report* (March 12, 1993).

23. *The Friday Report* (April 2, 1993): 5.

24. Popcorn, Faith. *The Popcorn Report: Faith Popcorn on the Future of Your Company, Your World, Your Life.* New York: Doubleday, 1991, pg. 6.

25. Only 8 percent of those surveyed had confidence in the advertising industry, according to "The 1993 Yankelovich MONITOR®," Yankelovich Partners, Westport, CT.

26. Popcorn, pg. 6.

27. Popcorn, pg. 76.

28. Ouelette, Laurie. "Smells Like Subversive Spirit." *Utne Reader* (March/April 1993): 32.

29. Data courtesy of Univisa Telemarketing Group, Culver City, CA. Univisa is a division of Univisa Inc., a Televisa Group of Companies.

30. "14th Annual Survey of Promotional Practices." Donnelley Marketing, Inc., Stamford, CT, 1992.

31. "Emerging Markets." *Direct* (January 1993): 38.

32. See note 31 above.

33. In 1993, 75 percent of women questioned said that "All things being equal, I prefer to buy products made by well-established companies." "The 1993 Yankelovich MONITOR®."

34. Natalie Perkins, VP, account supervisor at Trone Advertising, Greensboro, NC, quoted in "The Media Wakes Up to Generation X," *Advertising Age* (February 1, 1993): 16.

35. Stern, Aimee L. "To the Pacific," *Direct* (April 1992): 31.

36. Geddes, Andrew. "Asian airlines try loyalty offers." *Advertising Age* (December 14, 1992): 10.

37. *United States International Direct Marketing Guide.* Alexandria, VA: Braddock Communications, Inc., 1992.

38. Jeffe, Larry A. "HSN Will Enter Japan in a Venture with TCI." *DM News* (February 28, 1994): 1.

39. Jacob, Rahul. "India is Opening for Business." *Fortune* (November 16, 1992): 128.

40. See note 37 above.

41. See note 37 above.

42. Gattuso, Greg, "CompuServe Expands Support in Mexico." *Direct Marketing* (February 1994): 12.

Chapter 2

1. Jackson, Robert and Paul Wang. *Strategic Database Marketing.* Lincolnwood, IL: NTC Business Books, 1994, pg. 10.

2. The 1992 publication of a book by Don Schultz, Stanley I. Tannenbaum, and Robert F. Lauterborn (*Integrated Marketing Communications*, NTC Business Books), increased the visibility of the concept, which has been debated for years at marketing conferences and in the trade press.

3. Psychographics is a technique for defining market segments by life-style characteristics.

4. Jacobson Consulting Applications of New York, NY, commissioned by *Direct* magazine and reported in the January 1993 issue of *The Cowles Report on Database Marketing and Management*, pg. 10.

5. Hatch, Denison. "The Deathwatch at IBM." *Target Marketing* (February 1993): 6.

6. Mandese, Joe. "NBC dials interactive." *Advertising Age* (July 12, 1993): 1.

7. Bertrand, Kate. "Volcanic Activity: Customer-targeted magazines proliferate at big companies." *Business Marketing* (April 1992): 22.

8. Stan Rapp and Tom Collins first put forth this concept in *Maxi-Marketing* (New York: McGraw-Hill, 1987, pg. 171). They defined double-duty advertising as ". . . a way to maximize the power and synergy of your advertising which may not add a cent to your advertising budget. The secret is the extra value that can be extracted by arranging for a single advertising effort to accomplish two (or more) different jobs."

9. Source: Ogilvy & Mather, Los Angeles, CA.

10. *The Washington Post* (July 10, 1992): C1.

11. Balinger, Jerrold. "More Firms to Make Use of Tie-Ins and Mail for Marketing, Survey Says." *DM News* (March 8, 1993): 4.

Chapter 3

1. Hatch, Denison. "Buyer bonding: Some use flair, some use Big Mac." *Catalog Business* 3 (August 1, 1989): 22.

2. We ask our readers' indulgence in this oversimplification of the pronoun problem.

3. First described in Richard Cross's article, "The Five Degrees of Customer Bonding." *Direct Marketing* (October 1992): 33.

4. Liesse, Jill. "Private label nightmare." *Advertising Age* (April 5, 1993): 1.

5. See Chapter 3, "Hostage Brands," in David Martin's *Romancing the Brand: The Power of Advertising and How to Use It*, AMACOM, a division of the American Management Association, (New York, 1989). Excerpts printed with permission of the publisher. All rights reserved.

6. "The Eurosion of Brand Loyalty." *Business Week* (July 19, 1993): 22.

7. See note 5 above.

Chapter 4

1. Mayer, Martin. *Madison Avenue USA*. New York: Harper & Brothers, 1958, pg. 312. Copyright © 1958 by Martin Prager Mayer. Reprinted by permission of Curtis Brown Ltd.

2. For an excellent review of brand loyalty and brand awareness, see Aakers, David. *Managing Brand Equity: Capitalizing on the Value of a Brand Name.* New York: The Free Press, 1991.

3. Reprinted with permission of Cahners Publishing from "How Advertising Drives Profitability," a study commissioned by Cahners from the Strategic Planning Institute in Cambridge, MA.

4. According to an Avis spokesperson, market share dominance was not the goal of the campaign when it was launched, and financial measures of the campaign's impact are not available.

5. Company literature.

6. Grimm, Mike. "Coke Plans to Put Its Bears to Work." *Adweek* (July 21, 1993): 10.

7. Fahey, Alison. "Comeback Brands." *Adweek* (May 3, 1993): 1.

8. Hagstrom, Jerry. "Political Consulting: A Guide for Reporters and Citizens." The Freedom Forum Media Studies Center (1992): 14.

9. Colford, Steven W. "Clinton's forces score with tactical use of ads." *Advertising Age* (August 24, 1992): 3.

10. A 1992 study of consumer willingness to purchase insurance and financial services found that consumer interest increased by 50 to 100 percent when the brand was well-known. See Oren, Haim. "The New Demands of Brand-Equity Marketing." *DM News* (February 15, 1993):39.

11. Cox, Stephen. *The Mirror Makers.* New York: Vintage Book, 1985, pg. 231.

12. Bowes, Murray. "A World Without Borders." *Direct* (April 1992): 56.

13. Browning, E.S. "Eastern Europe Poses Obstacles for Ads." *The Wall Street Journal* (July 30, 1992):B6.

14. Alvarez, Paul H. Copyright © *Public Relations Journal* (August 1993): 14. Reprinted by permission of *Public Relations Journal*, published by the Public Relations Society of America, New York, NY.

15. "Managing Corporate Communications in a Competitive Climate." The Conference Board, (New York 1993): 22.

16. A reference from Philip Kotler and Gary Armstrong. *Marketing: An Introduction, 3rd Edition.* Englewood Cliffs, NJ: Prentice Hall, 1993, pg. 433. The authors were citing Tom Duncan, *A*

Study of How Manufacturers and Service Companies Perceive and Use Marketing Public Relations, Muncie, IN: Ball State University, December 1985.

17. Bauman, Risa. "Selling in the Long Form." *Direct* (January (1993):24.

18. Carmody, Deirdre. "New Guidelines Established for Magazine Advertising." *The New York Times* (October 21, 1992): D17.

19. Aakers, David. *Managing Brand Equity: Capitalizing on the Value of a Brand Name.* New York: The Free Press, 1991, pg. 72.

20. Roddick, Anita. *Body and Soul: Profits with Principles—The Amazing Success Story of Anita Roddick & The Body Shop.* New York: Crown Publishers, 1991, pg. 97.

21. *15th Annual Survey of Promotional Practices.* Stamford, CT: Donnelley Marketing Inc., 1993.

22. "Pontiac takes successful test drive on HSN." *Direct Marketing* (February 1994): 8.

23. *IEG Sponsorship Report*, a Chicago-based newsletter that tracks sports, entertainment, and cause marketing.

24. Fuhrman, Peter. "Welcome to the dollar bloc." *Forbes* (October 14, 1991):100.

25. Rose, Matthew. "Sharp Tests Viewcam in German Market Via Direct Selling System." *DM News* (December 27, 1993): 20.

26. Ogilvy, David. *Ogilvy on Advertising.* New York: Crown Publishers, 1983, pg. 201.

27. Levin, Gary. "Joe Camel can't light up children in 'Q' ratings." *Advertising Age* (March 1, 1993): 8. The article cites a November 1992 study by Marketing Evaluations showing that Joe Camel was recognized by 74% of its sample of 6- to 17-year olds. The camel figure is familiar to 58% of children ages 6 to 11, compared to 64% familiarity with average cartoon characters. (Significantly, however, the character's likability rating among children was low.) An RJR spokeswoman was quoted saying that "Our own research of adult smokers shows the campaign is very appealing and that's the only market we're interested in."

28. In the past five years, store brands have gained three percentage points in the battle for supermarket sales in all packaged-goods categories combined (18 percent). Some experts predict that by

1997 store brands will represent a quarter of the products on supermarket shelves and maybe even half by the year 2000.

29. The Coalition for Brand Equity is a trade group of North American advertisers and media groups chartered to "refocus attention on brand-building."

30. Light, Larry. "At the center of it all is the brand." *Advertising Age* (March 29, 1993): 22.

31. Aakers, David. *Managing Brand Equity: Capitalizing on the Value of a Brand Name.* New York: The Free Press, 1991, pg. 14.

32. For a good review of advertising frequency, see Naples, Michael J., *Effective Frequency: The Relationship Between Frequency and Advertising Effectiveness.* New York: Association of National Advertisers, 1979.

33. Mandese, Joe. "Home improvement wins $ race." *Advertising Age* (September 6, 1993): 3.

34. By 1910, with Procter & Gamble's introduction of Crisco, many of the techniques of modern marketing were already being modeled. The Crisco launch involved what may be the first carefully orchestrated national brand launch, involving a complex pattern of focus groups ("Criso teas"), trade promotions, mass advertising ("advertorial" style), product samples and promotions, publicity, consumer-information campaigns, and cooking schools. Source: Strasser, Susan. *Satisfaction Guaranteed.* New York: Pantheon Books, 1989, pg. 3.

35. According to Rob Jackson, author of "Close Encounters of the Fourth Kind," Don Schultz made this remark when addressing a Chicago direct-marketing group: "Technology has killed the mass market. With many nontraditional marketers developing databases, the more they know about their customers, the less they need rely on mass advertising communications. The more the consumer knows about your product, the less they need traditional advertising." *DM News* (February 8, 1993): 25.

Chapter 5

1. Popcorn, Faith. *The Popcorn Report.* New York: Doubleday, 1991.

2. Shapiro, Eben. "Cigarette Makers Outfit Smokers in Icons, Eluding Warning and Enraging Activists." *The Wall Street Journal* (September 27, 1993): B1.

3. Elliott, Stuart. "Marlboro's 2-Fisted Pitch." *The New York Times* (April 6, 1993): D1.

4. Co-branded MasterCard Fact Sheet.

5. "The Evolving Mind of Global Management—Part Two." Cross-Culture Communications, Ltd., Tokyo.

6. *IEG Sponsorship Report*, Chicago.

7. Gross, Jane. "Profile of Working Assets." *The New York Times* (November 7, 1993): 8.

8. Hume, Scott. "Marketers rally around school sponsorships." *Advertising Age* (June 1, 1992): 32.

9. Emerson, Jim. "Phone-Service Resale Prospects Adore Ben & Jerry's Ice Cream." *DM News* (June 14, 1993): 4.

10. For example, try talking to what *The Wall Street Journal* called the "puberty-something crowd" of 1993 without the right "slanguage," and you'll only turn off an already consumer-hostile audience. See Cooper, Helene. "Once Again, Ads Woo Teens With Slang." *The Wall Street Journal* (March 29, 1993): B1.

11. Company interview.

12. Dell-Apa, Frank. "Do Pro Sports Take Advantage of Their Fans?" *Public Citizen* (May/June 1993): 10.

13. Cohen, Roger. "The Calling Card." *The New York Sunday Times* (January 3, 1993): 3.

14. Spindle, William. "King of the Phone-Card Collectors." *Business Week* (January 10, 1994): 18E3.

Chapter 6

1. Levin, Gary. "Marketers flock to loyalty offers." *Advertising Age* (May 24,1993): 13.

2. Elliott, Stuart. "Consumer-product marketers are using premiums and incentives as rewards for customers' loyalty." *The New York Times* (May 4, 1993): D20.

3. The programs have become standard for all the airlines operating in Europe, according to Rapp & Collins/Piment. And a group of

Asian airlines have recently launched a cooperative frequent-flier venture to combat competitive inroads from Western airlines.

4. According to statistics provided by Burger King, children between the ages of four and twelve spend nearly $9 billion annually and influence another $82 billion in family food and beverage purchases, $1.14 billion on apparel, $797 million on movies and spectator sports, and $530 million on consumer electronics.

   But care must be taken when marketing to this age group. Parents are rightfully concerned about the impact of commercialism on kids. Marketers who want to form relationship bonds with children must be very sensitive to their responsibilities. According to *The Cowles Report on Database Marketing*, companies like Fox Children's Network (Fox Kids Club) and Lego Systems Inc. (Builders Club) are also building relationships that both kids and parents appreciate. "If kids are your target audience." *The Cowles Report on Database Marketing* (February 1993): 1.

5. "A candid conversation with frequent-flyer pioneer Michael Gunn." *Colloquy, The Quarterly Frequency-Marketing Newsletter* 3: 8.

6. Grosvald, Stevan A. "Ten Days Late, 5,000 Miles Better." *Frequent Flyer* (November 1992): 32.

7. See the discussion of "private money" and "breakage" in Chapter 2.

8. Grosvald, Stevan A. "Frequent Flyer Programs. The Inside Story." *Frequent Flyer* (November 1992): 28.

9. Rapp, Stan and Tom Collins. *MaxiMarketing*. New York: McGraw-Hill, 1987.

10. "American Airlines Digs Deeper for Gold." *Cowles Report on Database Marketing* (November 1992): 1.

11. These costs vary widely, depending upon your unique requirements. A recent survey of packaged-goods database marketers by *The Cowles Report on Database Marketing* found the upper end to be well over $300,000 for start-up costs and monthly maintenance costs of $115,000 plus $75,000 for each staff person required. On top of these costs you have to add ongoing costs for direct marketing programs including direct mail, telephone, and so forth. For a copy of this report, "Database Marketing and Promotion for Packaged Goods Manufacturers—Facts,

Myths, and Beliefs," contact Robert Cottrell of Clayton/Curtis/Cottrell in Boulder, Colorado, 303–444–2381.

Another excellent discussion of how to cost out your database and figure your payback can be found in Chapter 21 of Arthur Hughes's text, *The Complete Database Marketer*. (Chicago: Probus Publishing Company, 1991.) Hughes also offers the advice that "The database must be up and running in one year or less." This is true not only because you stand to lose internal support without early demonstrable results, but because each day lost means lost money and a greater chance that your competitors will beat you to it. The database contribution to customer lifetime value is further developed in Hughes's book *Strategic Database Marketing* (Chicago: Probus Publishing Company, 1994).

Frequency-marketing consultant Richard G. Barlow, president of Frequency Marketing, Inc., and publisher of *COLLOQUY, The Quarterly Frequency Marketing Newsletter*, cites the wide range of $5 to $15 per customer as the cost of doing frequency-marketing programs. It is true that the cost will vary tremendously depending upon your industry's cost structure, the complexity of your program, and how much of your database effort is managed in-house.

12. Elliott, Stuart. "A mail campaign helps SAAB find, and keep, its customers." *The New York Times* (June 21, 1993): D7.

13. See note 8 above.

14. See note 10 above.

15. "BA gets personal at the departure gate." *The Cowles Report on Database Marketing* (February 1993): 3.

16. Ballinger, Jerrold. "DowElanco, Crop-Protection Firm, Is Building a Centralized Database." *DM News* (May 10, 1993): 19.

17. Hansell, Saul. "American Express Shows Broad Improvement in Profit." *The New York Times* (July 27, 1993): D4.

18. General-purpose credit cards can be used to purchase goods and services anywhere the card is accepted; they differ from "private-label" cards, which can only be used to buy the goods of the issuing company. And general-purpose cards are quite a bit more lucrative with average balances running about $1,400, as opposed to $250. Source: Pae, Peter. "More Major Marketers Are Now Offering Their Own General-Purpose Credit Cards." *The Wall Street Journal* (August 26, 1992): B1.

19. "Banks' Airline Cards Keep Gaining Altitude." *Credit Card News* (February 1, 1993): 1.

20. Eisman, Regina. "Charge!", *Incentive* (November 1992): 42.

21. See note 18 above.

22. From company literature and selected publications, including:
Daly, James J. "Flooring it at GM." *Credit Card Management* (December 1992): 12.
Ballinger, Jerrold. "General Motors Credit Database Key to Future Promotions." *DM News* (April 26, 1993): 2.
Evans, David. "In the Driver's Seat." *Direct* (July 1993): 35.

23. "New Charge Cards Earn Cruises, Tours, Gasoline." *Consumer Reports Travel Letter* (March 1994): 49.

24. "GE Lights Up Its Rewards Card with a Refund." *Credit Card News* (March 15, 1993): 3.
"GE to Issue Credit Cards, Possibly Tied to Discounts." *The New York Times* (August 13, 1992): D12.
Quint, Michael. "New Credit Card from G.E. to Offer Merchant Coupons." *The New York Times* (September 3, 1992): D4.

25. See note 20 above.

26. "Ford Hitches a Ride on GM's Credit Card Concept." *Credit Card News* (February 15, 1993): 1.

27. Elliott, Stuart. "Consumer-product marketers are using premiums and incentives as rewards for customers' loyalty." *The New York Times* (May 4, 1993): D20.

28. Company correspondence and press reports.

29. Elliott, Stuart. "Cigarette makers encourage smokers to wear their favorite brands on their sleeves." *The New York Times* (February 10, 1993): D19.

30. "Camel Cash Program Extended." *Direct Marketing* (March 1993): 11.

31. See *The Friday Report* (March 12, 1993): 4 and "Marlboro Enters Catalog Arena." Gattuso, Greg, *Direct Marketing* (April 1993): 12.

32. Huttner, Richard. "The Basics of Continuity." Direct Marketing Association Resource Report (July 1989), Report 206.01.

33. *COLLOQUY, The Quarterly Frequency Marketing Newsletter* 3, Issue 3, pg. 1. Cited with permission of publisher Richard G. Barlow, president of Frequency Marketing, Inc.

Chapter 7

1. *Webster's Encyclopedic Unabridged Dictionary of the English Language*. New York: Portland House, 1989.

2. The Wally Byam Club actually began as a manufacturer-sponsored club. It was launched by Airstream Trailers back in the 1950s. It was, as far as we could determine, the first "users" club in the recreational industry and served as a model for clubs launched in the 1960s and 1970s by motor home manufacturers. In the course of company mergers, however, club management was taken over by Airstream owners and now restricts membership to only certain types of Airstream trailers. This demonstrates the fine line manufacturers face in community bonding: Control too hard and you may alienate. Lose control and your community will not necessarily serve *your* needs anymore.

3. The figures were provided by the companies mentioned.

4. *Online Services: 1990 Review, Trends and Forecast*, a report by SIMBA Information Inc., Wilton, CT.

5. Chris Elwell, editor of *Online Services: 1990 Review, Trends and Forecast*, a report by SIMBA Information Inc., Wilton, CT.

6. *Information Sources: Camping and the RV Lifestyle*, Recreational Vehicle Industry Association (RVIA), Box 2999, 1896 Preston White Drive, Reston, VA 22090-0999, 703–620–6003.

7. Tom Walworth, Statistical Surveys, Inc., Grand Rapids, MI.

8. Popcorn, Faith. *The Popcorn Report: Faith Popcorn on the Future of Your Company, Your World, Your Life*. New York: Doubleday, 1991, pg. 32.

9. Amelar, Sarah. "The Whole Earth Reader's Digest," *Magazine Week* (April 5, 1993): 18.

10. Holiday Inn revamped its plan in 1986 to get away from overreliance on rewards, adding the relationship element with a point-based reward system. In 1993, a plan to add mileage rewards in addition to points was scuttled when mileage broker *Air Miles* folded its North American operation. However, the company now offers mileage rewards through agreements with several major airlines.

11. Kim, Bryan. "Most sponsorships waste money." *Advertising Age* (June 21, 1993): S-2.

Chapter 8

1. Kotler, Philip and Gary Armstrong. *Marketing: An Introduction, Third Edition.* Englewood Cliffs, NJ: Prentice-Hall, 1993, pg. 150.

2. Spokespeople at UWSA are not revealing actual numbers, probably because the organization does not want to tip its hand about Mr. Perot's 1996 ambitions.

3. See note 1 above, pg. 142.

4. The information in this paragraph is drawn from an article by Keller, John J. "AT&T, MCI, Sprint Raise the Intensity of Their Endless War." *The Wall Street Journal* (October 20, 1992): A1.

5. President and founder Scott Cook, as quoted by John Case, "Customer Service: The Last Word." *Inc.* (April 1991): 88.

6. *The Cowles Report on Database Marketing and Management* (January 1993): 12.

7. An earlier organization formed by Mr. Perot, United We Stand, Inc., was also adept at grassroots activism. Back in 1969, UWSI was buying full-page ads in *The New York Times* and dropping 25 million postcard mailings to support the Nixon Administration's Vietnam policy. See Wilentz, Sean. "Pox Populi," *The New Republic* (August 9, 1993): 29.

8. According to a UWSA spokesperson.

Chapter 9

1. Hiam, Alexander. *Closing the Quality Gap.* Englewood Cliffs, NJ: Prentice-Hall, 1992, pg. 19.

Chapter 10

1. According to Philip Kotler and Gary Armstrong, VALS is the most widely used of the life-style measuring techniques (Kotler and Armstrong, *Introduction to Marketing:* Third Edition. Englewood Cliffs, NJ: Prentice-Hall, 1994, pg, 133. VALS was first introduced by SRI in 1978 and classified consumers as "experientials" (inner-directed), "belongers" (outer-directed), or "sur-

vivors" (need-driven). VALS 2, introduced in the late 1980s, re-vamped these classifications, grouping people by their consumption tendencies into life-style groups. For more information on psychographics, see Piirto, Rebecca. "Measuring Minds in the 1990s." *American Demographics* (December 1990): 35 and "VALS the Second Time." *American Demographics* (July 1991): 6.

2. According to a Direct Marketing Association study reported in *DM News*, "DMA: Over 90% of BTBers Use Databases" (January 31, 1992): 10.

Glossary

Advertorial. Print advertisements designed to resemble editorial matter.

Affinity Credit Card. Affinity credit cards are issued by a bank on behalf of a specific affinity group such as a nonprofit organization, a seniors' or employees' organization, a professional association, a fan club, or any identifiable group with a common interest or "affinity." An image depicting the focus of the affinity (a logo or other image) is prominently displayed on the card, and special benefits may be offered to cardholders by virtue of their membership in this group. (See also *Co-Branded Credit Card* and Chapters 5 and 6.)

Anticommercialism. The phenomenon, growing in some Western economies where advertising clutter is rampant, of consumer mistrust and hostility towards advertising.

Benchmarking. According to the American Productivity and Quality Center, benchmarking can be defined as "the process of continuously comparing and measuring an organization against business leaders anywhere in the world to gain information that will help an organization improve its performance." A useful concept to incorporate into your assessment and planning of customer bonding programs.

Breakage. The amount of a reward that customers will *not* use. Frequent-flier programs and other frequency programs figure an amount for breakage into their programs in order to determine how much they can afford to give away on a promotion. (See Chapters 2 and 6.)

Business-to-Business Marketers. Companies that sell business products or services to other businesses (as opposed to consumer or packaged-goods marketers that sell to the general public).

Cause Marketing. Investing the marketing in budget programs that benefit social, environmental, or other causes. If the causes selected are valued by your target audience, you can create strong awareness and identity bonds.

Co-Branded Credit Card.   An increasingly popular variant on affinity credit cards, co-branded cards are issued by a bank and marketed to the customer base of the co-brander. The co-brander might be an airline, automobile manufacturer, insurance company, retail chain, or telephone-service company. It is usually an organization with a recognized brand and/or logo. (See also *Affinity Credit Card* and Chapters 5 and 6.)

Consumerism.   Organized movements of consumers concerned with protecting their interests by disciplining and controlling the marketing and promotion activities of businesses.

Continuity.   A structural requirement for the reward component of relationship-marketing programs. Continuity means that each purchase the customer makes magnifies the value to the customer of the next purchase. It creates a cumulative reward system (also known as a progressive reward), in which consumers accumulate rewards such as points or miles to apply to various award levels. Successive award levels are easier to achieve than the first level, so consumers have an ever-growing incentive for continuing their business relationship with you. (See Chapter 6.)

Cross-Promotion.   See *Tie-in Promotion.*

Database Marketing.   The process of building, maintaining, and using computerized records containing the name and address and other relevant information about a company's prospects and customers. The database, when properly maintained, is continually replenished with new information each time the company interacts with a prospect or customer by phone, mail, or in person. Some companies maintain separate transaction and marketing databases, but both sets of information are useful when analyzing the lifetime value of a customer and developing strategies for increasing the value of the relationship.

Datamotion.   The dynamic movement of data between the marketplace and the marketer's database. By recording prospect and customer transactions, you pull new information about their needs and preferences into the database. This knowledge then informs marketing strategies and outbound communications back to the prospect or customer. (See Chapter 2.)

Dialogue.   The process of interacting directly with your prospects, customers, donors, or supporters. Dialogue requires a marketing database and some form of direct media.

Direct Mail. Marketing- or sales-related material sent by mail to a person's home or business address and usually addressed to the individual by name.

Direct Media. Communications channels that enable organizations to interact directly with their constituents. Outbound communications are directed to the individual constituents by name. The most common channels are direct mail, broadcast fax, and telemarketing. (See also *Private Media* and Chapter 2.)

Direct Sales. Selling done face-to-face, usually by a dedicated sales force. Aside from multilevel companies like Avon or Mary Kay, most direct sales practitioners are business-to-business companies.

Dollar Doublers. Techniques that magnify the impact of every marketing expenditure by adding value without adding cost. Effective Dollar Doublers include: double-duty advertising, private money, and tie-in promotions with marketing partners.

Donor Pyramid. A concept popularized by San Francisco-based fund-raising consultants, Robert and Joan Blum. It uses a pyramid image to describe the donor-acquisition process. Typically, many small donors are acquired (the bottom of the pyramid), and the traditional fund-raising strategy is to try to move them to the top of the pyramid, where there are fewer, but much larger dollar, donors.

Double-Duty Advertising. A term coined by Stan Rapp and Tom Collins in *MaxiMarketing* to describe the process of making a single ad do multiple jobs.

Enhanced Fax. Refers to an evolving set of facsimile applications made possible by integrating the fax with computerized databases and voice technologies to support the dissemination of advertising or other information. Includes one-way fax communications (fax broadcast), fax mailboxes, and the interactive capability known as fax retrieval or fax-on-demand.

Event Sponsorship. The underwriting by a commercial sponsor of an event such as a sports tournament, workshop, concert, or other life-style activity.

Fax Broadcast, Fax on Demand, Fax Retrieval. See *Enhanced Fax.*

Frequency-Marketing Program. A program that encourages customers to make repeated purchases, usually by offering a progressive reward. Airline frequent-flier clubs are a good example. (See Chapter 6.)

Frequent-Purchase Program. See *Frequency-Marketing Program.*

Home Shopping. A phenomenon that started in the United States with the Home Shopping Network and is quickly spreading to Europe and Asia. Home shopping programming is dedicated to the presentation of consumer goods available for purchase. Currently, buyers must call in credit-card orders by telephone. But developments in interactive television may turn the television itself into a device for placing orders.

Image Advertising. Advertising that is intended to create awareness and capture share of mind for a brand, a product, or an organization. Image advertising focuses on creating an image, a perception in the consumer's mind, rather than on *selling* products or services. (See Chapter 4.)

Image-Based Marketing Model. The predominant model in most consumer product categories throughout the century, this approach is losing ground as more companies turn to information-driven marketing. The goal of image-based marketing is to support a particular image for your product or service, cause, or candidate. As such, it is heavily weighted toward image-oriented advertising, often through mass media. Other activities are often budgeted and measured according to their ability to enhance the desired image. (See Chapter 2.)

Individualized Marketing. See *Targeted Marketing.*

Infomercial. A long-form television advertisement made to resemble program material.

Information Core. The database of information about individuals in your marketplace. It is created and continually replenished from a variety of sources, such as incoming calls to your sales- or customer-service departments, product-registration cards, and replies to surveys and promotional offers. (See Chapter 2.)

Integrated Marketing Communications. A marketing model that emphasizes the importance of delivering consistent messages through all of the elements in your marketing mix. In theory, each element—advertising, direct marketing, sales promotion, and publicity—is recognized as a legitimate contributor to an overall strategy of market penetration or defense. In practice, however, general advertising is often given more weight than other activities. The integrated approach is favored by the advertising industry, which has been experiencing sales declines for several years. (See Chapter 2.)

Interactive Marketing. A broad term that generally describes marketing techniques in which the buyer and the seller interact directly, often via a technological medium such as the telephone, fax machine, on-line network, or interactive television system. Used more loosely, interactive marketing can also describe any marketing program that encourages the consumer to make direct contact with the company through a survey, direct mail, or telephone response.

Interactive Shopping. A range of technological purchasing channels that give buyers a means to buy goods electronically, often without leaving their homes or offices. Some interactive-shopping services are offered through on-line computer networks such as CompuServe in the United States or Minitel in France. Television is another promising new vehicle for interactive shopping. Many consumers are already used to buying goods by telephone after seeing them demonstrated on home-shopping channels. Interactive television technology will soon make it possible to purchase goods and services seen on these channels without even making a phone call.

Loyalty Marketing. The process of initiating and sustaining a lasting relationship with each customer or prospect. (See Introduction.)

Marketing Database. A repository for the information you need in order to have a mutually rewarding relationship with your customers or supporters. To build such relationships, it should contain three categories of information: customer name and address; relevant information about each individual, such as age and income level; and any data captured whenever you and the individual interact. (See Chapter 2.)

Marketing Partners. Organizations that form an alliance for the purpose of improving marketing opportunities. The alliance may include offering the marketing partner's product as a reward for desired customer behaviors (tie-in promotions), co-operative advertising, sharing customer lists, and so on. (See Chapter 2).

Matrix Management. A management approach that involves assembling a team of key people from every department to handle a specific cross-organizational task. A useful approach for assessing your organization's marketing needs relative to customer bonding. (See Epilogue.)

Multilogue.   An extension of our concept of dialogue, which is two-way communication between the marketer and the prospect or customer. Multilogue involves communications among customers *and* between customers and the marketer.

Point-of-Purchase Politics.   See *Cause Marketing*.

Private Media.   Channels of communications with prospects and customers that are owned by the marketer. Newsletters, magazines, and catalogs are all examples of regular communications channels that can be privately sponsored. (See Chapter 2.)

Private Money.   A scrip or currency that is issued as a reward for desired behaviors by your customers and is exchangeable for products or services from you or your marketing partners. Examples include airline miles, hotel frequent-stay points, and frequent-shopper points from retail clubs. (See Chapter 2.)

Progressive Reward.   (See *Continuity*.)

Promotion.   A marketing program offering some sort of special deal in exchange for a requested action. Most promotions are designed to increase sales over a specified time. More and more, marketers are also using promotions to build databases of prospects and customers.

Psychographics.   The science of measuring and categorizing consumer life-style patterns. Marketers who collect psychographic data about the individuals in their database (or purchase it from another source when available) are able to refine their marketing strategies to fit their customers' needs and preferences more precisely.

Recognition.   An important element in relationship-bonding, recognition acknowledges the status of preferred customers or donors or supporters. This might include some combination of prestige (as in VIP frequent-flier clubs), dedicated communications channels (such as a members-only hotline), special treatment by your personnel, special services, or special purchasing options. (See Chapter 6.)

Relationship Marketing.   This term means different things to different people. But all definitions seem to share a common objective: keeping customers once you have them and increasing the value of your relationship with them. Some people talk about relationship marketing as providing good customer service. Others use it only to describe frequent-buyer programs. Database marketers use the term to describe the process of building ongoing relationships with customers based on direct, ongoing interaction. In customer bonding, we refine that definition to describe a set of activities that deepen your relationship with customers by offering recognition of the customer's status with you, rewards for desired purchase behavior, and continuity (each purchase increases the value of the next). (See Chapter 6.)

Reward. Something of value that your constituents get each time they buy your product or service, donate funds to your cause, or invest their time on behalf of your candidate. In promotional programs, rewards are given just for responding to the promotion and usually involve some sort of discount, premium, or other giveaway. In relationship-marketing programs, rewards are generally given in the form of reduced prices on future purchases or totally free products or services (your own or those of a marketing partner who wants to reach your customers). The customer earns them by accumulating coupons, points, or miles each time a purchase is made. (See also *Continuity* and Chapter 6.)

Skunkworks. An organization team created by management and given a mandate to accomplish a specific task in the best and simplest but most effective way, at the cheapest cost, in the quickest time. A useful approach to consider when assessing and planning your organization's customer bonding strategy. (See Epilogue.)

Social-Cause Marketing. See *Cause Marketing.*

Targeted Marketing. The process of targeting your advertising and marketing communications to individual recipients. Typically, targeted marketing is done by direct mail or telemarketing and is supported by a list of prospect and customer names and addresses. The list may be rented from an outside source such as a magazine, catalog, or credit card company. Or it may be a customer list maintained in a computerized database by the company doing the marketing. (See also *Database Marketing.*)

Tie-in Promotion. A promotion in which another company's goods or services are offered as a reward for a consumer's purchase behavior. Also known as "cross-promotion." (See Chapter 2.)

Index

About the Authors

Richard Cross is president of Cross•Rapp•Associates, a strategic database marketing consulting company co-founded with Stan Rapp.

Through the years, Cross has earned a reputation for outstanding entrepreneurial abilities and broad expertise in marketing. Since launching his own consulting concern in 1987, Cross has helped in the design and implementation of innovative marketing programs that build profitable customer relationships. Cross•Rapp•Associates' clients include Fortune 100 companies from such diverse fields as broadcasting, publishing, insurance, financial services, packaged goods, and business-to-business. Clients also include leading nonprofit organizations and U.S. government agencies.

Prior to starting his own firm, Cross was Associate Director of Consumers Union, where he pioneered new marketing strategies for *Consumer Reports* magazine. Under Cross' direction, Consumers Union launched numerous new products and services directed to its subscriber database, including a travel newsletter, a new car price information service, a children's magazine, a publication for consumer affairs professionals, and a nationally syndicated radio series and newspaper column.

Cross is a regular speaker at publishing, fund-raising, and marketing events. He holds both bachelor's and master's degree from Cornell University and lives in Tarrytown, N.Y.

Janet A. Smith is a veteran marketing communications consultant who creates marketing solutions for Fortune 50 companies in computers and telecommunications, pharmaceuticals and healthcare, petrochemicals, and financial services. She also aids smaller firms, nonprofit organizations, and individuals in creating marketing communications programs.

A former marketing manager with Digital Equipment Corporation, Smith is broadly versed in marketing technologies and writes on these and other topics for Enterprise, *Profit, Beyond Computing,* and *Direct Marketing* magazines. She holds a bachelor's degree with honors in languages from Brandeis University, and an MBA in marketing from Babson College.

Please introduce yourself!

Your name _____

Your position _____

Company or organization name _____

Street address _____

_____

_____

_____

City _____ State _____ Zip _____

Telephone (switchboard) _____

Telephone (direct line or voice mail) _____

Fax _____

What business are you in?

I would like to apply ideas from this book to my company or organization.

1	2	3	4	5
Strongly disagree		Neither agree nor disagree		Strongly agree

I will recommend this book to others.

1	2	3	4	5
Strongly disagree		Neither agree nor disagree		Strongly agree

Please tell us how this book could be made more useful to you.

Would you like to learn how to put customer bonding to work in your situation? Yes, I am interested in (check all that apply):

☐ Public seminars.   ☐ Telephone consultation.
☐ Private in-house training seminars. ☐ Future customer bonding faxletters.
☐ On-site consultation.

Please mail, fax, or e-mail your information to:

Richard Cross and Janet Smith
Cross • Rapp • Associates
32 Park Avenue
Tarrytown, NY 10591
Fax: 914 332 8807
Internet address: cbonding@aol.com